BRITISH TRACTORS
1945-1965

By Stuart Gibbard

Herridge & Sons

Published in 2013 by
Herridge & Sons Ltd
Lower Forda, Shebbear
Devon EX21 5SY

ISBN 978-1-906133-52-8
Printed in Hong Kong

CONTENTS

FOREWORD

David Brown introduced its first tractor, the VAK1 model, in 1939. Production commenced at Meltham in Yorkshire, but was limited by the company's commitments to the war effort.

Growing up on a farm in the late 1950s and early '60s, some of my most vivid memories are of being taken to the agricultural shows. As a youngster with a fascination for all things mechanical, I was mesmerised by the colourful lines of tractors; each having its own individual identity and distinctive livery – a visual treat that represented the very best that the British tractor industry had to offer.

And I could take it home with me – not the actual tractors (my father didn't have very deep pockets when it came to replacing farm machinery) – but the sales literature that related to it. By stuffing a carrier-bag with brochures I could at least relive the scene when I got home. The pile of brochures continued to grow as I visited more shows, but was eventually consigned to a cupboard and forgotten as I discovered other, albeit less ingenuous, attractions in my later teenage years.

Several years later I came across the brochures while clearing out the cupboard and my interest was reawakened. I began adding to the collection and what started out as a hobby became an obsession and eventually a business and even a profession. I divided my time between farming, trading in tractor literature and writing books on the subject.

In due course the journalism, historical research and literature business took precedence and farming became the loss-making hobby. I devoted my time to documenting the history of the British tractor industry – and what a story it is of mechanical achievement and human endeavour. Condensing two decades of that story into one volume hasn't been easy, but a least I knew how it needed to be illustrated.

The brochures issued by the British manufacturers encapsulate the ethos of the industry – the colour, the passion and the excitement. I've drawn heavily on my own collection sourcing images from sales literature, advertisements, instruction and parts books, but I've also been helped by a number of people. I'd like to thank Rory Day (Classic Tractor magazine), Brian Bell, Peter Longfoot, David Fenton, Peter Anderson, Richard Hayfield, John Goldup, Martyn Henderson, Ian Halstead, Malcolm Robinson and Jim Russell for rummaging through their collections to fill in the gaps; also Sean Philips (AT Graphics) for enhancing some of the illustrations.

Deciding what to put in and what to leave out has not been easy. I've tried to make the story as inclusive as possible, but documenting every single make and model would have been an impossible task. The major players are all there, and most of the minor manufacturers get at least a mention. The result is an overview of a magnificent industry that grew from almost nothing to become a global influ-

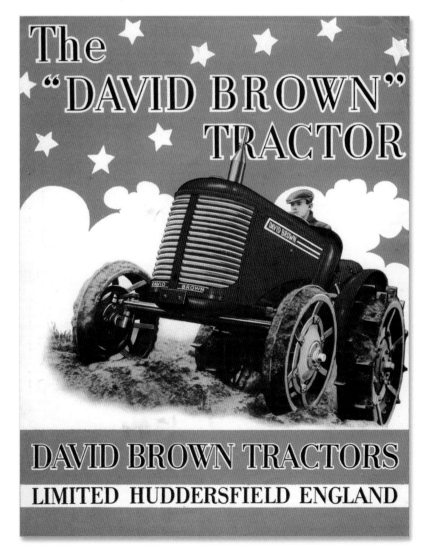

The "DAVID BROWN" TRACTOR

DAVID BROWN TRACTORS
LIMITED HUDDERSFIELD ENGLAND

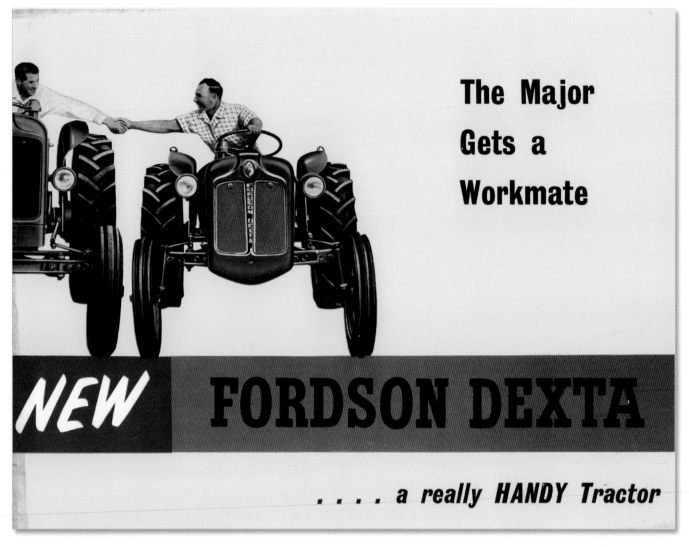

The Major
Gets a
Workmate

NEW FORDSON DEXTA

. . . . a really HANDY Tractor

ence in world agriculture.

The year 1945 has to be an obvious place to start because it represented the dawn of a new era for both the British tractor industry and agriculture in general as the country emerged from the dark days of the Second World War. There was a sea change in tractor development in the mid-1960s with a new and more modern breed of machines for world markets, so 1965 is the ideal cut-off point.

The new ranges from Ford and Massey Ferguson appeared at the end of 1964, while David Brown launched its 'white' tractors the following year. However, the Nuffield line didn't really change until 1968, and the last of the 'old guard' of International tractors wasn't swept away until the 1970s, so no dateline is ever going to be perfect. In places I've strayed outside the parameters, usually going backwards in time, in order to tell the complete story.

Sorting out the terminology for weights and measurements has been another problem, but I haven't

been too pedantic about this. Metrification was still several years away, so most figures are given in imperial because this was the system still in common usage during the period covered by the book. However, all rules are there to be broken.

In one of those anomalistic situations that only Britain can engender, several manufacturers preferred to give the bore and stroke of their engines in millimetres and the displacement in cubic centimetres or litres. To avoid confusion, I have followed their lead because these would be the terms that enthusiasts for any given make of tractor would expect to see and be most familiar with. Where I felt it was relevant, I have given the capacity in both cubic centimetres and cubic inches.

Dagenham operated a one-model policy for its tractor line until the Fordson Major got a workmate. The new Dexta model was launched in 1957 after Ford became fearful of the rising tide of grey Ferguson tractors that were beginning to populate British farms.

Stuart Gibbard
May 2013

BACKGROUND

Ford's wartime production programme at its Dagenham plant was immense and it included military trucks and tracked Bren-gun carriers. Between 1939 and 1945, Ford also managed to produce a massive 137,483 tractors, accounting for 85 percent of all the tractors on British farms.

The years between 1945 and 1965 represented a golden age for the British tractor industry with a plethora of new makes and models that fulfilled the needs of both home and export markets. To borrow a phrase that was much used by David Brown at the time, it was an era when Britain mechanised the world's farms.

The emergence of new manufacturers and factories was driven by the demand for greater agricultural mechanisation, but the makeup and rapid expansion of the British tractor industry was very much shaped by the events surrounding the Second World War. Prior to the war, the industry had become fragmented and was almost inconsequential as far as the global stage was concerned. Many of the British pioneer tractor manufacturers had fallen by the wayside in the 1920s as agriculture dropped into depression.

In 1932 there was just one model of wheeled tractor in production in Britain – the Marshall 18/30. The following year, the Fordson began to roll out of Dagenham and it wasn't long before thousands of Model N tractors began to flood onto British farms. But there wasn't much else on the market; the shortfall being made up by the large number of (often superior) tractors being imported from North America.

There simply wasn't the demand to warrant the

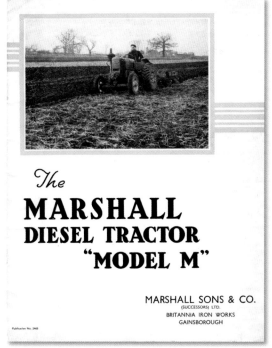

Marshall tried to keep its Model M tractor in production at Gainsborough during the Second World War, but was restricted by a large number of contracts for munitions work.

investment needed to stimulate increased tractor production. The amount of land in arable use, which had peaked at nearly 16 million acres at the end of the First World War, was less than 13 million acres by the end of the 1930s.

Harry Ferguson tried to interest farmers in a new system of mechanised agriculture, but his Type A tractor was dismissed as a novelty. Built for Ferguson by David Brown from 1936, it arrived in a frenzy of media speculation and then quietly disappeared just three years later.

The Second World War changed everything with the need to safeguard Britain's food supplies. The ploughing campaigns to bring more acres into arable production and the drive towards increased farm mechanisation as men were drafted into the armed forces led to a growing demand for tractors. During the conflict Britain's tractor population rose from 55,000 in 1939 to stand at 140,000 by D-Day in 1944.

Ford, which had been awarded the principal Ministry of Supply contract for the manufacture of tractors, rose to the challenge with production at Dagenham peaking at one tractor rolling off the line every 17 minutes 36 seconds. David Brown entered the fray after launching its first tractor in 1939, but the company was juggling lots of balls in the air with numerous government contracts in place so production of its new VAK1 model was limited. Production of Marshall's Model M tractor at Gainsborough was also curtailed by the company's munitions work.

Again, the American manufacturers had to step in and make up the deficit. On 11 March 1941, the Lend-Lease Act was passed by US Congress, giving President Franklin D Roosevelt the power to loan Britain and its Allies equipment and supplies from the USA with payment deferred until after the war. Under the agreement, Britain received around 30,000 wheeled tractors and 5,000 crawlers.

VE Day on 8 May 1945 was a time for celebration. However the return to peace was fraught with difficulties and Britain was facing a prolonged period of austerity with shortages of food, petrol and tobacco. Six years of war had seriously affected the global agricultural economy and trade. The situation was made more critical by a succession of droughts during 1945 in many of the main production areas leading to a worldwide shortage of grain at harvest time. After Clement Attlee's Labour government swept to power in July, bread rationing was introduced in Britain for the first time and remained in place for another two years.

Farmers now had to address a world food shortage that threatened at least a quarter of the

Harry Ferguson brought mechanised farming to the masses and his TE-20 tractor has been cited as the machine that finally replaced the horse. He introduced not just a new system of farming, but also a new way of selling tractors with extensive marketing campaigns, finance deals and an integrated dealer network offering after-sales service

entire population of the globe with starvation and disease. The battle for the land was far from over; in fact, it was probably only just beginning. The policy of livestock restoration was postponed in favour of ploughing up more grass for the growing of cereals in an attempt to alleviate the wheat shortage.

During the war, around 40,000 men had been lost from the farms to the armed forces or industry. Soon the Land Army girls and the prisoners of war would also leave the land and the shortage of

Crawlers were in short supply on the post-war UK market, but Fowler was one manufacturer that met the challenge of producing an all-British tracklayer. Its VF model, developed in conjunction with its sister firm, Marshall, was unveiled in 1947 with a single-cylinder diesel engine.

Nuffield was a newcomer to the market when its 'Universal' model was launched in 1948. The tractor was met with great acclaim and the organisation quickly became a major player in the British tractor industry with substantial sales both at home and abroad.

manpower would become critical. Now more than ever, machinery was needed to fight the renewed crusade for food production.

The major factor that led to the expansion of the British tractor industry was the decision made by

Marshall was one of the pioneers of diesel tractors, but its single-cylinder design probably outstayed its welcome. The Field Marshall Series 3 was already looking outdated at the time of its launch with more modern multi-cylinder diesel tractors appearing on the market.

the incoming US president, Harry S Truman, to terminate the Lend-Lease agreement, which happened unexpectedly and without warning in August 1945. There would be no more deferred payments, and with the country facing a severe dollar-shortage, the British government reacted quickly to place import restrictions on American wheeled tractors.

With no more tractors coming in from the USA, although crawlers were exempt from the restrictions, Britain now had to go it alone and stimulate home production. The demand was insatiable, but UK manufacturers rose to the challenge. Within just three years, the output of the industry had doubled its wartime peak.

The American manufacturers weren't going to be left out in the cold. Several got around the restrictions by establishing satellite production in the UK, which also gave them access to the Commonwealth's lucrative sterling markets. Before long the North American names of Allis-Chalmers, International Harvester, Massey-Harris and Minneapolis-Moline were manufacturing in the UK alongside major British newcomers such as David Brown and Nuffield.

Harry Ferguson also returned to the UK and his TE-20 tractor flipped the industry on its head with a completely new system of marketing, sales and on-farm service. The established firms, notably Ford and Marshall, soon realised that they had a fight on their hands to retain their market positions. But when it came down to building tractors to a price in volume production, Ford was unassailable.

The exigencies of war had restricted tractor development, but the years that followed were a time for change. Most tractors had spark-ignition engines running on petrol or a cheaper distillate such as paraffin or kerosene. The distillate had to be vaporised before it would burn, so the tractors were fitted with a vaporiser manifold that heated the fuel for efficient combustion.

Most major oil companies offered a special distillate tractor fuel known as vaporising oil. Shell and BP actually branded their fuel as Tractor Vaporising Oil, and the acronym TVO became the generic term for the distillate. Tractors were started on petrol with the changeover to TVO being made once the engine was warm.

The compression-ignition or diesel engine offered better economy, greater longevity and was more reliable, but it was also more complicated and costlier to build. Several manufacturers developed their own diesel engines, but a cost-effective alternative was to adopt one of the proven high-speed power units developed by Perkins of Peterborough. Most tractor firms were offering a diesel option by the early 1950s, and during the next 10 years the petrol/TVO engine all but disappeared from the market.

In 1945 most tractors were still supplied with a belt pulley to drive a threshing drum, but it was becoming an archaic feature as the combine took over harvesting duties on most farms. What farmers now wanted was a power take-off shaft to match the new breed of power-driven implements, and this soon became a standard feature on most tractors.

After the arrival of the Ferguson tractor most customers demanded a hydraulic lift and linkage for mounted implements. The Ferguson system of hydraulic draft control, which controlled the depth of the implement in work, was protected by patents so the other manufacturers could only offer a basic lift that went up, down or would hold at any position in between (position control). The lapse of certain Ferguson patents in the early 1960s saw many manufacturers add draft control to their specification list.

The pumps powering most hydraulic systems were driven from the power take-off (pto). If the driver depressed the clutch to halt the forward motion of the tractor, then the lift and pto would also stop working. Tractors fitted with engine-mounted hydraulic pumps didn't have this problem and offered what was known as 'live' hydraulics. On other tractors the introduction of a two-stage clutch, which allowed the power take-off to be controlled independently of the tractor's forward motion, gave both 'live' pto and 'live' hydraulics.

Other features that became norm during the period included electric starting and lighting, a greater number of transmission speeds and differential lock. This latter feature locked the differential so that the rear-axle shafts became a solid axle to prevent wheel-spin in soft or sticky conditions. Normal service was resumed automatically for turning on headland after the pedal was released.

The tractors evolved from a functional design with bolt-on bits into stylish machines with flowing lines and integrated components. Greater thought was given to operator comfort and safety with improved accessibility and ergonomic controls. In the 20 years between 1945 and 1965 the tractor changed dramatically from a mere replacement for the horse into a feature-laden motive powerhouse at the centre of a modern agricultural system.

Things would change even more dramatically in the next decade with the arrival of the so-called

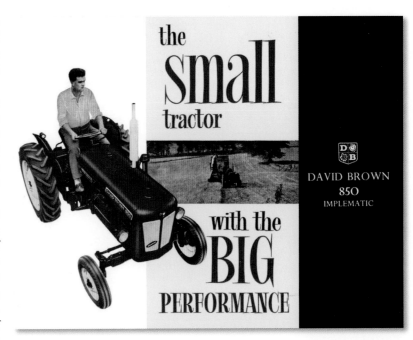

'second generation' of post-war tractors. The mid-1960s was a watershed period of tractor design with new and more modern machines offering sleeker styling, multiple-speed transmissions and more sophisticated hydraulic systems.

Most significantly the new ranges were homogonous products, produced as worldwide models for global markets. They lacked the character and pioneering spirit of what had gone before, and the golden age of the British tractor industry was over.

David Brown packed its tractors with novel features including high-speed direct-injection diesel engines, six-speed gearboxes and two-speed power take-off. The 850 Implematic model was introduced in 1960 with draft control hydraulics and a differential lock as standard.

Launched in 1961, the new International B-414 sported a modern appearance and its extensive list of features included 'Vary Touch' draft control hydraulics, an eight-speed gearbox, differential lock, disc brakes and 'live' power take-off. The power came from a new 40hp four-cylinder diesel engine fitted with the latest CAV rotary pump.

ALLIS-CHALMERS

Allis-Chalmers was one of several American tractor builders that established a manufacturing base in post-war Britain to circumvent import restrictions imposed because of dollar shortages. The Allis marque from Milwaukee had a tremendous following in the UK and a large number of A-C's 'Persian Orange' tractors had been imported under Lend-Lease during the Second World War.

Wartime sales were handled by a British subsidiary, the Allis-Chalmers Manufacturing Company, under the management of Mr H S Brayshaw with offices at Abbeydore in Herefordshire. The imports arrived via a British distribution depot that had been established in 1936 at Totton, near Southampton.

Between 1947 and 1949, some 2,000 Allis Model B tractor skid units (engines and transmissions) were shipped from Milwaukee to be assembled at Totton using locally-sourced wheels, tyres and electrical components. The tractor was

British Allis-Chalmers production had begun with the English Model B tractor. Some 2,000 of these were assembled at Totton between 1947 and 1949 using engines and transmissions shipped from Milwaukee. Wheels, tyres and electrical components were sourced in the UK.

supplied with the more powerful CE engine (as fitted to the American Model C tractor) and was fitted with an adjustable wide-front axle.

In February 1950, the Allis-Chalmers Manufacturing Company acquired the former Minneapolis-Moline factory at Essendine near Stamford. Production lines for both the Model B and a British version of the All-Crop 60 combine were laid down with the first English tractor engine, based on the CE power unit with a 3⅜in bore, being completed at Essendine on 13 November of that year.

The English B, with an EB prefix to its serial number and a price of £335, was now an all-British product. The engine was manufactured at Essendine with the final assembly still carried out at Totton. Production of the All-Crop 60 combine at the new factory began in early 1951 with a target of 500 machines for that year's harvest.

Essendine was now employing 400 staff under the leadership of the works manager, Mr C A Morris. A sales meeting was held at the factory in April 1953, which saw the launch of an English version of the Roto-Baler and an improved version of the EB tractor with a pan seat and the option of hydraulic three-point linkage. The following year, the British subsidiary was reorganised as Allis-Chalmers Great Britain Ltd with Mr E J Mercer as its general manager.

Assembly of the English Model B tractors was eventually moved entirely to Essendine, where they were built at a rate of about 100 per week. During 1954 a diesel version of the Model B, priced at £483 10s, was introduced using the Perkins P3 engine. Some of the very last EB tractors had four-speed gearboxes in readiness for the launch of the new D270 tractor.

The D270, which replaced the English Model B in July 1954, was essentially the same tractor with a four-speed gearbox, revised tinwork, improved linkage and more power. The D272, introduced in 1957, was yet another revamp of an ageing design and did nothing to improve Allis's

sales, which were struggling in the face of competition from the Massey Ferguson 35 and Fordson Dexta.

Work began on a new British tractor, which was designed 'in-house' with the project led by Essendine's chief engineer, Jack Eames. However, finances were tight because the company was negotiating the purchase of Jones Balers at Mold in Clwyd (finally acquired in 1961).

The new tractor, known as the ED-40 (English diesel 40hp), was launched in 1960. Designed on a shoestring with several features copied from the American D-14 model, it had a selective weight-transfer hydraulic system and an eight-speed gearbox. The tractor's four-cylinder 23C diesel engine was supplied by Standard-Triumph of Coventry.

Sales were disappointing: the ED-40 had inherited an engine with a reputation for poor starting and farmers were unimpressed with its basic hydraulic system. To address the problems with the hydraulics, a new system called Depthomatic Control was launched in December 1965, but it was too little too late.

The ED-40's new hydraulic system was complicated and the tractor was outclassed by its rivals. Production ended in March 1969, but stockpiles of unsold machines meant that the last tractor was not delivered until 1971. The model that had been expected to be Essendine's saviour became its downfall.

Allis-Chalmers had pinned its British hopes on the ED-40 but internal communications citing 'troublesome' hydraulics and an engine 'of questionable durability' suggested that its failure to establish worthwhile sales totals contributed to the disposal of A-C's UK farm machinery division to Bamfords of Uttoxeter in 1971.

In February 1950 Allis-Chalmers acquired the former Sale-Tilney factory at Essendine near Stamford. The first English tractor engine, based on the CE power unit with a 3⅜in bore, was built here on 13 November. Essendine was also home to production of the British All-Crop 60 combine and A-C Roto-Baler.

The Allis-Chalmers D270, which replaced the English Model B in July 1954, was essentially the same tractor with revised tinwork, improved linkage and more power. The petrol/paraffin version developed 22hp as opposed to the EB's 19hp. Again a diesel option was available using the 27hp Perkins P3(TA) engine.

An improved version of the Allis Model EB tractor with a pan seat and the option of hydraulic three-point linkage was launched in April 1953. During 1954 a diesel version was introduced with a three-cylinder Perkins P3 engine offered as an alternative to the four-cylinder petrol/TVO power unit (shown).

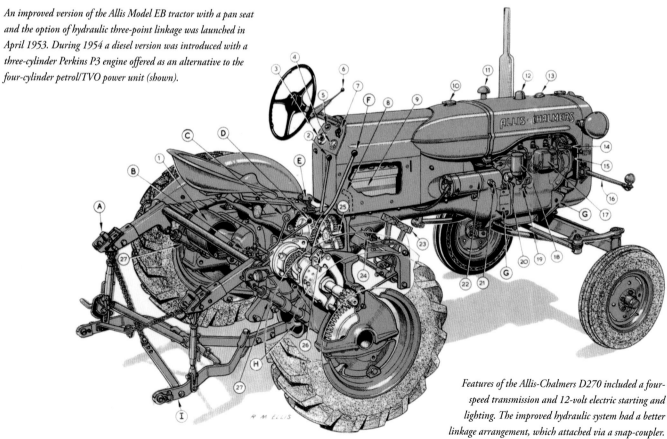

Features of the Allis-Chalmers D270 included a four-speed transmission and 12-volt electric starting and lighting. The improved hydraulic system had a better linkage arrangement, which attached via a snap-coupler.

FOR
BETTER LIVING
BETTER FARMING
MORE PROFIT

ALLIS-CHALMERS D272

The Allis-Chalmers D272 arrived in 1957 and promised much, however in reality it was only really a revamp of the earlier D270 with improved styling. The sheet-metal was bulkier, but beneath the tinwork there were few mechanical changes.

The D272 was offered with similar engine choices as the earlier models. The three-cylinder Perkins P3/144 diesel delivered 31hp, while the tried and trusted four-cylinder CE engine gave 30hp on petrol or 26hp when running on TVO.

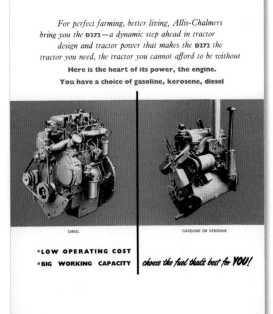

For perfect farming, better living, Allis-Chalmers bring you the **D272**—a dynamic step ahead in tractor design and tractor power that makes the **D272** the tractor you need, the tractor you cannot afford to be without

**Here is the heart of its power, the engine.
You have a choice of gasoline, kerosene, diesel**

DIESEL

GASOLINE OR KEROSINE

• **LOW OPERATING COST**
• **BIG WORKING CAPACITY** *choose the fuel that's best for YOU!*

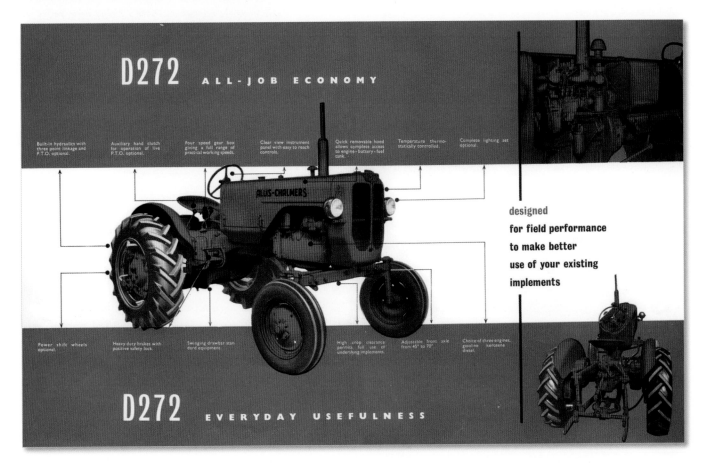

D272 ALL-JOB ECONOMY

Built-in hydraulics with three point linkage and P.T.O. optional.

Auxiliary hand clutch for operation of live P.T.O. optional.

Four speed gear box giving a full range of practical working speeds.

Clear view instrument panel with easy to reach controls.

Quick removable hood allows complete access to engine-battery-fuel tank.

Temperature thermostatically controlled.

Complete lighting set optional.

designed
**for field performance
to make better
use of your existing
implements**

Power shift wheels optional.

Heavy duty brakes with positive safety lock.

Swinging drawbar standard equipment.

High crop clearance permits full use of undersling implements.

Adjustable front axle from 45" to 70".

Choice of three engines. gasoline kerosene diesel.

D272 EVERYDAY USEFULNESS

The specification of the Allis-Chalmers D272 included a four-speed transmission, built-in hydraulics, heavy-duty independent brakes, a swinging drawbar and electric starting and lighting. An independent power take-off and PAVT (power-adjusted variable-tread) wheels were optional.

ALLIS-CHALMERS **MODEL D272 HIGH CLEARANCE TRACTOR**

ALLIS-CHALMERS GREAT BRITAIN LIMITED • ESSENDINE • STAMFORD • LINCOLNSHIRE • ENGLAND • TELEPHONE: STAMFORD 2471 • GRAMS: GYRATING, STAMFORD.

Variations on the D272 design included a 'High-Clearance' model giving more than 27in of under-axle clearance for specialist rowcrop operations. The tractor was ideal for cultivating vegetables or spraying fruit bushes. A special low orchard version of the D272 was also offered as Allis-Chalmers tried to find new markets for its products.

Allis-Chalmers' all-new British model, the ED-40 tractor, was unveiled at a dealer conference at Harrogate on 22 November 1960, followed by a public launch at that year's Smithfield Show. The initial list price was £610 for the standard tractor and £622 for the 'De-Luxe' model with a cushioned seat, a swinging drawbar and a tractormeter (combined rev counter and hour-meter).

The Allis ED-40 was powered by a 2.3-litre Standard 23C diesel engine, which featured the Comet indirect-injection system developed by Sir Harry Ricardo. A similar engine had until recently powered the Ferguson 35 tractor. The version fitted to the ED-40 developed 37hp running at 2,000rpm. With its indirect-injection system the engine was a poor starter from cold and was by no means the best power unit on the market

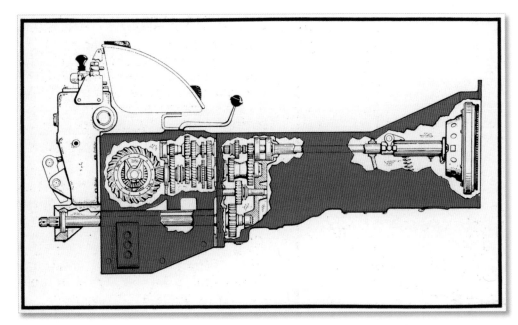

The ED-40's transmission was copied from the American Allis D-14 model. It was basically a four-speed gearbox with dual ranges giving eight-forward and two-reverse speeds. 'Live' power take-off with a separate hand clutch was also offered as an optional extra. Other options included a belt pulley, a differential lock, electric lighting and a swinging drawbar.

The New **ED·40**

Allis-Chalmers presents today's finest All-Duty Tractor...Handsome! Versatile! Economical!

ALL THE ADVANCED FEATURES

GREATER VERSATILITY

NEW SELECTIVE WEIGHT TRANSFER

The New ED-40 is the finest and most versatile all-duty Tractor in its class...the Tractor that has a place in every farming operation. The Tractor is the outcome of Allis-Chalmers world-wide experience. It brings you all the well-proved modern developments including the Allis-Chalmers <u>Selective Weight Transfer</u> which minimises wheel slip in the worst conditions.

In the ED-40 you have a farm proved 4-cylinder power unit; high and low transmission range giving 8 forward and 2 reverse speeds; 'live' hydraulic system with category 1 three-point linkage. Category 2 conversion set available as optional extra; depth control; adjustable front axle and rear wheels for convenient spacing; ideal clearance permitting the use of mid-mounted implements; controls and instrument panel placed for operator comfort and convenience.

Nothing of practical value has been overlooked, and the styling matches the up-to-date mechanical features. Notice the sleek, handsome, functional lines.

We urge you to examine the ED-40 for yourself at your nearest Allis-Chalmers Dealer.

'LIVE' HYDRAULIC LIFT
Engine mounted hydraulic pump. Separate oil reservoir for hydraulic system.

SMOOTH RUNNING POWER UNIT
4-cylinder Diesel Engine for smooth running operation— good lugging characteristics.

FULL RANGE TRANSMISSION
High and low range system giving a total of 8 forward and 2 reverse speeds—and correct P.T.O. speed. A speed for every job.

CONVENIENT CONTROLS
Controls and instrument panel designed for operator comfort. Hand throttle and hydraulic control levers mounted on steering column.

ADJUSTABLE FRONT AXLE
Front and Rear choice of Wheel Widths from 48" to 72" in 4 inch steps.

BIG TRACTION INCREASE
Selective Weight Transfer gives maximum traction in bad conditions without affecting implement working depth.

CROP CLEARANCE
The traditional Allis-Chalmers crop clearance permits use of mid mounted implements.

The ED-40's selective weight-transfer hydraulic system incorporated a category 1 and 2 three-point linkage and had an adjustable stop to act as a form of depth control by limiting the downward movement of the linkage. An accumulator valve in the system could be set to exert a lifting effort on the implement to transfer weight onto the tractor's rear wheels. The hydraulic lift lever was mounted on the column under the steering wheel opposite the throttle lever. The system was a crude attempt at controlling the depth of the implement because automatic draft control was still covered by Ferguson patents.

BMB

BMB was the acronym for the British Motor Boat Manufacturing Company, which was founded in the 1930s by Jack Shillan. As well as making its own Rytecraft boats, the company imported small marine power units from the USA, including Evinrude and Elto outboard motors and Solo inboard engines. BMB's offices were in London at Britannia House in Ampton Street near Kings Cross.

Shillan had started out as a designer of fairground rides and had established connections in the USA while exhibiting his Rocket Speedway at Dallas and New York's World's Fair. BMB built its first motor vehicle, the Rytecraft Scootacar, in 1934. Designed by Shillan, it was a micro-car based on a fairground dodgem fitted with a single-cylinder Villiers engine.

In the early 1930s Shillan was joined by Charles Henry Harrison, a keen motorcyclist and prominent powerboat racer. Harrison, who had served his apprenticeship with J A Prestwich Industries Ltd (manufacturers of JAP engines) was a skilled engineer in his own right. Appointed BMB's technical director, he developed the company's Britannia outboard motor.

Harrison also had an interest in horticultural machinery and persuaded Shillan to become an agent for two-wheel garden tractors produced in the USA by the Simplicity Manufacturing Company of Port Washington, Wisconsin. The

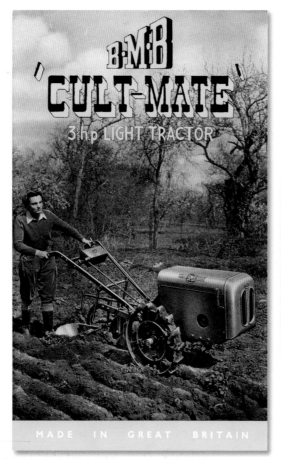

Production of BMB's two-wheel garden tractors was transferred to Crossens in 1949 after the range was acquired by Brockhouse Engineering (Southport) Ltd. The Cult-Mate was powered by a BSA engine – an air-cooled single-cylinder unit rated at 3½hp. The machine was available with various attachments. When fitted with an 8in plough, it would turn over up to 1½ acres per day.

The BMB Hoe-Mate was built at Crossens with a Brockhouse 'Spryt' air-cooled engine. This single-cylinder two-stroke unit developed 1¾hp and the petrol consumption was less than one pint per hour. Ideal for cultivating in restricted areas, the machine's V-belt transmission gave operating speeds of 1-2½mph.

Simplicity machines were initially sold as the BMB 'Light Tractor', but the range was later extended to include the BMB Plow-Mate and Cult-Mate. The Plow-Mate was based on the Simplicity Model C garden tractor fitted with a 6hp JAP engine. The Cult-Mate was powered by a 3hp JAP engine.

In 1938 Shillan and Harrison went their separate ways. Harrison took over the British Anzani Engineering Company and introduced its Iron Horse tractor. His former partner established Shillan's Engineering with manufacturing facilities in Oxfordshire at Crouch Street in Banbury.

The outbreak of war curtailed the import of Simplicity machines so Shillan's Engineering began making its own components to continue production of the Plow-Mate and Cult-Mate. It also introduced a garden tractor of its own design: the Hoe-Mate with a 1⅓hp JAP engine.

Despite wartime shortages, limited production of BMB's pedestrian-controlled machines continued at Banbury until about 1948. During 1949, the Agricultural Division of the British Motor Boat Manufacturing Company was still advertising the Hoe-Mate for £55, the Cult-Mate for £85 and the Plow-Mate for £129 10s, but a deal had been struck for the BMB tractor line to be sold to Brockhouse Engineering (Southport) Ltd.

Brockhouse operated from the former Vulcan lorry factory at Crossens near Southport. The company had become involved with tractors during the Second World War after it developed a torque-converter transmission that was fitted to a number of Fordsons for the Royal Navy's Fleet Air Arm.

Production of the BMB 'Light Tractors' continued almost unchanged at Crossens. The only amendment to the specification was that the Cult-Mate now had a 3½hp BSA engine and the Hoe-Mate was fitted with Brockhouse's 1¾hp 'Spryt' power unit. However Brockhouse had ambitious plans to capture a larger share of the market with a conventional four-wheel tractor.

The four-wheel tractor was still a lightweight machine aimed primarily at the smallholder and market gardener. Following rigorous testing it was launched at the 1950 Royal Show as the BMB President. Priced at £239 it was powered by an 8hp Morris car engine mated to a three-speed transmission.

The President was an unprecedented success and a number were exported with significant sales to Ceylon and Turkey. Production was a drop in the ocean compared to the all-conquering Ferguson, but for a time it was the TE-20's main competitor and sales continued to rise until 1954.

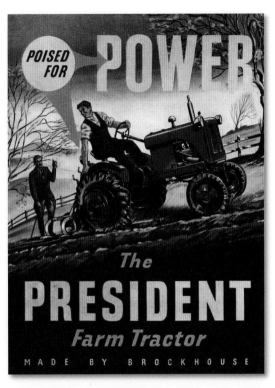

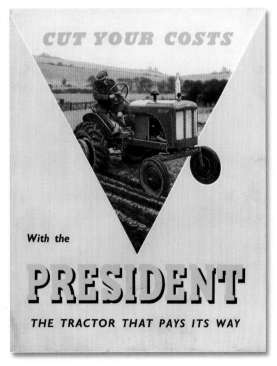

During 1954 vineyard and orchard versions of the President were introduced, but by this time the UK market for small tractors had become oversaturated. Sales began to decline and in 1956 Brockhouse took the decision to end all tractor production and concentrate on its torque-converter transmissions.

Launched in 1950, the BMB President was fitted with an 8-10hp Morris car engine. This economical four-cylinder power unit was fitted with a Solex updraught carburettor for running on petrol, but could be ordered with an additional vaporiser for burning TVO. The three-speed transmission gave speeds of 1.8mph, 3.4mph and 8.3mph with 2.9mph in reverse. Electric starting and lighting using 6-volt equipment was later changed to 12-volt.

The BMB President was aimed at smallholders and market gardeners or larger farmers wanting a spare tractor as a handy runabout. The concept was a lightweight machine for light operations with the emphasis on low running costs. However sales were starting to decline by 1954 when the price of the tractor had risen to £293.

BRISTOL

The Bristol tractor was conceived in the early 1930s as a project developed by Roadless Traction Ltd of Hounslow to find an application for its rubber-jointed tracks. The aim was to provide a lightweight crawler for cultivating market gardens and orchards or for ground-care work on golf courses and in parks.

Roadless had two prototypes running by 1932 when it entered into an agreement for the tractor to be built by the motorcycle manufacturers, Douglas Motors. Douglas's factory was at Kingswood on the outskirts of Bristol – hence the name. The plan was for the crawler to be fitted with Douglas's own flat-twin engine, but just one

'BRISTOL' HAULING 2 FURROW RANSOME "MOTRAC" PLOUGH

The Bristol TRACTOR

THE NEW IMPROVED

BRISTOL TRACTOR

A TRULY REMARKABLE TRACTOR

100% BRITISH IN DESIGN MATERIAL LABOUR AND CAPITAL

The early Bristol tractor was fitted with rubber-jointed tracks supplied by Roadless and had tiller-controlled clutch-and-brake steering. The first 60 built by Bristol Tractors Ltd during 1933 were fitted with V-twin British Anzani engines. The gearbox gave three forward speeds and reverse.

The 'New Improved' Bristol tractor was launched in 1937 with a price of £195. The capacity of the Jowett flat-twin power unit had been upped to 946cc and the three-speed gearbox gave forward speeds of 1.66mph, 2.5mph and 4.9mph. Soon afterwards Bristol offered another Jowett engine, a flat-four 1166cc 10hp unit.

The Bristol '20' was announced in June 1948 with a 2,197cc Austin engine that gave 22hp at a governed speed of 1,500rpm. The engine was modified to run on TVO and changes were made to the sump to prevent oil starvation to the engine bearings when the tractor was operated on steep inclines. The foot-operated 9in Borg & Beck clutch could be operated from the rear of the tractor by a lever-operated cable to assist the driver when coupling up to implements. The gearbox was still a three-speed, single-reverse unit.

tractor had been built before the company went into receivership.

In 1933, Roadless helped finance a new concern, Bristol Tractors Ltd, to build the crawler from premises at Sunbeam Road in Willesden using a V-twin British Anzani engine. This was later changed to a flat-twin sourced from Jowett Cars Ltd of Idle in Bradford with a Coventry-Victor diesel offered as an alternative.

The new company still didn't prosper – the problem being the prohibitive royalties it had to pay Roadless for the design – and was again running into financial difficulties. On 4 July 1935 Bristol Tractors Ltd was sold to William Jowett of Jowett Cars and production was moved to Idle. The buyout was almost certainly an attempt by Jowett to recoup some of the money he was owed for engines.

Bristol flourished under Jowett's ownership. A 'New Improved' model was launched in 1937 and production continued using both Jowett flat-twin and flat-four petrol engines. The Second World War saw Jowett power units in great demand for fire pumps and the company was left with virtually

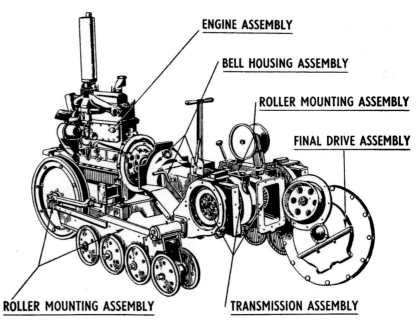

ENGINE ASSEMBLY

BELL HOUSING ASSEMBLY

ROLLER MOUNTING ASSEMBLY

FINAL DRIVE ASSEMBLY

ROLLER MOUNTING ASSEMBLY

TRANSMISSION ASSEMBLY

The Bristol '20' tractor's main components: the bell-housing was specially designed to allow the Austin engine to bolt to the transmission case without the need for underbelly or side-rail supports. Each steering clutch was operated by a separate lever and an independent foot pedal operated each steering brake. The track frames were also greatly improved and incorporated three bottom rollers.

The tracks fitted to the Bristol '20' were now manufactured in-house at Earby following the termination of the agreement with Roadless on 1 July 1946. The '20' was designed to be fitted with three-point linkage, which could be held rigid by the use of stabiliser bars to provide a drawbar for draught implements.

ADJUSTABLE DRAWBAR FOR DRAUGHT IMPLEMENTS

THE BRISTOL '20'

THE TRU-TRAC PLOUGH
(Patented in all countries)
KEEPS ALL FURROWS EVEN WIDTH

Ploughing to match standards with every furrow of even width comes almost automatically to the new BRISTOL '20'. Hitherto, a disadvantage of any crawler tractor has been the difficulty of ploughing a furrow of even width. Crawlers ride with both tracks on the land—and the plough's side draught has made the tractor difficult to steer.

All that is done away with by this unique patented BRISTOL feature. The plough is unit-attached, and side draught is automatically corrected by a guide wheel running against the land side of the furrow. Provided that the first furrow of each bout is opened up accurately, the BRISTOL Plough does the rest.

Illustration on the right shows frontal view of plough at work

no spare engines for its tractors. In 1942 an agreement was reached for Bristol to be supplied with four-cylinder Austin engines from Longbridge.

In 1945 the Jowett family sold Jowett Cars Ltd and its Idle factory. Bristol crawler production was relocated to Earby, near Colne in Lancashire. William Jowett's son, Clarence W Jowett, was now running the tractor business as joint managing director with his father. A new model, the Bristol '20', was announced on 1 June 1948.

The Bristol '20' was a great improvement on what had gone before. The TVO engine, rated at 22hp, was derived from the power unit for the Austin 16 car. The gearbox gave three speeds and the tracks, which were still rubber-jointed, were now built in-house at Earby.

Successive designs brought even greater improvements as the Bristol tractor was transformed from a lightweight machine for market gardeners into a proper crawler capable of true agricultural or industrial applications. In 1952, the '20' was replaced by the Bristol '22' with four bottom rollers and improved tracks. A Perkins P3(TA) diesel option was offered the following year.

The Bristol '25' of 1955 was the first of the company's crawlers to be offered with conventional pin-and-bush tracks. The Austin TVO engine was dropped with the arrival of the Bristol Series D tractor in 1959, which was only available with the Perkins P3/144 diesel power unit.

In 1961 the Jowett family relinquished control of Bristol Tractors Ltd to H A Saunders. Clarence Jowett stayed on as a director, manufacture remained at Earby and a new sales company, Bristol-Saunders Sales Ltd, was established in Worcester.

The Bristol Taurus, powered by a Perkins 3.152 engine developing 44hp, was launched in 1964.

A two-furrow plough was specially built to accompany the linkage fitted to the Bristol '20', but the company hadn't solved the problem of how to steer a tracklayer when so equipped. Much was made in the sales literature of this 'Tru-Trac' plough being fitted with a guide wheel that ran against the furrow wall and kept the front furrow at the correct width; the tractor, of course, was running on the land. It was claimed that the guide wheel also prevented the inevitable side-draught being transmitted to the tractor during steering. The literature was very careful to state that 'provided the first furrow of each bout is opened accurately' the Bristol plough did the rest. What it was trying to say was that if the furrow was dead straight, then the tractor and plough would work; if not, then any attempts to steer went out the window!

The new tractor was marketed with various industrial attachments including a front loader. However the writing was now on the wall for Bristol's future. Compact wheeled tractors had captured the orchard and market garden sales, and Bristol's other key markets were being eroded. The construction industry was increasingly turning to wheeled backhoe-loaders from firms such as JCB and others.

On 2 January 1970 it was announced that the Thomas W Ward Group was taking over production of the Taurus and incorporating it into its Track-Marshall range. Production was transferred to Marshall's factory at Gainsborough and the Taurus loading-shovel, the only product that could offer any real sales potential, became the Track-Marshall 1100.

THE NEW BRISTOL '20' ORCHARD MODEL

The Bristol '22', launched at the 1952 Royal Show, had a four-roller track frame that incorporated a conventional spring-release mechanism. With the lengthened track frame came, for the first time on a Bristol tractor, a top roller. The tracks were still rubber-jointed, but the links were a combination of fabricated steel and forgings. From 1953 the Bristol '22' was offered with a 23hp three-cylinder Perkins P3(TA) engine as a diesel alternative to the Austin petrol/TVO unit. This is the wide-gauge version of the '22'.

The Bristol '20' was also produced as an orchard model with enclosed fenders to prevent the tracks damaging overhanging branches or young saplings. With an overall width of just over 3ft and a height of less than 4ft it was ideal for this type of work.

Continual development saw the arrival the Bristol '25' in 1955 – the first of the company's models to use conventional steel pin-and-bush tracks. However the '25' only had three bottom rollers, but with larger spaces between them; no doubt done on the grounds of cost – a perfect example of the penny-pinching that typified most British engineering products as the 1960s approached.

The Bristol Series D tractor of 1959 was only available with the Perkins P3/144 diesel engine, which developed 32hp. The Series D featured lengthened track frames to accommodate four bottom rollers while still retaining the wider spacings introduced on the previous '25' model.

The 1964 Bristol Taurus was powered by the 44 bhp Perkins 3.152 engine. The previous three-speed gearbox was finally updated to a six-forward and four-reverse unit. The tractor was given a more modern appearance with greatly improved operator comfort. The loading-shovel version offered the most sales potential.

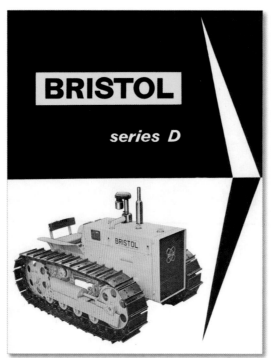

The D33 (33in gauge) version of the Bristol Series D was designed for orchards and vineyards. Equipment included track guards, hydraulic lift, three-point linkage, power take-off, belt pulley and lighting.

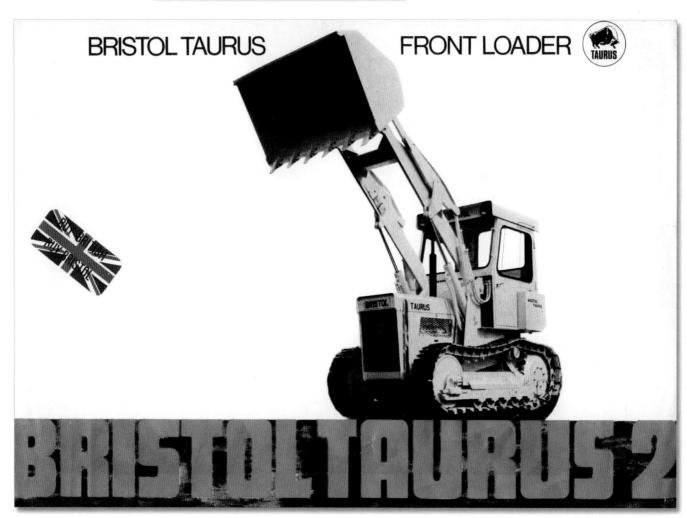

COUNTY

ounty, based at Fleet in Hampshire, almost got into the tractor market by default. County Commercial Cars Ltd, as its name suggests, was established to manufacture lorry conversions and vehicle bodies. Founded in 1929 by two brothers, Ernest and Percy Tapp, it had no connection with agriculture prior to the Second World War. During the war, County was involved in a massive production run for six-wheel versions of Ford trucks for military use. Its vital war work also included the development of a two-man tank.

The end of wartime production left a big gap in County's business. It continued to build truck conversions, but on a much smaller scale. New opportunities came in the form of orders for high-clearance spraying machines and narrow-gauge crawler tractors for Pest Control of Cambridge. Standard-gauge crawlers followed heralding a change of direction for the company.

The crawlers, which were based on the Fordson

E27N Major skid-unit, were developed jointly by Ernest Tapp and County's chief engineer, Joe Davey. Ernest came from an engineering background while his brother, Percy, was the businessman with a sharp commercial mind. Initially the tractors were only thought of as a stop-gap product until the truck business picked up again. In the beginning there was no real tractor assembly line at Fleet and some of the manufacture was subcontracted out to Kennedy & Kempe, suppliers of grain driers and wheel strakes at Longparish near Andover.

County now found itself on unfamiliar ground. The company had traditionally been a product-led manufacturing concern – developing and building for third-parties (usually Ford) who had handled the sales and marketing. The crawler was County's own product and it had to do the selling. The company managed to make the transition and skilfully handled the marketing to the point where home and export sales of the tractor soon eclipsed all the truck business.

Sales of the crawler, which was modified to take the new Fordson E1A Major skid-unit in late 1951, went from strength to strength. Agricultural, industrial and low ground-pressure versions were produced and the tractors were exported as far afield as the West Indies – the sugar-cane industry being one of County's largest customers.

In 1954 County received a request from sugar-cane growers in Puerto Rica to supply a wheeled tractor that had the performance of a crawler in the field. This resulted in the Four-Drive; essentially a crawler on rubber tyres with the front wheels chain-driven from sprockets on the rear axle. The tractor sold well in the West Indies, but enjoyed only limited success on the home market.

The Four-Drive highlighted the potential in terms of performance of having four equal-size driven wheels. Taking the concept one step further, County launched its first four-wheel drive tractor with conventional front-wheel steering in 1961. Designated the Super-4, it introduced a ground-breaking four-wheel drive system that was to feature on all future County tractors.

The County Full Track crawler, based on the Fordson E27N Major, went into production in 1949 at the rate of 10 machines per week. Early examples had solid pressed-steel front idlers. The four-cylinder side-valve petrol/TVO Fordson engine lacked power and its outdated gravity-fed lubrication system gave problems when the tractor was working on slopes. Many farmers preferred the optional Perkins P6 diesel engine, which was more refined, more powerful though more expensive.

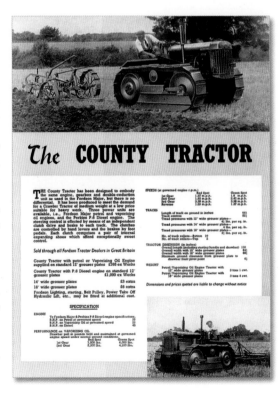

The County Full Track had a unique steering mechanism operated by internal-expanding Girling shoes enclosed in a brake drum. Pulling on either steering lever released the internal shoes from the drum, disengaging drive to the appropriate track. The heavier cast front idlers with spoked centres were fitted from 1950.

The Super-4 was based on the Fordson Super Major with the power to the front wheels being transmitted by twin propeller-shafts driven by bevel gears off the Fordson bull-pinion shafts. The advantage of the system, which was conceived by Joe Davey, was that it kept the tractor's centre-of-gravity low and the standard differential would operate on all four wheels. A six-cylinder version, the Super-6, appeared in 1962.

The Super-4 and Super-6 pushed County into volume production and the firm expanded into a new factory complex across the road from the original site. The crawlers were eventually phased out, but the company's other projects included the Hi-Drive high-clearance tractor and an industrial version of the Fordson Dexta.

Ernest and Percy Tapp were now taking a back seat. Ernest's eldest son, Geoffrey, and Percy's son, Raymond, were appointed as joint managing directors. They were joined by Geoffrey's younger brother, David, as engineering liaison and technical director.

The County range was revised to embrace the new Ford models launched in late 1964. Production peaked in 1977 when the company's annual turnover reached £18 million, but by 1980 world recession was hitting the firm's important export trade.

The final blow came in 1981 when Ford announced that it was introducing four-wheel drive versions of its own tractors. Two years later, in February 1983, County Commercial Cars Ltd went into receivership.

Following the launch of the new E1A version of the Fordson Major in November 1951, the County Full Track was redesigned to suit the new skid unit. The new crawler was designated Model Z and very little was changed apart from the adoption of the new engine and six-speed transmission. Most customers ordered the crawler with the superb new 40hp Fordson diesel engine. Although petrol and TVO options were still available, they were rarely specified.

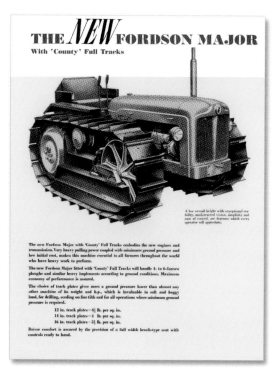

The County Mark lll industrial crawler was introduced in 1954. At the same time the agricultural Model Z became known as the Mark ll. Attachments for the industrial crawler included a Bray hydraulic angledozer. Problems with stress fractures on the Mark lll led to the introduction of the strengthened Mark IV in 1956 with eight-stud rear axles in heavy-duty cast-steel housings.

THE **County** *Ploughman*

51.8 B.H.P. diesel Crawler for Agriculture

Designed especially for agricultural use the County Ploughman combines an exceptionally high performance with economy of operation. This is achieved by the highly efficient track and transmission design which allows the astounding output of the Fordson Power Major engine to be utilized to the full.

Correct balance of power and weight gives the Ploughman a performance unsurpassed in its class.

Steering is by independent clutches and brakes to each side. Fingerlight County multiplate steering clutches allow maximum manoeuvrability for turning at tight headlands with minimum driver fatigue.

Roller bush tracks, a unique County feature, give longer life than ever before, especially on abrasive soils.

The County Ploughman combines all these advantages with the amazing economy and long life of the Fordson Power Major diesel engine to give better value than any other agricultural crawler.

The County Ploughman was introduced in 1957 to replace the agricultural Mark ll crawler. Following the launch of the Fordson Power Major skid unit in 1958, it became known as the Ploughman P50 and was rated at 51.8hp.

The County Ploughman was fitted with improved roller-bush tracks and had the option of multi-plate steering clutches. Features included an extended air intake and a cast guard to protect the radiator.

County CD-50

ENGINE: 51.8 B.H.P. Fordson Power Major Diesel.

TRANSMISSION: Through Borg and Beck 13" Heavy Duty Clutch and 5 forward, 2 reverse speed gearbox.

STEERING CLUTCHES: Multiplate, self adjusting.

TRACKS: 'County' special roller bush for Long Life.

ANCILLARY EQUIPMENT: Dozers, Winches, Toolbars, Sideboom Cranes.

And supported by a World Wide Sales and Service Organization.

Manufactured by
COUNTY COMMERCIAL CARS LTD.
FLEET, HANTS

Telephone: FLEET 1155   Cables: COUNTY FLEET TELEX

The CD50, introduced in 1959 to replace the Mark IV tractor, was the ultimate version of County's industrial crawler. A quality machine designed for heavy-duty applications, it was available with a wide range of ancillary equipment. The sister machine to the agricultural Ploughman model, the CD50 was fitted with the same 51.8hp engine from the Fordson Power Major.

ROLLER BUSH TRACKS
Additional free rolling bushes encircling the fixed bushes give increased life to Tracks and Sprockets.

TRACK ROLLERS

Steering clutches positioned outside the transmission housing make maintenance easier and cheaper. Steering brakes are of the external contracting band type and can be removed and replaced without interference to the steering clutches.

The County CD50 boasted roller-bush tracks and multi-plate steering clutches as standard. Both features were a great improvement on the earlier models: the steering clutches were self-adjusting and required less maintenance, while the roller-bushes were more hard-wearing and gave longer life to the tracks and sprockets.

the County Ploughman 55

- 55 B.H.P. engine for greater pulling power
- Heavy-duty transmission for longer life
- Cast sprocket and roller bush tracks to reduce maintenance costs
- Multiplate steering clutches for ease of control
- Luxury seat to better driver's comfort
- Two headlamps and one rear ploughing lamp, as standard

The County P55 Ploughman was the final version of County's agricultural crawlers. Introduced in 1960 it was based on the Fordson Super Major, but was fitted with an up-rated 55hp industrial version of the tractor engine. The P55 was finished in the same yellow colour scheme as the industrial crawlers.

The new "FOURDRIVE"

40.5 H.P. (BRAKE)   34.3 H.P. (DRAWBAR)

7,750 lbs. MAX. SUSTAINED DRAWBAR PULL

COUNTY TRACTOR

Manufactured by
COUNTY COMMERCIAL CARS LTD., Fleet, Hants.
Telephone No. FLEET 1155 (4 lines)

Introduced in 1954, the Four-Drive was essentially a County crawler on rubber tyres. The tractor had four driven wheels; the front wheels being chain-driven from sprockets on the rear axle via articulated chain-cases. The crawler's expanding-shoe steering system was retained, and the machine was skid-steered by relying on the flex in the tyre-walls to slew the tractor round. The Four-Drive met the needs of the sugar-cane industry, but home-market sales were disappointing.

SUPER MAJOR/
COUNTY SUPER 4

*The Super 4 has many features that make
it attractive for work under extremely
difficult conditions.*

★ Four wheel drive with interchangeable equal-size wheels.
★ Wide choice of wheel and tyre
equipment.
★ Only one differential; cuts out
wheel spin and fight between
back and front.
★ Steering brakes operate on all
four wheels.
★ 18 ft. turning circle.
★ Full power available on front
wheels—no slip clutch.
★ Power assisted steering,
standard.
★ Front axle positioned for
maximum weight distribution
and traction.
★ Full range of Fordson hydraulic lift linkage and equipment
can be fitted.
★ Maximum wheel grip at all
times means lower fuel consumption and less tyre wear.

*The Super-4's rugged front-axle improved stability and
added weight to the front wheels to increase traction. The
tractor had a low centre-of-gravity with the advantage
that the twin propeller-shafts meant that the brakes and
differential lock operated on all four wheels. The Super-4
was priced at £1,470.*

County
SUPER – 4

DESIGNED FOR WORLD FARMING

*The County Super-4, based on the Fordson Super Major, was
launched in 1961. It was a conventional four-wheel drive
tractor with four equal-size wheels and front-wheel steering.
The twin propeller-shafts – one to each front hub – were
driven by bevel gears off the tractor's bull-pinion shafts. The
design made full use of proprietary Ford parts. The front hubs
contained Fordson Dexta crown-wheels with modified
pinions, while the propeller-shafts and universal joints came
from a Ford Thames Trader truck. This reduced the dealers'
stock inventories, simplified servicing and cut the cost of
production at a stroke.*

County
SUPER

*The County Super-6 was a six-cylinder version of the Super-4
with 95hp available from its Ford 590E engine. The tractor was
launched in 1962 with a price tag of £1,950. The following year
the Super-6 was given a styling makeover with a fibreglass bonnet
and a new and protruding front cowl. The restyling was done to
emphasise the difference between the six-cylinder model and its
four-cylinder Super-4 counterpart.*

95 BHP GROSS FOUR WHEEL DRIVE TRACTOR

Four large Wheels
Four Wheel Braking
Wheel adjustment
Choice of Wheels and Tyres
Full ground clearance
Power assisted Steering

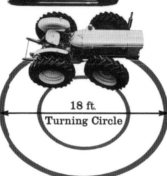

18 ft. Turning Circle

Heavy Duty Rear Linkage
Heavy Duty Gearbox
Heavy Duty Clutch
Heavy Duty Rear Transmission
Protected Sump
Rest-O-Ride Seat

No other Tractor has all these features

Full Torque Front Axle
Single Differential
Differential Lock on all wheels
Correct weight balance
Front Towing Eye

Big Tractor performance Small Tractor versatility

To cope with the extra power, the County Super-6 was fitted with a strengthened gearbox and clutch. Heavy-duty linkage, power steering and a sprung Rest-O-Ride seat complete the specification. The tractor remained in production until 1965.

Developed for the sugar-cane industry in the West Indies, the County Hi-Drive was launched in 1958. A new axle gave 30in ground clearance, and the rear axle was raised using drop-casings with a vertical train of three gears. Hi-Drive versions of the Fordson Diesel Major, Power Major and Super Major (shown) were built.

HIGH CLEARANCE TRACTOR

The high clearance version of the Super Major by 'County' gives a crop clearance of 30 in. overall. It has a normal drive to short axle shafts to a train of three gears to a stub axle for wheel fitment 13½ in. below normal size.

The front suspension is centrally pivoted on the normal adjustable front axle but of very rigid construction with an overall ground clearance of 30 in.

The drawbar assembly is of rugged construction with two towing heights; either 33 in. or 17 in. from the ground. It has a reversible jaw to give horizontal coupling in either position and normal 3-point linkage can be fitted. Front and rear tracks are adjustable.

The high clearance of 30 in. overall can clearly be seen from this view.

DAVID BROWN

Of all the companies extant during the period covered by this book, David Brown was probably the most prolific in terms of models produced. It was by no means the largest manufacturer and its output was undoubtedly eclipsed by that of Ford at Dagenham and Ferguson/MF at Coventry. But DB was the little company with big ideas, and the bewildering array of different models it launched between 1945 and 1965 can only be described as overwhelming.

David Brown was first and foremost a gear manufacturer with roots dating back to the mid-nineteenth century. The man with the vision to propel the organisation into tractor building was the founder's grandson, who was also called David Brown. In 1936, David Brown 'the younger', as he was known by some of the older employees at the company's Park Works gear factory in Huddersfield, entered into an agreement to build Harry Ferguson's Type A tractor.

The venture was short-lived and at times acrimonious, ending in 1939 after Ferguson formed a new partnership with Ford to manufacture tractors in the USA. However it did give young David (later Sir David) Brown a taste for tractor production. In 1939 David Brown Tractors Ltd was formed to build a new model at a former cotton mill in nearby Meltham.

Painted in what would become DB's trademark colour of 'Hunting Pink', the new David Brown tractor (later designated VAK1) was modern in appearance and had a four-cylinder overhead-valve petrol/TVO engine mated to a four-speed gearbox. The exigencies of war limited production as the Meltham Mills factory became involved in making tank gearboxes and aero gears, but it was sufficient to secure David Brown's future as a mainstream tractor manufacturer.

Minor improvements saw the VAK1 upgraded into the VAK1/A model in 1945. More radical changes, including the introduction of a multi-piece mainframe, resulted in the VAK1/C – the famous Cropmaster – which was built from 1947-53 and enjoyed a phenomenal production run of nearly 60,000 tractors sold worldwide. Variations on the Cropmaster theme included diesel, narrow, industrial and prairie variants, as well as the more powerful Super Cropmaster.

The first tractor to be built at Meltham under the David Brown name was launched in 1939. It was later designated VAK1 (Vehicle Agricultural Kerosene) to differentiate it from the industrial models the company produced for the RAF during the Second World War. Although DB's facilities were primarily tied up with defence contracts, it still managed to produce more than 5,000 VAK1 tractors.

The general layout of the VAK1 tractor set the design of all future David Brown models with the mainframe forming a horizontal joint to which the engine and transmission were bolted. This simplified servicing and overhauls because the main assemblies could be removed without splitting the tractor or disturbing other components. The four-cylinder overhead-valve power unit was derived from a Bedford truck engine. The four-speed gearbox incorporated the spiral-bevel wheel and differential. The optional U36 power lift was introduced in 1941.

The Cropmaster's intended replacement – designated VAK3 – was stillborn, but a spin-off from the project was the Trackmaster crawler (TAK3), which was introduced in 1949. Another development of the VAK3 project was a six-cylinder wheeled tractor – the VAD6 Cropmaster 50 of 1951.

David Brown had a small and highly skilled engineering team, headed-up by its technical director, Herbert Ashfield, and chief engineer, Charles Hull. Both were truly inventive engineers and they made their engineering budget go a long way as the company quickly expanded its tractor range, ensuring that it lived up to its motto of mechanising the world's farms.

The early 1950s line-up included the 25, 25D, 30C, 30D and 50D wheeled tractors; the 30T, 30TD and 50TD crawlers; and a whole host of industrial models. David Brown had built aircraft-towing tractors for the RAF during the Second World War and this association continued into peacetime with a number of specialist models for both military and civilian use.

Many of the features taken for granted on tractors by the 1950s, such as the turnbuckle top-link and dished wheel-centres for altering track width, were all David Brown 'firsts'. The company also pioneered high-speed direct-injection diesel engines, six-speed gearboxes and the two-speed power take-off.

Perhaps the most exciting development of this period was the introduction of the innovative 2D rowcrop tractor with its ground-breaking air-operated lift. The company also diversified into the manufacture of farm machinery after purchasing the Lancashire firm of Harrison, McGregor & Guest Ltd and its Albion range of implements in 1955.

David Brown now had the largest tractor range in Britain, but it was pretty obvious that the product line was becoming unwieldy and the company was in danger of putting too much of a burden on its own resources. Some rationalisation was needed and the tractor line was somewhat slimmed down during the late 1950s and early '60s.

The rationalisation began with the launch of the 900 tractor in 1956 – a much more modern machine in appearance with new styling and, in a break with tradition, blue wheel-centres to liven-up the 'Hunting Pink' livery. The 900 promised much, but sadly delivered little and was plagued by reliability problems. Many of the troubles were due to the diesel version

Introduced in 1945, the David Brown VAK1/A was an upgrade to the VAK1 with improvements to the vaporiser, carburettor and governor. The transmission was strengthened and the front axle was turned around to give a longer wheelbase.

being used as a test-bed for the new and as yet untried CAV rotary fuel pump.

The woes connected with the 900 were swept away in 1958 with the launch of the 950 tractor, which addressed all of the earlier model's failings. The 950 was similar in design to the 900, but to avoid the association the wheel colour was changed to yellow.

The Implematic version of the 950 arrived the following year. Implematic was a more sophisticated hydraulic system incorporating selective draft control; now possible because of the lapse of certain Ferguson patents. Further Implematic models – the 850, 880 and 990 – were launched over the next couple of years. The later models were only produced with diesel engines, including a new three-cylinder unit introduced for the 880 in 1964.

The next step was the Selectamatic hydraulic system that simply tidied up the Implematic arrangement by putting all the valves into a single cast-iron body with a single switch for the driver to dial-in the required hydraulic service. The first Selectamatic model was the three-cylinder 770, which was launched at the 1964 Smithfield Show. It was also the last DB tractor to be produced in 'Hunting Pink'. The following year, the full Selectamatic range was unveiled in a new white livery that represented the beginning of a new era for David Brown tractors.

The Cropmaster, designated VAK1/C, was one of the most successful David Brown tractors ever built. Launched in 1947, the standard four-speed model was priced at £446. Nearly 60,000 were built before production ended in 1953.

*The Cropmaster featured
a number of improvements
over the VAK1/A, but the
most significant was a
longer multi-piece
mainframe that
incorporated an integral
hydraulic lift. The power lift
on the earlier tractors had
been a simple bolt-on unit.*

*The Cropmaster 6S was
fitted with a six-speed
gearbox. The 'S' suffix
denoted that the tractor also
had electric starting. The
optional six-speed
transmission only cost £25
more than the four-speed
gearbox, which was phased
out in January 1949.
Tractors built after this date
also had a square front-
extension to the mainframe.*

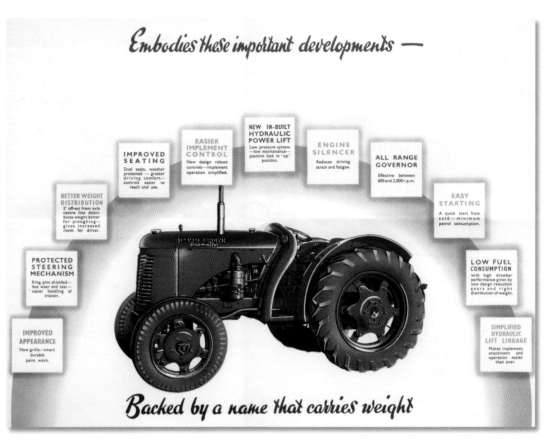

Embodies these important developments —

Backed by a name that carries weight

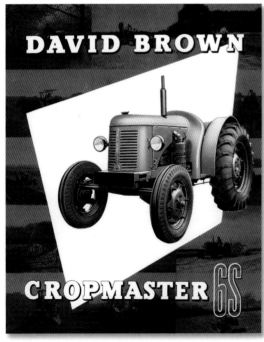

DAVID BROWN
CROPMASTER 6S

CROPMASTER DIESEL

INCORPORATING all the exclusive design features of the standard Cropmaster, this Diesel model has been developed to meet the big demand for this type of engine, especially from overseas. Power unit is of David Brown design and manufacture, notable for its compactness and light weight. Direct injection into the special toroidal combustion chamber ensures complete burning of fuel, saves oil and cuts maintenance costs. Other features include full force feed lubrication, C.A.V. injection equipment, replaceable wet liners—all calculated to prolong life and cut upkeep costs.

ENGINE. 4-cylinder monobloc; wet liners; overhead valves. Bore: 3½". Stroke: 4". Direct fuel injection using equi-spaced sprays into toroidal form combustion chamber, promoting maximum turbulence. C.A.V. pump and injectors. Decompressor for easy starting.
OUTPUT. 22 belt h.p. at 1,400 r.p.h., developing 27·5 belt h.p. at 1,800 r.p.m.
TRANSMISSION. Identical with standard petrol/paraffin model.
EQUIPMENT. 12-volt starting; universal lighting optional, as also safety overload release top link. Tyre sizes to specification. 2-speed P.T.O. and pulley available.
SPEEDS. 1·35 m.p.h. in 1st Low; 15·6 m.p.h. in 3rd High (on 11·00 x 28 tyres).
DRAWBAR H.P. – On pneumatics, 19·25 d.h.p. at 1,400 r.p.m.

*The Cropmaster Diesel was launched in 1949. Its direct-injection
power unit had the same dimensions as the petrol/TVO engine and it
developed nearly 30hp. It had CAV injection equipment and 12-volt
electric starting as standard. In 1952, the bore of the engine was
increased from 3½in to 3⅝in, which upped the power to 34hp.*

DAVID BROWN

★ 20% more POWER
★ More GRIP
★ More WORK per gallon

WITH **SUPER CROPMASTER**

Appearing in 1950, the Super Cropmaster was fitted with a more powerful version of the original petrol/TVO engine used in the standard Cropmaster. The revised power unit, which had been developed for the Trackmaster crawler, had a 3⅝in bore and a number of other modifications that increased the available horses to 38hp. The tractor also had a strengthened steering box, a higher-capacity hydraulic lift, louvered bonnet panels and a chaff screen fitted to the front grille. The price was £565.

DAVID BROWN

Trackmaster

The idea of the VAK3 project was to develop a common frame that could be used to provide general-purpose, rowcrop, industrial and tracked tractors. The TAK3 (Tracklayer Agricultural Kerosene) was the only element of the original project to come to fruition, and was launched at the 1949 Royal Show as the David Brown Trackmaster with a similar petrol/TVO engine as fitted to the Super Cropmaster. The Trackmaster Diesel version of the crawler went into production in September 1953.

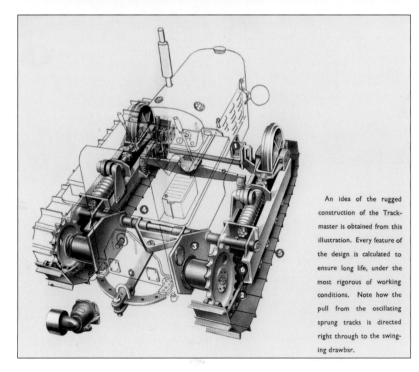

An idea of the rugged construction of the Track-master is obtained from this illustration. Every feature of the design is calculated to ensure long life, under the most rigorous of working conditions. Note how the pull from the oscillating sprung tracks is directed right through to the swing-ing drawbar.

All of David Brown's post-war crawlers adhered to the same design with alignment of the track frames maintained by a square pin riding in a slotted bracket (1). Conventional pin-and-bush tracks (2) were fitted and massive steel plates (3) supported the pivot shaft (4) and the sprockets. The track-profile (5) was flat for stability and the track-rollers (6) were supported by heavy ball-bearings.

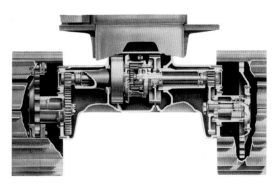

David Brown's experience with tank transmissions during the Second World War was reflected in the design of its crawler tractors. The steering system, like the tanks, was by controlled differential. Unlike the clutch-and-brake system, this kept both tracks under power when turning.

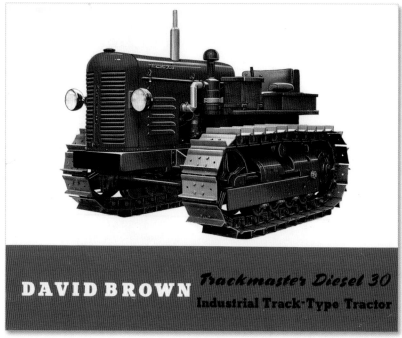

In 1952 David Brown's four-cylinder Trackmaster crawlers were given the '30' suffix to differentiate them from the new six-cylinder model coming onto the market. The Trackmaster Diesel 30 was a 34hp machine with a six-speed gearbox and a four-speed power take-off.

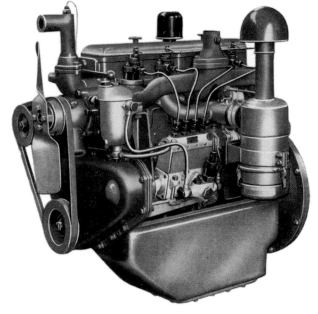

The Trackmaster Diesel 30's four-cylinder diesel engine was a direct-injection unit with a CAV inline pump. Designated AD4/30, it had a 3⅝in bore and a 4in stroke giving a capacity of 165cu in (2,705cc). A similar power unit was fitted to the Diesel Cropmaster from 1952.

David Brown's six-cylinder crawler went into production in April 1952 as the Trackmaster Diesel 50. It was the same basic design as the four-cylinder crawlers except for a larger diameter clutch and minor modifications to accommodate the longer engine.

DAVID BROWN CROPMASTER 50

Designed primarily for heavy work with pull type implements the Cropmaster "50" with its powerful David Brown Diesel Engine is capable of handling 4–6 furrows, and has ample horse power in reserve for driving P.T.O. driven combines, balers, and other heavy machinery.

Especially suited to wide open fields where multi-furrow ploughs and wide implements are used, the Cropmaster Diesel is ruggedly built to withstand the toughest conditions.

* AMPLE POWER
* 6 FORWARD SPEEDS
* DIESEL ECONOMY
* 4-SPEED P.T.O.
* SIDE MOUNTED PULLEY

LOW COST DIESEL POWER FOR FASTER, CHEAPER WORK

David Brown's six-cylinder wheeled tractor was a spin-off from the VAK3 project and utilised similar transmission and axle casings to those used on the crawlers. Designated VAD6, it was first announced as the Cropmaster 50 in November 1952 with a price of £967 10s. Full production began the following January.

The Cropmaster 50 shared its AD/6 six-cylinder engine with the Trackmaster 50 crawler. Rated at 50hp it had the same bore and stroke dimensions as the four-cylinder engines. The power unit was developed by Meltham's engine designer, Stanley Mann, and his assistant, Maurice Jones.

DAVID BROWN 50 D
DIESEL

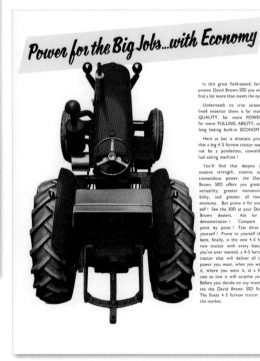

Power for the Big Jobs...with Economy

In this great field-tested, farm proven David Brown 50D you will find a lot more than meets the eye.

Underneath its trim streamlined exterior there is far more QUALITY, far more POWER, far more PULLING ABILITY, and long lasting built-in ECONOMY.

Here at last is dramatic proof that a big 4-5 furrow tractor need not be a ponderous, unwieldy, fuel eating machine !

You'll find that despite its massive strength, stamina and tremendous power, the David Brown 50D offers you greater versatility, greater manoeuvrability, and greater all round economy. But prove it for yourself ! See the 50D at your David Brown dealers. Ask for a demonstration ! Compare it point by point ! Test drive it here, finally, is the new 4-5 furrow tractor with every feature you've ever wanted, a 4-5 furrow tractor that will deliver all the power you want, when you want it, where you want it, at a fuel cost so low it will surprise you ! Before you decide on any tractor, see the David Brown 50D first. The finest 4-5 furrow tractor on the market.

The 50D was designed primarily for overseas markets, specifically for heavy-duty work and road haulage. The specification included a six-speed transmission, a four-speed power take-off, a swinging drawbar and a side-mounted belt pulley; but no differential lock, hydraulic lift or linkage was offered. The lack of hydraulics restricted sales in the UK and the model was phased out in June 1958 after a production run of just 1,260.

In April 1953 the Cropmaster 50 became the 50D following a revamp of the entire DB range. The 50D was essentially the same tractor with minor detail changes including the provision of a side-mounted Burgess oil-bath air cleaner.

earns its place on every farm

Launched in early 1953, the David Brown 25 was an 'economy' model stripped of all the frills including the dual-seat, wide fenders and horseshoe scuttle that typified the earlier four-cylinder wheeled tractors. The petrol/TVO engine had a 3½in bore and a 4in stroke giving 31.7hp at 2,000rpm. The price in 1955 was a miserly £470 15s.

The David Brown 25 was marketed as a 'no-frills' tractor, but it was by no means basic and had a six-speed gearbox, two-speed power take-off and a hydraulic lift as standard. The most noticeable changes to the design were the shell mudguards and the provision of a single seat. The clutch pedal was moved to the left and the driver now sat astride the transmission unlike the earlier tractors, which had an offset driving position.

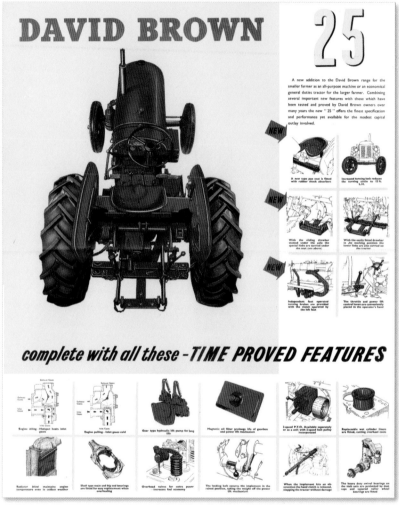

The diesel-powered David Brown 25D was the sister tractor to the petrol/TVO 25 model. Built from October 1953 to June 1958, it was a particularly popular tractor for the company and more than 13,000 were sold.

The petrol/TVO David Brown 30C model replaced the Cropmaster in 1953. Early 30C tractors had the same tinwork as the Cropmaster, but from 1954 the model adopted the same styling as the 25. A new weight-transfer hydraulic system called TCU (Traction Control Unit) was also introduced in 1954, allowing the tractors to make greater use of their implements. The 30C models had the same engine as the Super Cropmaster.

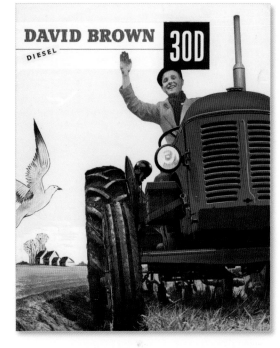

The David Brown 30D also arrived in 1953 and was the diesel version of the 30C. It underwent the same styling changes and was powered by a similar power unit to that fitted to the Diesel Cropmaster and the Trackmaster Diesel 30.

The revamp of the David Brown range in 1953 saw the crawlers given new identities to bring them into line with the wheeled tractors. The Trackmaster Diesel 30 became the David Brown 30TD while the petrol paraffin model was renamed 30T. The specification remained the same.

The enlarged tractor range that emanated out of the 1953 revamp was dubbed 'Field Force'. As part of the changes, the six-cylinder Trackmaster Diesel 50 was became the David Brown 50TD in 1953. An industrial model of the six-cylinder crawler was also released as the 50ITD.

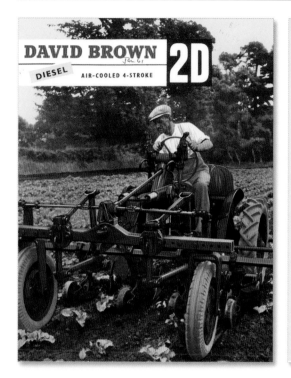

1. Rack and pinion steering.
2. Tubular frame and air reservoir.
3. 'Air-light' pneumatic lift.
4. Twin finger-tip lift control.
5. Pneumatic tyre inflator point.
6. 2-cylinder 4-stroke diesel engine.
7. Wheel-mark eliminator.
8. 4-speed gearbox.
9. Air compressor.
10. Forward P.T.O.
11. Wheel width settings from 40 in. to 68 in.
12. Fully adjustable linkage and single self-locking pin.

The David Brown 2D was an exciting addition to the range. Introduced in 1956, it was a specialist rowcrop tractor aimed at market gardeners and sugar beet and vegetable growers. It had a 14hp engine, a four-speed gearbox and weighed less than a ton. Production continued until 1961 and more than 2,000 were built.

The 2D rowcrop tractor was a marvel of engineering with an air-operated lift powered by a compressor with the tubular frame acting as an air-reservoir. The two-cylinder air-cooled diesel engine had a third opposed idler-cylinder to balance out any vibration.

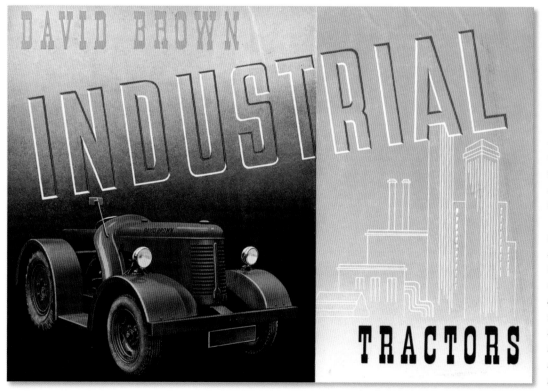

In addition to the agricultural tractors there was an extensive range of David Brown industrial models. These included the Taskmaster for light haulage, the 'Heavy Industrial' for a variety of municipal and commercial enterprises, plus tractors for aircraft-towing and military applications. Some of the tractors supplied to the RAF had fluid-drive torque-converter transmissions.

Launched in late 1956 the 900 brought a more modern era of styling to the David Brown range. The diesel version was the first British tractor to be fitted with a CAV rotary pump. Unfortunately this new injection pump had not been thoroughly tested in the field and problems were rife. The 900 was by no means an unmitigated disaster, but it did cause the company some headaches.

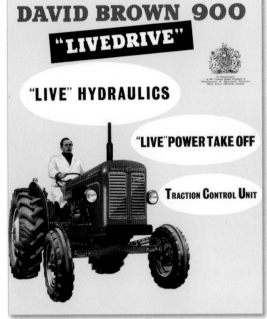

From 1957 the 900 became the first David Brown model to have 'Livedrive' – a dual clutch allowing the power take-off and hydraulics to operate independently of the tractor's forward motion. Note the blue wheels and radiator grilles – a break from the tradition of an all-over 'Hunting Pink' livery.

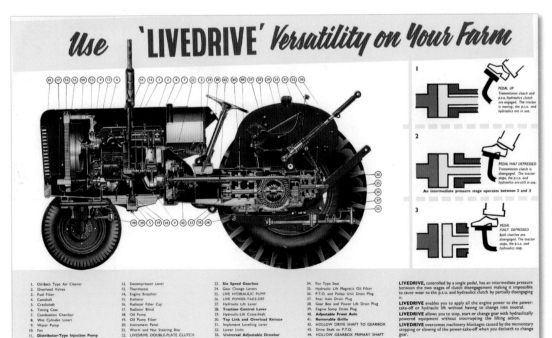

The David Brown 900 was mechanically similar to the 30C/30D models. It had a six-speed gearbox and was available with four engine options: diesel, TVO, petrol and high-compression petrol. 'Livedrive' added a new dimension to the tractor's versatility.

The 950, launched in November 1958, was everything the 900 should have been. The appearance was similar, except for the new yellow wheels, but beneath the paintwork several revisions and improvements had been made to address the problems that had plagued 900 production.

The David Brown 950 boasted several new features including an up-rated diesel engine developing 42.5hp; a petrol unit was also offered but was rarely specified except for export. Both 'Livedrive' and 'non-live' versions were available.

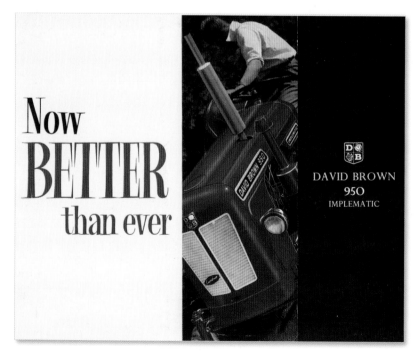

The 950 Implematic model arrived in 1959 with a more advanced hydraulic system with single-lever control. Advertised as 'all-purpose hydraulics', the Implematic system featured selective draft control, TCU, position control and a three-way isolator valve for external services. The tractor also had differential lock as standard.

ALL-PURPOSE HYDRAULICS

One control lever—any hydraulic system. This is Implematic achievement in a nutshell.

Movement of this one control lever enables you to operate either with standard hydraulics using positive wheel depth control or with draft hydraulic equipment. By means of the same single lever you can engage Traction Control when required . . . and the same lever is used to operate tipping trailers and loaders.

Implematic Controls

Conveniently grouped at the driver's right hand are (1) the all-purpose control lever; (2) a pre-set guide which ensures return to the same working depth when using draft control implements; (3) the hand wheel which regulates the degree of Traction Control required; (4) the differential lock pedal which is foot-operated.

When you buy a David Brown Implematic tractor you do not need to change your implements. Any Implematic tractor will handle all linkage-mounted equipment, thus widening your choice when it comes to the time for replacements.

2 SYSTEMS IN ONE

The new Implematic system was developed by David Brown's hydraulics expert, Harry Horsfall, who was working under the guidance of Charles Hull. It was not a completely new system, but rather a modification of the old layout with changes to the valves and linkage to automatically control the working depth of the implement. The selective draft control had top-link sensing via a Bowden cable from a telescopic top-link.

The Small Implematic

DB The **DAVID BROWN** 850

ALL-PURPOSE HYDRAULICS · TRACTION CONTROL UNIT · DIFFERENTIAL LOCK

Rated at 35hp, the 850 Implematic had the four-cylinder (3½in bore) engine as was fitted to the previous 25/25D tractors, but the remainder of the specification including the Implematic system was more akin to the 950. A six-speed gearbox and differential lock were standard, and the options included power steering, a three-way isolator valve for the hydraulics, a belt pulley, lighting and tractormeter (combined tachometer and hourmeter). Launched in February 1960, the standard 850 Implematic cost £614 15s with the 'Livedrive' model priced at £644 15s.

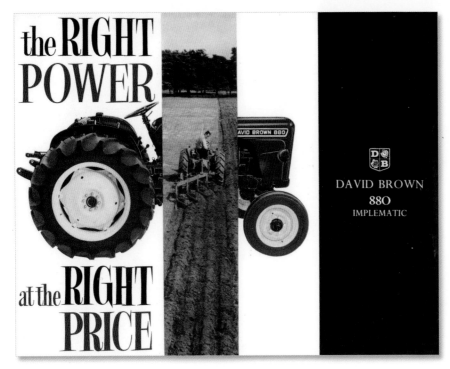

In 1961 David Brown introduced its four-cylinder 880 Implematic tractor; essentially a stop-gap machine because a new three-cylinder version was in the pipeline. Its 3⅝in bore diesel engine, as fitted to the 30D, was now rated at 42.5hp. The 850 remained in production alongside the 880 as a lower-cost alternative.

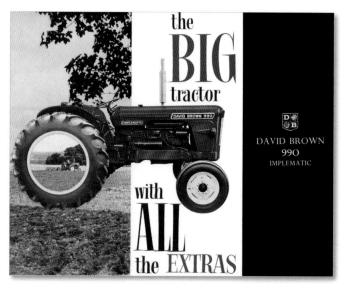

the
BIG
tractor

DB

DAVID BROWN
990
IMPLEMATIC

with
ALL
the EXTRAS

David Brown claimed that the 880 Implematic offered the farmer all-round versatility with extra under-axle clearance and extra power both at the drawbar and the power take-off. Both 'Livedrive' and 'non-live' versions were available. Customers were now fully attuned to the advantages of diesel engines and it was the first four-cylinder David Brown wheeled tractor to be launched with no petrol or TVO alternatives.

The 990 Implematic went into production in September 1961 with a new 52hp four-cylinder AD4/47 diesel engine. Its most notable feature was a cross-flow head with separate inlet ports for each cylinder on the right-hand side of the head and the exhaust ports on the left. The cross-flow arrangement optimised the swirl rate in the cylinders to ensure clean combustion while keeping the exhaust heat away from the induction side of the engine, thus allowing a full charge of cool air with the air cleaner repositioned in front of the radiator.

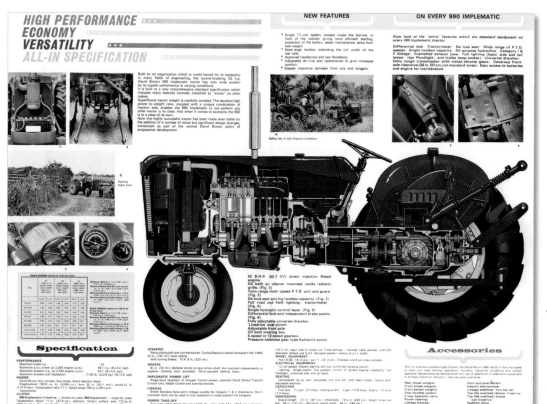

The 990 Implematic came in for a number of small improvements in September 1964 with the battery relocated in front of the radiator, improved lighting and a larger toolbox. An optional 12-speed transmission was also introduced.

The three-cylinder 880 Implematic also arrived in September 1964 and the company claimed that the tractor had been completely redesigned from bonnet to drawbar. It had a longer wheelbase and tidier lines with the air cleaner and battery mounted beneath the bonnet and in front of the radiator. The 880 had all the usual David Brown features plus the option of a 12-speed gearbox.

The AD3/40 three-cylinder engine fitted to the 880 was a direct-injection unit engine with a cross-flow head and the injection-pump mounted vertically and driven by spiral gears from the camshaft. The new power unit was a lively performer and its 154cu in (2,526cc) displacement gave 42.5hp.

The 770 Selectamatic was launched at the 1964 Smithfield Show and went into production the following January. Its three-cylinder AD3/30 engine was a development of the AD3/40 unit with a shorter stroke. The tractor's styling differed little from the existing Implematic models, but it was the last DB model to be finished in the traditional 'Hunting Pink' livery with yellow wheels.

Another David Brown first

SELECTAMATIC

...4-in-1 hydraulics at the flick of a switch

The 770's Selectamatic hydraulics had all the features of the Implematic system, but tidied up the arrangement by putting all the valves into a single cast-iron body with a single switch for the driver to dial-in the required hydraulic service. The system would become the focus of a new range of white David Brown tractors launched at the end of 1965.

DOE

Today, Ernest Doe is a long-established machinery dealership with a network of branches in the south and east of England. It is also a family firm with roots dating back to 1898 when the company's founder began trading as a blacksmith in the Essex village of Ulting. This business prospered and after Ernest was joined by his three sons, it also moved into repair, retail and contracting.

Ernest Doe & Sons was formed in 1937 by which time the firm was advertising itself as 'The Tractor Specialists' with agencies for several leading

makes. The post-war boom in sales led to an increased turnover and the decision was made to incorporate the business into a limited company. Ernest Charles Doe, the eldest son of the founder, was appointed chairman and managing director.

By this time the company was manufacturing a number of specialist machines for local farmers. These included orchard and high-clearance conversions of the Allis-Chalmers Model B tractor, a 'silage combine' and even the 'Doe Wild Oat & Weed Seed Collector'. By the 1950s Ernest Doe & Sons Ltd was selling more Fordson tractors than any other make, and on 1 February 1956 the company was appointed a Ford main dealer.

During 1957 one of Doe's customers, George Pryor of Navestock, began experimenting with two Fordson Diesel Major tractors joined together in tandem. Pryor's goal was to provide a powerful four-wheel drive machine that would plough or cultivate his large acreage of heavy Essex clay.

After much experimentation Pryor arrived at a workable pivot-steer design. The front axles were removed from the two Majors and the tractors were joined together using a turntable arrangement. The combination of the two 52hp power units provided a four-wheel drive machine with more than 100hp available.

The vehicle was steered by two pairs of two hydraulic rams working in tandem on either side of the turntable. The result was probably one of the most unorthodox tractors ever built, but it was surprisingly manoeuvrable. More importantly, it had tremendous traction and unbeatable pulling power.

The tractor became the talk of the area. Ernest Charles Doe could see it had great potential and he entered into an agreement with George Pryor for Ernest Doe & Sons Ltd to put the design into

PATENT NO. 6777/58

Doe's Dual Drive...

The introduction of the Triple-D in June 1959 marked the official entry of Doe's tandem tractor into the marketplace and brochures were issued for the first time. The Triple-D incorporated a number of steering improvements over the previous Doe Dual Drive, including mounting the steering pump on the rear skid unit to satisfy the taxation rulings, but it still had rod-linkage gear-change mechanism.

production. Doe's works manager, Charles Bennett, was put in charge of adapting Pryor's ideas and refining the design.

The clutch operation on the two units was synchronised through the pedal on the rear tractor using a hydraulic master cylinder and slave ram for remote control. The throttles were connected together by a wire cable. A system of link-rods running across the rear tractor's bonnet allowed the driver to operate the high/low gear lever on the front unit. With this in neutral, he had to dismount to manually select the gear ratio on the front tractor for the job in hand. It was not a satisfactory arrangement, but it worked.

The production tractor, based on two Fordson Power Major skid units, was launched in 1958 as the Doe Dual Power. Just six were made before the Motor Taxation Department requested changes. To satisfy the rulings for the machine to be classified and taxed as one vehicle, the ancillaries, including the power steering pump, had to be moved from the front to the rear tractor unit. At the same time, the opportunity was taken to improve the steering system.

The tandem tractor reappeared in June 1959 as Doe's Dual Drive, better known as the 'Triple-D' for short. Only another 14 were sold before the design again fell foul of officialdom after Health & Safety officials became concerned about the method of gear selection on the front unit using the rod-linkage arrangement.

Production was suspended while a number of modifications were made to allow the high/low lever on the front unit to be operated by a hydraulic master cylinder and slave assembly. The Triple-D was re-launched in May 1960 and now looked a sleeker machine without the rod-linkage cluttering the rear bonnet. Doe also introduced its own colour scheme of blue with orange bonnets and radiator shrouds.

By the time the Super Major version of the Triple-D was introduced towards the end of 1960, Ulting's engineers had further improved the control layout. Now all the gears on the front tractor could be selected from the driver's seat on the rear unit using a system of master and slave cylinders. Another master cylinder and slave ram assembly synchronised the differential locks on the two Super

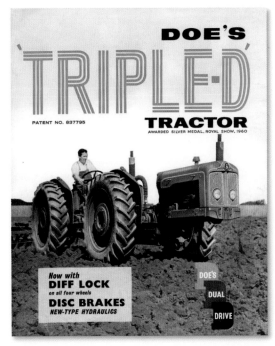

The Doe Triple-D was re-launched in May 1960 with an improved gear-change mechanism. The basic price of £1,950 included an assister ram and a solenoid-type starter for remote starting of the front unit from the rear seat. When the new Fordson Super Major skid units became available later in the year, the Triple D gained the advantage of disc brakes and differential lock on all four wheels.

The improved gear-change mechanism fitted to the Triple D in 1960 used a hydraulic master cylinder and slave assembly to operate the high/low lever on the front tractor. A full hydraulic gear-change was also developed to give the driver complete control over the front unit. The throttles were linked by a heavy-duty Bowden cable, which at £100 was the most expensive component on the tractor.

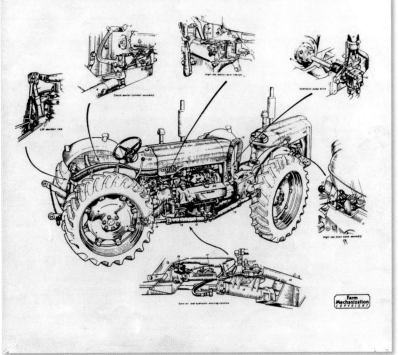

1. Assister ram to boost three-point lift.
2. Master clutch pedal.
3. Clutch hydraulic cylinders.
4. Rear of left-hand pair of steering rams.
5. Brake lever.
6. Master high-low gear lever crank.
7. High-low hydraulic cylinders.
8. Fan belt pulley on rear engine.
9. Hydraulic pump drive flexible coupling.
10. Hydraulic pump for power steering.
11. Conduit carrying clutch, high-low, throttle and pump cut-off controls to front unit.
12. Hydraulic slave cylinders for remote control of front high-low lever.
13. Front high-low lever.
14. Front of right-hand pair of steering rams.
15. Turntable assembly.
16. Pivot shaft connecting front unit to turntable.
17. Linkage between steering wheel and steering hydraulic control valve.
18. Steering hydraulic control valve.
19. Rear steering ram.
20. Hydraulic steering oil-supply tank.
21. Turntable pivot shaft.
22. Throttle control lever coupled to both engines.

DOE'S
DUAL
DRIVE

The manœuvrability of the **"TRIPLE-D"** is demonstrated by this practical illustration of turning at a headland with the heavy disc harrow.

Ernest Doe AND SONS LTD
ULTING MALDON ESSEX
Tel: HATFIELD PEVEREL 311

Despite its ungainly appearance, the Doe Triple D was very manoeuvrable and had a turning circle of just 21ft. Not bad for a tractor that was over 20ft long!

Major skid units.

To make use of the Triple-D's full power, Ernest Doe & Sons Ltd began making its own implements. The range was eventually extended to include ploughs, cultivators, toolbars, harrows and disc harrows. Interest in the Triple-D was shown world-wide with shipments to Europe, Scandinavia, Israel, North and South America, Africa and even Russia.

The final incarnation of the Triple-D was the blue/grey model, based on the 'New Performance' Super Major and launched at the Royal Show in July 1963. The eventual demise of the Triple-D was brought about by the end of Fordson production at Dagenham. Doe's engineers had to go back to the drawing board and come up with a new design to suit the Ford 5000 that was to be built at Basildon from late 1964.

More than 280 Triple-Ds were built and the last was dispatched from Ulting on 3 October 1964 by which time the tractor had achieved legendary worldwide status. It successor, the Doe 130, never attained the same level of recognition.

The Doe Triple-D had its own colour scheme of blue with orange bonnets and radiator shrouds. Ernest Doe & Sons Ltd was an agent for Fritzmeier cabs, which were available as optional equipment. The basic price of the tractor in 1961 was £2,350.

The version of the Triple-D based on the 'New Performance' Super Major, introduced in 1963, featured stronger bearings and bushes for the turntable. A steel valance was also fitted beneath the front tractor unit to protect the sump. The price was now £2,450 and Doe offered an optional heavy-duty linkage assembly for an extra £100.

FERGUSON

In his acclaimed biography of Harry Ferguson, the late Colin Fraser called the Ulsterman an inventor and pioneer. There is no more apt description of the man who in 1909 built and flew the first aeroplane in Ireland, was a keen racing motorcyclist and in the late 1950s championed several ground-breaking automotive developments – including traction control, anti-lock braking and safety belts. But he is best remembered for his tractor – the archetypal 'little grey Fergie' – which of all the machines featured in this book is probably the one most familiar to the layman.

And yet Ferguson never set out to build a tractor. His ambition was to develop a better hitch – a safer way to attach a plough other than using a drawbar or chain. Through the 1920s he strived to make the plough an integral part of the tractor and his experi-

The Ferguson tractor was part of a comprehensive farming system that included a full range of implements, equipment and accessories designed to meet the farmer's every need. It was the culmination of Harry Ferguson's ambition to make mechanised agriculture both better and safer by developing a three-point linkage that saw the plough become an integral part of the tractor.

ments culminated in his revolutionary converging three-point linkage, which incorporated hydraulic draft control to regulate the depth of the implement in work. Despite the advantages of the system, Ferguson was unable to find a manufacturer to adopt his ideas and so his only option was to build his own machine.

Ferguson's first tractor, the Type A (Ferguson-Brown), was manufactured for him by David Brown at its Park Works factory in Huddersfield from 1936-39. Harry was a somewhat mercurial and single-minded character and the partnership with DB was never harmonious. Ferguson's subsequent arrangement with Henry Ford to build the 9N and 2N (Ford-Ferguson) tractors in the USA ended in an even more acrimonious split in 1946. The fallout from this was the famous legal battle in which Ferguson sued Ford for patent infringement and was eventually awarded an out-of-court settlement of $9.25 million.

Harry had proved that he was not a man to be dallied with, but one British captain of industry, Sir John Black of the Standard Motor Company, was prepared to accept the challenge. Standard, a leading motor manufacturer, had an unused factory at Banner Lane in Coventry. The plant had operated as a wartime shadow factory for aircraft production, but now lay empty.

Sir John was a similar strong personality and he shared Harry's engineering ideologies and welcomed an approach to build Ferguson's new British tractor. Standard had a new car, the Vanguard, under development and the plan was that both it and the tractor would use the same four-cylinder power unit to save on manufacturing costs.

Although Ferguson was the driving force behind his many developments, much of the design work was attributable to his stalwart band of engineers – notably Willie Sands, Archie Grier and John Chambers who had all been with him since the days of his early experiments with ploughs in Northern Ireland. The same three men, assisted by Alex Patterson, were responsible for bringing the new British tractor to production while Harry fussed over every tiny detail.

The new FERGUSON TRACTOR with MORE power... MORE speeds... STILL GREATER fuel economy!

YEARS AHEAD! FERGUSON ENGINEERING PAYS OFF WITH →

Launched in 1946, the Ferguson TE-20 was powered by a four-cylinder Continental Z-120 overhead-valve petrol engine developing 23hp. Visually and dimensionally, the Continental unit was very similar to the Standard petrol engine fitted to the later Ferguson TE-A20 tractor and is identified by the slight kink in the pipe where the exhaust leaves the manifold.

The tractor, designated TE-20 (Tractor England 20hp) had similar dimensions and layout to the American Ford-Ferguson models. The TE-20 had a four-speed transmission and naturally incorporated the Ferguson System of hydraulic lift and three-point linkage. As Standard's engine was not yet ready for production, an American Continental Z120 power unit was temporarily adopted for production to begin on 6 July 1946.

Priced at £343, the TE-20 was an enormous success. Ferguson had brought affordable power farming to masses. It was the tractor that finally ousted the horse on smaller farms while on marginal land the TE-20's inherent stability on hillsides made it an indispensable tool. It was sold as part of a complete package, the Ferguson System, which included a full range of implements (the manufacture of which was subcontracted to outside suppliers across the UK) and accessories, plus an integrated dealer network offering on-farm service and even a hire-purchase plan.

The Standard Motor Company's own petrol engine came on-line during 1948. Tractors fitted with the Standard engine, which had similar dimensions to the Continental unit, were designated TE-A20. A petrol/TVO version, the TE-D20, arrived the following year with the diesel TE-F20 model introduced in 1951. Narrow and vineyard versions of the agricultural tractors were also produced as was a lamp oil model for burning low-octane distillates in countries where TVO wasn't available.

Industrial and semi-industrial variants of the TE-

20 series tractors were very popular with building trades and municipal corporations. Councils and local authorities found the economical Ferguson tractor the ideal machine for general transport, refuse collection, mowing roadsides and maintaining parks and playing fields.

By 1953 Harry Ferguson was again becoming characteristically restless. He felt that he had achieved many of his lifetime's ambitions as far as farm machinery was concerned and was becoming disillusioned with the business. Keen to amalgamate with a global corporation, he opened a dialogue with the Canadian Massey-Harris Company with proposals for a merger.

The negotiations led to Massey-Harris acquiring Ferguson's tractor and implement business and merging it into a new concern to be known as Massey-Harris-Ferguson. The joint company came into being on 30 January 1954. Harry was offered the position of chairman, but resigned six months later to devote his time to new interests within the motor industry.

For a time the red Massey-Harris and grey Ferguson lines were retained and the two franchises were kept strictly separaTE- The TE-20 series continued in production and its worldwide popularity was undiminished. During 1956 the half-millionth tractor was driven off the Banner Lane assembly line, and TE-A20 models were even chosen for Sir Edmund Hillary's Antarctic expedition to the South Pole.

A new model, however, was in the pipeline. The last of the TE-20 series was built in October 1956 following the launch of its replacement – the Ferguson FE-35. Finished in a distinctive grey and bronze livery, the FE-35 inherited the TE-20's DNA and incorporated it with a number of new and more modern features including a six-speed gearbox, two-speed and 'live' power take-off, and a more sensitive hydraulic system controlled by two quadrants. Engines were again sourced from the Standard Motor Company with petrol, TVO, lamp oil and diesel versions offered.

The logistics of running two separate ranges were putting a financial burden on the company, so the decision was taken to rationalise the product lines into one corporate identity. In December 1957 the board of Massey-Harris-Ferguson Ltd sanctioned the renaming of the company as Massey Ferguson. In the same month the FE-35 was re-launched at the Smithfield Show as the Massey Ferguson 35 tractor in a new red and grey livery. The Ferguson legend had ended.

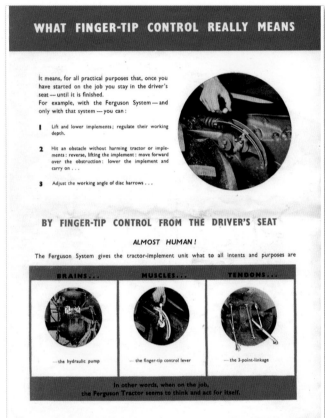

The Ferguson System combined draft control – using the tractor's hydraulics to automatically control the depth of the implement in work – with three-point linkage consisting of two converging lower links and a single top-link. The hydraulic system raised and lowered the implement and controlled its working depth. The converging linkage also ensured that the plough remained centred and followed a straight course behind the tractor with no lateral movement.

The three-point linkage provided a triangulation of hitch points that attached the plough to the tractor. A lever on a quadrant to the right of the driver's seat provided fingertip control over the implement's working depth.

The Ferguson Tractor carries as well as pulls the plough or other unit. As most Ferguson implements have no wheels, *all* their weight must be carried by the tractor. The weight of wheeled implements — such as trailers — is distributed over the four wheels of the tractor and the two wheels of the implement.

The weight of the plough, the suck of the plough, the weight of soil on the plough all add weight to the tractor's rear wheels (shown by dotted arrows). At the same time, through the Ferguson System of 3-point linkage, the natural tendency of the implement to revolve as it is pulled into the ground is converted into a strong forward-slant-thrust which holds the front wheels down too (shown by white arrow).

A deeper cut, or heavier going, merely increases these natural forces, adjusting the traction to the job — instantly, automatically.

Forces acting on the implement in work put the lower-link arms in tension and the top-link in compression. The linkage lifted the plough in and out of the ground and both pulled and carried it in work, transferring its weight on to the tractor's rear wheels to aid traction. The line of pull of the implement in work extended through the converging linkage to a theoretical hitch point just behind the tractor's front axle. This created a strong downward thrust on the front wheels to keep the tractor stable.

The TE-20's simple hydraulic system consisted of a pump driven off the gearbox countershaft through a dog-clutch. It sucked oil from the rear-axle housing and passed it through a control valve and bush to an internal ram cylinder. When the ram was pressurised its piston operated on a cross-shaft to raise the lift arms, which were connected to the lower links via lift rods. The control valve, operated by a single lever in the quadrant beside driver's seat, received signals via the top-link to monitor the depth of the implement.

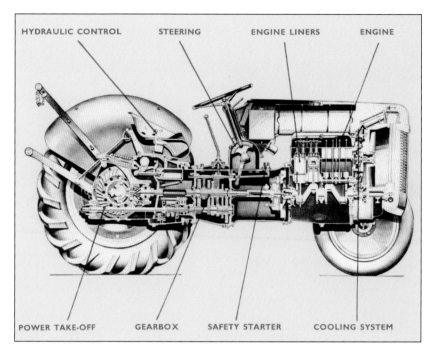

The Ferguson TE-A20 tractor with the Standard Motor Company's petrol engine was phased in during 1948. For a time both it and the Continental-powered TE-20 were built alongside each other until Standard's engine manufacturing plant got up to full speed. Developing 25hp, the engine was a 1,849cc unit with wet liners and an 80mm bore and 92mm stroke.

Harry Ferguson Ltd offered a full line of equipment for the TE-20 series tractors with the implements being manufactured by a number of outside suppliers. The manure loader and spreader were added to the range in 1949. The loader was made by Steel's Engineering Products of Sunderland.

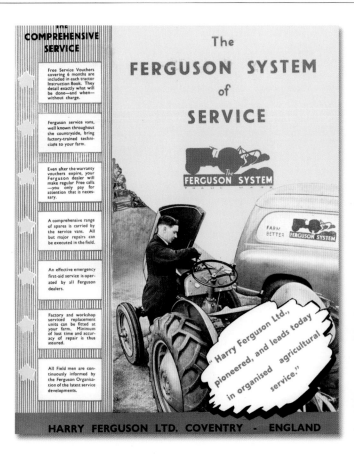

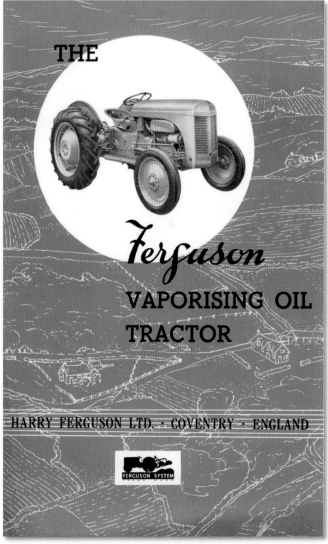

Ferguson offered a complete system of farming and great importance was placed on having a fully-trained and fully-stocked network of dealerships. A fleet of vans provided on-farm service – still something of a novelty in the late 1940s.

With a four cylinder engine developing 25 belt horse power, the Ferguson Diesel Tractor incorporates all the features of the Vaporising Oil and Petrol Models—built-in hydraulic system, safety self-starter, adjustable wheel widths, four forward speed and reverse gears, power take-off, pneumatic tyres, adjustable drawbar, internal expanding brakes, exceptional easy handling and manoeuvrability with complete safety. This Ferguson Tractor is the lightest diesel on the market in relation to its output.

Easily started in cold weather, the engine, notably quiet and smooth running, is built to the same high standards of engineering as the other Ferguson Tractors and has been designed to give the Ferguson System the advantages of another low-priced fuel.

Following the withdrawal in 1949 of the 'red petrol' scheme that allowed the fuel to be rebated for agricultural use, Ferguson rushed to introduce its vaporising oil model to run on TVO. Designated TE-D20, the tractor had a larger 85mm bore to compensate for the loss of efficiency resulting from the lower-grade fuel. An aluminium heat-shield was fitted to the manifold to vaporise the distilla TE-

Harry Ferguson was vehemently against diesel engines believing them to be dirty, noisy, complicated and expensive to manufacture. But eventually the company had to yield to the demand and introduce its TE-F20 model in March 1951. The Standard 20C diesel engine was an indirect-injection unit with spherical combustion chambers developed by Arthur Freeman Sanders.

51

The Ferguson narrow tractor was developed for the hop and fruit growing areas of the country. Shortened rear-axle housings and half-shafts were fitted with extensive modifications made to the front axle, radius arms and brake pedals. Alterations were also made to the linkage, and steel hub-caps were fitted to protect the crop from damage by the wheel-nuts. This TE-C20 model was the narrow version of the TE-A20 petrol tractor.

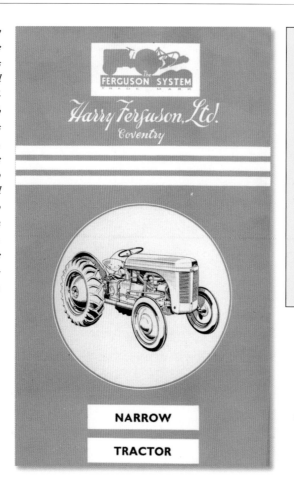

NARROW

TRACTOR

VINEYARD TRACTOR
Available for Petrol, Lamp Oil or V.O engine as shown. For certain agricultural applications the Narrow tractors are not narrow enough, especially for the cultivation of Vineyards, Sugar Cane, and similar crops, so this extra narrow version of only 46″ overall width was developed and has met with tremendous success.

The vineyard tractor was an extra-narrow and low-profile tractor for specialist applications such as wine producing and sugar cane. Introduced in May 1952 it had an extra support casting to move the radiator forward by 4in and give the front wheels greater clearance for turning. The tractor was only 46in wide and had a wheel-track of 37in. It was fitted with smaller diameter wheels (24in rear and 15in front) to lower the profile by some 2in. The TVO vineyard tractor was designated TE-L20.

The Ferguson industrial tractor range was designed to conform to the legal requirements for public road work and had two independent braking systems – hydraulic foot brakes and a mechanical handbrake. Various models were offered with a range of equipment including a heavy-duty front bumper with a radiator guard, enclosed industrial mudguards, industrial tyres, power take-off, lights, horn and rear-view mirror.

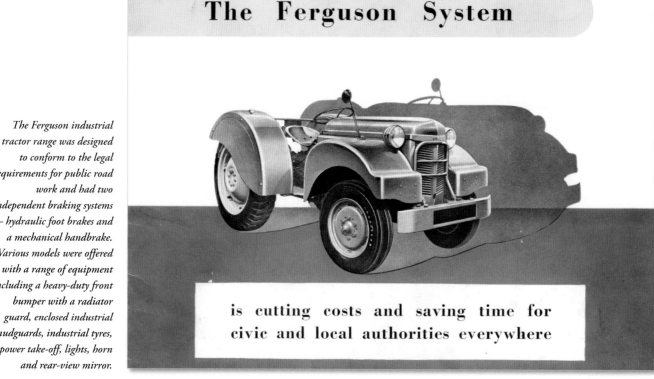

The Ferguson System

is cutting costs and saving time for civic and local authorities everywhere

The last of the British Ferguson tractors, the FE-35 model, replaced the TE-20 series in October 1956. Changes included a new bonnet with a detachable front grille and a hinged top panel for easy servicing, as well as a revised instrument panel with an ammeter, oil pressure or temperature gauge. Often referred to as the 'grey and gold' Ferguson, the tractor was finished in a distinctive metallic bronze and grey livery.

The Ferguson FE-35 was offered with a choice of diesel, petrol, TVO or lamp oil engines manufactured by the Standard Motor Company. The new 23C diesel engine had a Ricardo Comet head, but lacked torque and was sometimes temperamental when it came to starting on a cold morning. The tractor also featured a Burman recirculating-ball type steering mechanism.

The FE-35 boasted a new six-speed gearbox and a more advanced hydraulic system with two control levers in a dual quadrant. Other features included a stronger front-axle support, new implement location pads, a larger fuel tank and improved brakes. A two-speed power take-off (540rpm and ground speed) was fitted with 'live' drive optional via a dual clutch.

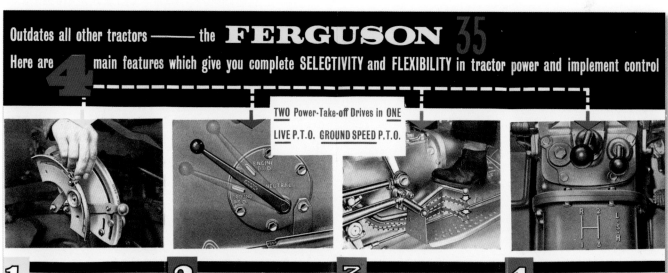

FORDSON

Fordson was the name given to the line of tractors built in Britain by Ford during the period of this book. The name dates back to 1917 when Henry Ford began building his first tractor, the Model F, at Dearborn in the USA. At the time, his fellow directors of the Ford Motor Company were opposed to the idea of building tractors and so Henry set up a separate venture in partnership with his wife and son. Henry Ford & Son was the name of the venture and Fordson their cable address.

The production of the Model F was later moved to Ford's mighty Rouge River plant in Michigan, where it was built until 1927 when the company exited the tractor market in the USA. Satellite production of the Model F was also carried out at Cork in Ireland from 1919-22. Cork also became the manufacturing centre for the improved Fordson Model N from 1929 until 1932 when production was transferred to the new Dagenham plant in England.

The Fordson tractor was now a product of the British Ford Motor Company. Production of the Model N commenced at Dagenham in 1933 and continued until the end of the Second World War. Although various improvements were made to the N during its lifetime, the design was getting a bit long in the tooth by the outbreak of the Second World War. Various upgrades were planned, including an overhead-valve engine, but had to be shelved when the urgency to produce as many tractors as possible to mobilise British agriculture in its time of need took precedence over any new design considerations.

Between 1939 and 1945, Ford's Dagenham plant produced nearly 140,000 Model N tractors – some 95 percent of all the wheeled models made in the UK. The factory operated a seven-day week and, at peak times, one tractor came off the line every 17 minutes 36 seconds.

The Fordson Major was introduced in 1945 to replace the Model N. The engine was the same side-valve unit, but Ford's engineers had managed to coax 27hp out of it by increasing its governed engine speed by 350rpm. This horsepower rating was reflected in the E27N label with 'E' denoting made in England and 'N' being Ford's tractor designation.

In 1944 the Ministry of Agriculture asked Ford to develop a more efficient model with greater horsepower and lower fuel consumption. The new tractor also had to be capable of handling a three-furrow plough. The result was the Fordson Major (designated E27N); the first of which rolled out of Dagenham on 19 March 1945.

The Major was by no means a completely new tractor. It inherited the N's petrol/TVO engine and three-speed gearbox, but the transmission was greatly modified. The earlier Fordson worm-drive had been dispensed with in favour of a crown-wheel and pinion final-drive, which was both quieter and more efficient. A little extra power was also coaxed out of the old side-valve engine by increasing its governed speed by 350rpm.

The Fordson E27N Major is not always remembered with great affection. It was indeed an old-fashioned design and could at times be temperamental, but it was ruggedly reliable and eminently affordable at just £237 for the basic agricultural model on steel wheels. It was the saviour of British agriculture in a time of austerity and more than 230,000 were built.

The E27N's outdated engine was almost unchanged since the inception of the Model F in 1917, and its biggest let down was its gravity-fed lubrication system. The introduction of the Perkins P6 diesel as a factory-fitted option in 1948 went someway towards alleviating the problem, but Dagenham's engineers were well aware that a better power unit was needed.

One of Dagenham's car engineers came up with an outstanding design of four-cylinder overhead-valve engine that could be produced as a petrol, TVO or diesel unit. This was mated to a new six-speed gearbox developed from the old E27N transmission by John Foxwell from Ford's tractor division – and the 'New' Fordson Major was born.

Launched in November 1951, the 'New' Major – designated E1A – was a world beater in every sense and the diesel model ranks as one of the best tractors ever made. The petrol and TVO variants were eventually dropped and the Fordson Diesel Major reigned supreme with sales to almost every corner of the globe.

In 1957 the Major got a workmate in the form of the Fordson Dexta, introduced as Ford's answer to Ferguson's 'grey menace'. The layout of the Dexta was based on the American Ford 8N, and John Foxwell was charged with ensuring the design didn't infringe any Ferguson patents; several of which had now lapsed.

By changing the hydraulic control-valve from

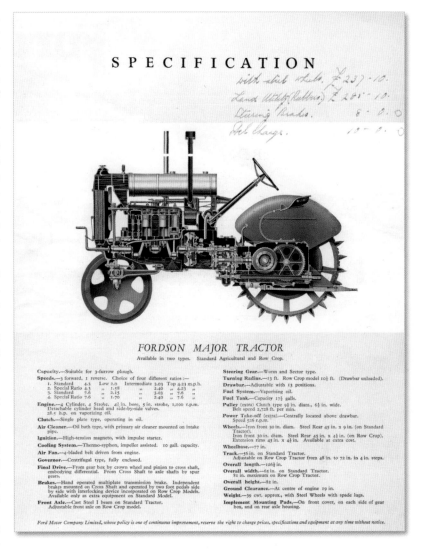

the suction to the delivery side of the pump, Ford was able to introduce draft control on the Dexta – a first for a Fordson tractor. The three-cylinder diesel engine was jointly developed with Perkins and was a Ford version of the P3(TA) unit.

The Diesel Major was revamped into the Power Major in 1958, with even more improvements heralding the arrival of the 'Super Class' in October 1960. The most obvious changes with the introduction of the Super Major were differential lock, independent disc brakes and a revised hydraulic system incorporating draft control.

At the same time the Dexta was given a facelift with minor changes. This model continued in production alongside the more powerful Super Dexta, which arrived in late 1961 with an enlarged version of the Dexta power unit.

The era of the 'Super Class' was probably the greatest period in the history of Fordson farming. Output at Dagenham had risen to over 350 trac-

The E27N Major still used the N's three-speed gearbox, but the transmission was greatly modified. The earlier Fordson worm-drive had been dispensed with in favour of a crown-wheel and pinion final-drive, which was both quieter and more efficient. Early examples of the Major, which were only available on steel wheels, had several features carried over from the wartime Model N, including the manifold, heat-shield and cast-iron air cleaner.

Two important extras were offered for the Major from 1946: rubber tyres and a hydraulic lift assembly. The lift assembly incorporated three-point linkage and allowed the tractor to be used with a variety of mounted implements. Two types were available: the Smith lift with one control lever or the Varley, which had two.

Further options introduced for the E27N Major included an electrical system with a 12-volt battery, generator and starter motor. By 1946 many of the earlier Model N features had disappeared and the tractor was now fitted with a Burgess oil-bath air cleaner.

tors a day and annual production was exceeding 71,000. Ford was in an unassailable position as Britain's number one tractor manufacturer.

But changes were afoot and Ford Tractor Operations was being restructured with a brief to recreate a worldwide range of Ford tractors. Production would be centred in the USA, in Belgium and at a new British plant in Basildon. The space currently occupied by tractor assembly in Dagenham would be given over to 'Project Archbishop' – the proposed new Ford Cortina.

The first step towards integrating Ford's worldwide tractor production was the introduction of a new corporate blue/grey colour scheme. This was applied to the existing Fordson models with the launch of the 'New Performance' range in 1963. 'New Performance' was little more than a facelift of the run-out of models from Dagenham. The Super Major and the Super Dexta received small power increases while the standard Dexta continued unchanged except for the new blue/grey livery.

The new worldwide Ford range, designated 6X, was unveiled with great flamboyance in New York in October 1964. Meanwhile, the British Fordson tractors had slipped quietly away a few months earlier. Production of the Dexta models had ended in June with the last Super Major built just four weeks later. The era of Fordson farming was over.

THE MAJOR POWER ON THE LAND

Three models of E27N Major were offered from 1946. The basic agricultural model had a fixed front axle and no steering brakes. The rowcrop model had independent steering brakes, an adjustable front axle and the rear tread could also be altered by turning the dished rear-wheel centres. The Land Utility model, only available on pneumatic tyres, had the fixed front axle, steering brakes and the adjustable rear wheel centres.

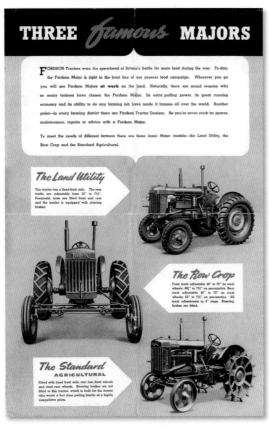

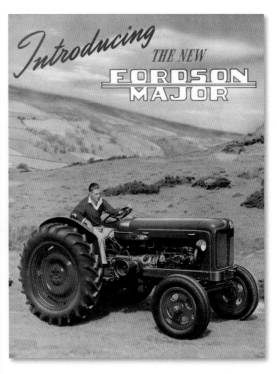

The 'New' Fordson Major, designated E1A, was launched in November 1951. It was a great leap forward in styling compared to the previous E27N model. The new tractor had a more modern appearance with uncluttered lines and the air cleaner tucked away neatly under the bonnet. The pre-production models that featured in the launch brochure were finished in a darker blue to the actual 'Empire Blue' paint used on the production tractors.

Customers who wanted their E27N Major to have more power and greater refinement were able to specify the Perkins P6 diesel from February 1948. This six-cylinder engine developed a useful 45hp and had a pressurised lubrication system, but there was a price to pay. The Land Utility model with the P6 engine would have cost £595 compared to £303 for the TVO version.

Designed by Laurie Martland, the new OHV engine for the E1A Major was produced in petrol, TVO and diesel versions. Many components were common to all three power units including a strong five-bearing forged-steel crankshaft. The valves were push-rod operated. Another advanced feature was the use of centrifugally-cast wet cylinder liners that were easy to service and gave exceptionally low oil consumption.

The engine fitted to the diesel version of the 'New' Major, designated E1ADDN, was an absolutely superb power unit – reliable, economical and easy to start. It had a 100mm bore, 115mm stroke and a Simms inline injector pump incorporating a pneumatic governor and an excess-fuel button for cold starting.

THREE *NEW* ENGINES

Modern in design

Economical in fuel consumption

Sectional view of the new petrol engine. Parts common to all three engines are picked out in red.

Petrol, Vaporising Oil, Diesel . . . the new Major gives farmers the choice of three entirely new Ford produced O.H.V. 4-cylinder engines. Good designing has made it possible to give power with economy and to use many components which are common to all three. Many desirable features have also been introduced to ensure the greatest efficiency on each of the three separate fuels. The use of common parts simplifies service—reduces the cost of spares and makes the New Fordson Major more economical to buy. This is just one example of how Major Farming Leads in Value.

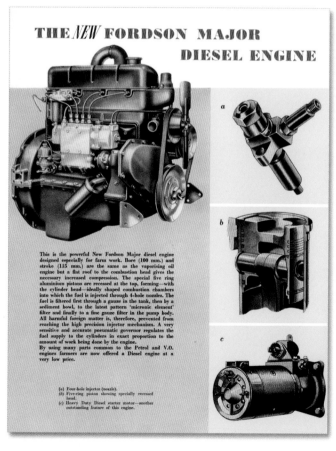

THE *NEW* FORDSON MAJOR DIESEL ENGINE

This is the powerful New Fordson Major diesel engine designed especially for farm work. Bore (100 mm.) and stroke (115 mm.) are the same as the vaporising oil engine but a flat roof to the combustion head gives the necessary increased compression. The special five ring aluminium pistons are recessed at the top, forming—with the cylinder head—ideally shaped combustion chambers into which the fuel is injected through 4-hole nozzles. The fuel is filtered first through a gauze in the tank, then by a sediment bowl, to the latest pattern 'micronic element' filter and finally to a fine gauze filter in the pump body. All harmful foreign matter is, therefore, prevented from reaching the high precision injector mechanism. A very sensitive and accurate pneumatic governor regulates the fuel supply to the cylinders in exact proportion to the amount of work being done by the engine.
By using many parts common to the Petrol and V.O. engines farmers are now offered a Diesel engine at a very low price.

(a) Four-hole injector (nozzle).
(b) Five-ring piston showing specially recessed head.
(c) Heavy Duty Diesel starter motor—another outstanding feature of this engine.

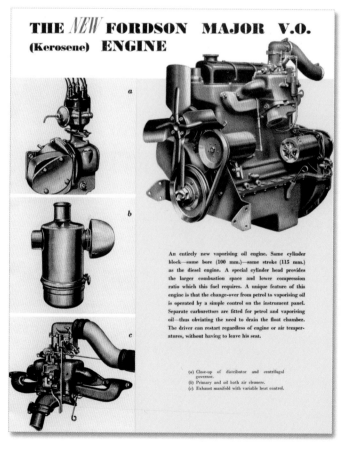

THE *NEW* FORDSON MAJOR V.O.
(Kerosene) ENGINE

An entirely new vaporising oil engine. Same cylinder block—same bore (100 mm.)—same stroke (115 mm.) as the diesel engine. A special cylinder head provides the larger combustion space and lower compression ratio which this fuel requires. A unique feature of this engine is that the change-over from petrol to vaporising oil is operated by a simple control on the instrument panel. Separate carburettors are fitted for petrol and vaporising oil—thus obviating the need to drain the float chamber. The driver can restart regardless of engine or air temperatures, without having to leave his seat.

(a) Close-up of distributor and centrifugal governor.
(b) Primary and oil bath air cleaners.
(c) Exhaust manifold with variable heat control.

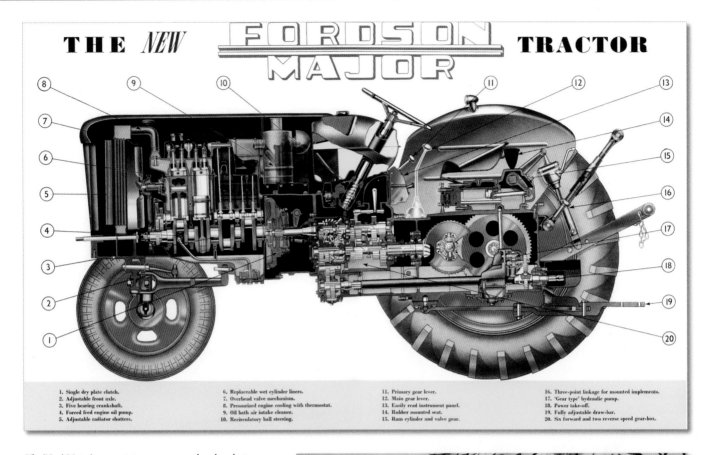

THE *NEW* FORDSON MAJOR TRACTOR

1. Single dry plate clutch.
2. Adjustable front axle.
3. Five bearing crankshaft.
4. Forced feed engine oil pump.
5. Adjustable radiator shutters.
6. Replaceable wet cylinder liners.
7. Overhead valve mechanism.
8. Pressurized engine cooling with thermostat.
9. Oil bath air intake cleaner.
10. Recirculatory ball steering.
11. Primary gear lever.
12. Main gear lever.
13. Easily read instrument panel.
14. Rubber mounted seat.
15. Ram cylinder and valve gear.
16. Three-point linkage for mounted implements.
17. 'Gear type' hydraulic pump.
18. Power take-off.
19. Fully adjustable draw-bar.
20. Six forward and two reverse speed gear-box.

The 'New' Major's transmission was arranged so that the input shaft from the engine to the E27N gearbox could drive both the top-shaft and lower-shaft independently of each other. This allowed six speeds to be obtained with the high and low ratios selected by a primary gear lever mounted above the gearbox. The transmission incorporated a dry clutch.

The TVO version of the engine was a decent power unit, but was thirsty and could be temperamental. It was outclassed by the diesel power unit and had nowhere as much torque. The TVO version of the 'New' Major was designated E1ADKN while the petrol model was E1AD. The TVO unit had coil ignition, an upright distributor (with automatic advance and retard) and a centrifugal governor.

By the mid-1950s, the Fordson Diesel Major dominated sales and more than 100,000 had been built. The petrol and TVO versions were eventually dropped. The importance of the compression-ignition power unit was now signified by a new style of bonnet badge with a big 'D' for diesel.

D·B·H·P

DRAWBAR POWER IS THE POWER THAT PAYS!

Under N.I.A.E. tests, the Fordson Major Diesel showed 31.4 d.b.h.p. ! This is the power that pays for hauling, for heavy three-furrow ploughing, and for most jobs on your land.

FORDSON MAJOR DIESEL

FORD MOTOR COMPANY LIMITED · DAGENHAM · ESSEX

LEADS IN VALUE

The year 1957 saw the launch of the Mark 2 Diesel Major with improved fuel injection and lubrication systems. The engine also had a new cylinder head with inline ports. An optional two-stage clutch gave 'live' power take-off and hydraulics.

The option of the two-stage clutch had been introduced in December 1956. This meant that the hydraulic lift and power take-off now operated independently of the tractor's forward motion.

Without 'live' power take-off it was almost impossible to operate a combine or baler. When harvesting, halting the tractor would also stop the drive to the threshing mechanism, usually resulting in a blockage. The two-stage clutch eliminated this problem. The driver could stop the tractor by depressing the clutch pedal halfway and the power take-off would continue to run.

The Major got a workmate in 1957 in the form of the new Fordson Dexta – Ford's answer to the dominance of the Ferguson TE-20 in the lightweight sector of the marketplace. Much of the design of the Dexta was based on the American Ford 8N tractor. During its development John Foxwell was charged with ensuring the design didn't infringe any Ferguson patents.

The Dexta's three-cylinder power unit was a Ford version \ of the Perkins P3 diesel. The castings for the engine were manufactured in Ford's foundry at Dagenham, while the internal components were fitted at the Perkins factory in Peterborough. Known as the F3 engine, it had an inline Simms injection pump and developed a handy 32hp.

Four bearing Crankshaft—steel forged. Bearings copper-lead lined thin wall type. Static and dynamic balance ensures smooth performance.

Pistons—Connecting Rods—five rings fitted, top ring chrome plated for long bore life. Thin wall big end bearings and steel backed small end.

Engine Oil Pump—high pressure, forced lubrication throughout. Pump is driven from the crankshaft. There is a full flow filter.

Overhead Valve-gear—enables the easily detachable head to be removed without disturbing the timing. Fewer parts—fewer adjustments—easy maintenance.

NEW-EFFICIENCY 3 CYLINDER DIESEL ENGINE

NEW TRANSMISSION

The Transmission for the new Fordson Dexta has been designed for great strength and long life and offers six forward and two reverse speeds.

The compact new gearbox is of the constant mesh type which means the elimination of much tooth wear due to crash changes. Initial gears are helically cut, giving greater strength coupled with silent operation.

As clearly indicated on the speed overlap chart there is a speed for every job. The operator is always able to select the most economical gear.

Crown wheel and pinion of the final drive are accurately matched in manufacture to ensure long life and quiet troublefree operation. Both run on heavy duty taper roller bearings, while the axle shafts have semi-floating tapered bearings at each wheel to carry the load.

Clutch is of 11 in. diameter with light pedal action and is fitted with nine pressure springs enabling it to withstand heavy shock loads.

There is also a "double" clutch when live p.t.o. is fitted. This is described on another page.

Road speeds at 2,000 engine r.p.m.

Gear	m.p.h.	k.p.h.	Gear	m.p.h.	k.p.h.
1st	1.72	2.77	5th	10.26	16.52
2nd	3.68	5.92	6th	16.8	27.05
3rd	4.80	7.33	High rev.	7.42	11.95
4th	6.03	9.7	Low rev.	2.66	4.28

The Dexta's six-speed gearbox was designed by John Foxwell and was based on the Major's configuration. The four highest gears (3, 4, 5 and 6) and high reverse had two reductions, while the two lowest gears and low reverse underwent four reductions. The gearbox was operated by two levers.

A special version of the Dexta for golf courses, parks and playing fields was introduced in 1959. Fitted with grassland tyres it could be supplied with or without hydraulics or power take-off.

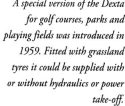

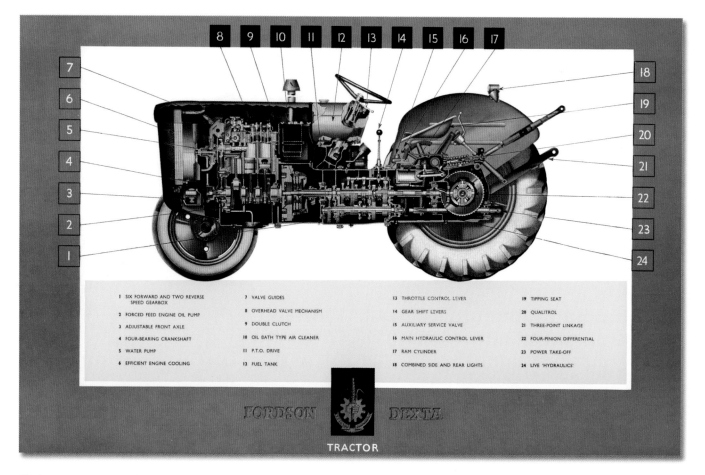

FORDSON DEXTA TRACTOR

1 SIX FORWARD AND TWO REVERSE SPEED GEARBOX	7 VALVE GUIDES	13 THROTTLE CONTROL LEVER	19 TIPPING SEAT
2 FORCED FEED ENGINE OIL PUMP	8 OVERHEAD VALVE MECHANISM	14 GEAR SHIFT LEVERS	20 QUALITROL
3 ADJUSTABLE FRONT AXLE	9 DOUBLE CLUTCH	15 AUXILIARY SERVICE VALVE	21 THREE-POINT LINKAGE
4 FOUR-BEARING CRANKSHAFT	10 OIL BATH TYPE AIR CLEANER	16 MAIN HYDRAULIC CONTROL LEVER	22 FOUR-PINION DIFFERENTIAL
5 WATER PUMP	11 P.T.O. DRIVE	17 RAM CYLINDER	23 POWER TAKE-OFF
6 EFFICIENT ENGINE COOLING	12 FUEL TANK	18 COMBINED SIDE AND REAR LIGHTS	24 LIVE 'HYDRAULICS'

The Dexta was a very neat package with a lively and economical three-cylinder diesel engine mated to a six-speed gearbox. A dual-clutch with 'live' power take-off was optional. The basic tractor was priced at £525 with the 'live' model costing an extra £30.

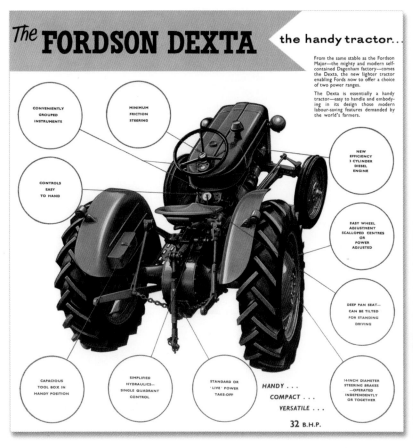

The FORDSON DEXTA — the handy tractor...

From the same stable as the Fordson Major—the mighty and modern self-contained Dagenham factory—comes the Dexta, the new lighter tractor enabling Fords now to offer a choice of two power ranges.

The Dexta is essentially a handy tractor—easy to handle and embodying in its design those modern labour-saving features demanded by the world's farmers.

CONVENIENTLY GROUPED INSTRUMENTS

MINIMUM FRICTION STEERING

CONTROLS EASY TO HAND

NEW EFFICIENCY 3 CYLINDER DIESEL ENGINE

EASY WHEEL ADJUSTMENT SCALLOPED CENTRES OR POWER ADJUSTED

DEEP PAN SEAT— CAN BE TILTED FOR STANDING DRIVING

CAPACIOUS TOOL BOX IN HANDY POSITION

SIMPLIFIED HYDRAULICS— SINGLE QUADRANT CONTROL

STANDARD OR 'LIVE' POWER TAKE-OFF

14-INCH DIAMETER STEERING BRAKES —OPERATED INDEPENDENTLY OR TOGETHER

HANDY . . .
COMPACT . . .
VERSATILE . . .

32 B.H.P.

By changing the hydraulic control-valve from the suction to the delivery side of the pump, Dagenham's engineers were able to bypass any Ferguson patents and introduce draft control for the first time on a Fordson tractor. The system was known as Qualitrol and had top-link sensing.

The E1A Major received a facelift in 1958 when it was upgraded into the Fordson Power Major. Outwardly not much of the tractor had changed, but several internal improvements had been made to the engine, hydraulics, transmission and differential.

new big engine

NOW, the Fordson Major, world-famous for its outstanding Diesel engine, becomes the Fordson Power Major, with a new, more powerful engine to do more work, all day, every day

The Power Major was indeed the Major with more power. The tractor had the Mark 3 engine, which was an evolution of the Mark 2 Major with modifications to the camshaft and injection timing. It developed 51.8 brake horsepower.

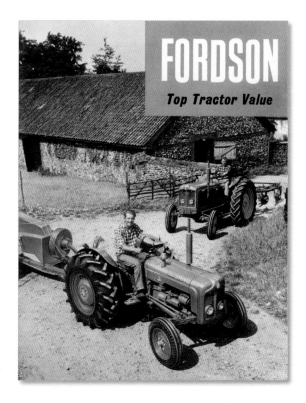

In October 1960 Ford introduced its 'Super Class' of Fordson tractors with the Super Major replacing the Power Major. At the same time, the Dexta was given a makeover to bring its styling inline with the Super Major with minor changes to the specification.

Apart from the engine changes, the Power Major also featured a strengthened transmission and differential. The lift capacity was also increased and the throttle was now next to the steering wheel with a new instrument panel that contained a tachometer indicating pulley and PTO-speeds. The stylish new wheel designs included scalloped rear centres that were designed to make it easier to adjust the wheel track.

The Super Major was the first E1A model to have a draft control hydraulic system. Its Qualitrol system incorporated a flow-control valve and top-link sensing. Other new features included a differential lock and independent disc brakes.

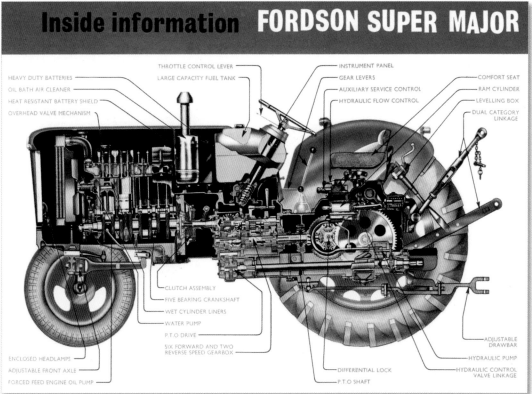

The Fordson Super Major is world famous for its basic design, its proved ruggedness and stamina. To that basic design the Super Major adds every worthwhile modern feature—disc brakes, differential lock, dual linkage, flow control, etc. Each designed to match the high standards of Fordson reliability and efficiency, to match the big tough design of the tractor. And the wide range of optional features, tyre sizes, etc., enables the buyer to have a tractor designed for his farm, giving every facility he needs without paying for things which he will never use. The Super Major is the acknowledged world leader in its class and has an unrivalled success story all over the world.

Making light work of PTO powered baling.

4 furrow ploughing in most conditions.

Super Major with 4 furrow FR reversible plough.

Rotavating, a tough job made easy with the Super Major

The Super Major—World leader in power for production.

The Super Major was more than just a facelift and the new model featured a large number of revisions. Styling changes saw the headlights set into the grilles. The tractor also had a heavier front cross-member and larger chrome handles for the bonnet.

Most of the changes made to the Dexta in 1960 were cosmetic with the most noticeable being the relocation of the headlights from the sides of the radiator cowling into the front grilles. New chrome badges were affixed to the bonnet sides and the vertical emblem on the front cowling's centre-strut was deleted.

Mowing with the FR Power take-off driven mower.

Disc harrowing—double acting ram control.

Hoeing is easy with quick change track width.

Handy work around the farm—linkage mounted lift box.

3 furrow ploughing—Dexta logging power.

Tough work rotavating—handled in Dexta's long stride.

Because the Fordson Dexta is designed for the man in the seat, with modern and simple hydraulics, high efficiency P.T.O. and all-crop gearbox, it makes it easy to produce more at less cost with less time lost. The Fordson Dexta is without doubt the top light tractor value on the market today.

Fordson Dexta—Fordson Farming Puts the Farmer First.

Take a look inside the FORDSON DEXTA

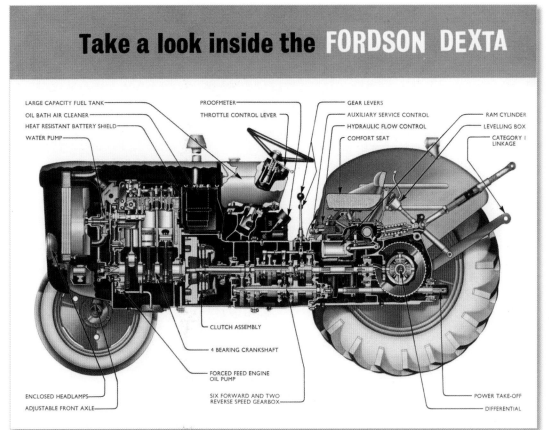

LARGE CAPACITY FUEL TANK
OIL BATH AIR CLEANER
HEAT RESISTANT BATTERY SHIELD
WATER PUMP

PROOFMETER
THROTTLE CONTROL LEVER

GEAR LEVERS
AUXILIARY SERVICE CONTROL
HYDRAULIC FLOW CONTROL
COMFORT SEAT

RAM CYLINDER
LEVELLING BOX
CATEGORY I LINKAGE

CLUTCH ASSEMBLY

4 BEARING CRANKSHAFT

FORCED FEED ENGINE OIL PUMP

ENCLOSED HEADLAMPS
ADJUSTABLE FRONT AXLE

SIX FORWARD AND TWO REVERSE SPEED GEARBOX

POWER TAKE-OFF
DIFFERENTIAL

Mechanically the 1960 Dexta was the much the same as the previous model. A deep-pan cushioned seat was now standard equipment and a flow-control valve was incorporated into the hydraulic system. The gearbox ratios had been revised earlier in the year and a handbrake had been added to the specification in 1959. Differential lock was introduced in 1961.

A narrow version of the Dexta was introduced in 1960 for working in hop-fields, vineyards and orchards. The conversion was done by Stormont Engineering in Kent and the tractor was just 52in wide.

TOP TRACTOR VALUE

The Fordson Super Dexta with 39.5 b.h.p. puts new power into light tractor farming.

Designed for the man who wants his light tractor to do really hard work fast, and to match the power of modern PTO driven implements the Super Dexta measures up to all these requirements sensationally.

The new 39.5 b.h.p. Super 3 engine fitted with Super Response Injection Pump with mechanical governor immediately meets changes in power demands, and ensures smooth engine performance, high quality work and long engine life. *All Fordson Tractors are now equipped with this latest injection system.*

In sheer farming value the Super Dexta, the powerful yet light tractor, shows a handiness and versatility unmatched in farming today.

SUPER DEXTA OFFERS TOP VALUE IN ITS CLASS
* More power with light tractor versatility
* Greater power available at PTO
* Designed for the man in the seat with comfort, convenience and safety
* Modern and simple hydraulics
* Unmatched Service

SUPER DEXTA OFFERS TRADITIONAL FORD VALUE AND RELIABILITY
* A low initial price
* Low running costs

SUPER DEXTA OFFERS BETTER VALUE
* More comprehensive range of optional equipment
* Backed by the resources of Ford

TRACTOR GROUP   FORD MOTOR COMPANY LIMITED   .   DAGENHAM

Ford

FORDSON NARROW DEXTA ONLY 52" WIDE

Designed for a host of jobs in plantations, vineyards, orchards, hop fields and for all soft fruit work, the narrow Dexta will work harder, more profitably for you than any competitive machine. With its low centre of gravity, essential on such narrow track widths when working across hillsides, the Dexta is the most versatile tractor for this type of work.

The Narrow Dexta's precision matched ratio 6-speed gearbox gives the operator the ideal speed for every cultivation and the simple, single quadrant control hydraulics allow the operator to give his full concentration to the job in hand.

More than a specialist machine, the Narrow Dexta can be easily adjusted for normal farm work up to 76 in. overall width.

TRACK ADJUSTMENT.
Rear wheels 42 in.-66 in. in 4 in. steps (10 x 28 tyres).
Front wheels 44 in.-60 in. in 4 in. steps (4.00 x 19 tyres).

The more powerful Super Dexta was unveiled at the Royal Show in July 1962. A larger capacity radiator was provided to improve cooling, and this was accommodated by a new nose-cone that somewhat altered the tractor's frontal appearance compared to the standard Dexta, which still remained part of the Fordson range.

MORE POWER ALL ROUND

39.5 BHP

THE new Super 3 engine, a development from the proved and style setting Fordson Dexta motor, has been engineered to match the requirements of modern PTO driven machines. Its three cylinders ensure maximum output of 39.5 b.h.p. at 2,000 r.p.m. with ample power at the drawbar, hydraulics, pulley or PTO (available power at PTO 34 b.h.p.). Lift the bonnet of the Fordson Super Dexta and see how much more accessible the new Super 3 engine is than those of its competitors. This means easier routine servicing, quicker, less expensive workshop repairs and in the engine itself there are many more long life features such as : 4-bearing crankshaft for trouble-free performance, high pressure engine lubrication and full fuel filtration, etc.

THE NEW SUPER RESPONSE PUMP

with its mechanical governing of the Super 3 diesel engine greatly improves the response of the governor to changes in engine load. It not only gives a quicker but a more accurate response enabling the operator to attain a smoother work rate together with higher quality work.

Mechanical governors have the advantage of being completely contained in the injection pump and as such are accurately pre-set before assembly to the engine.

An additional important feature of this new Super Response Pump is that reduced run out revs are obtained thereby enabling more accurate governing throughout the engine speed range.

* Enables tractor operator to attain smoother work rate with higher quality work.
* Governor completely self-contained in pump.
* Factory pre-set before assembly for maximum service-free performance.
* Flange mounted to ensure permanent alignment and longer life.

quicker more accurate response to changing engine load

The Super Dexta had the new 'Super 3' engine – a larger version of the standard Dexta power unit bored out to 152cu in (2,500cc). A mechanically-governed Simms Minimec pump was fitted and the engine developed 38.9hp. The gearbox and rear axle were also strengthened to cope with the extra power.

NEW SUPER DEXTA   NEW SUPER MAJOR   DEXTA

The final incarnation of the Fordson line from Dagenham was the 'New Performance' range of 1963. This facelift to the existing Super Major, Super Dexta and Dexta models included a change of colour to the new corporate blue/grey livery.

FORDSON SUPER MAJOR

THE
NEW PERFORMANCE
FORDSONS

NOW WITH
MAX 47 HP AT PTO

The 'New Performance' Super Major was launched in June 1962. Apart from the obvious change to a new blue and grey colour scheme, the tractor also featured a number of modifications including slightly more power and a strengthened gearbox and power take-off.

Continual development during the Super Major's production run had seen a number of other modifications made to the engine, including changes to the cylinder liners, timing gears, oil pump, exhaust valves, camshaft and lift pump. A Simms Minimec pump had also been fitted in July 1962. With the launch of the 'New Performance' model, the engineers tweaked the Minimec pump to deliver 53.7hp.

BIG PULLING POWER

PRACTICAL - PROVED POWER

With feature after feature - in engine design, in advanced hydraulics, in its tough reliable transmission, in comfort and safety a Fordson Super Major offers you far more than any other tractor in its power/price class.

Fordson Super Major power is PRACTICAL, PROVED POWER, designed for dependable operation with features so basically sound in design and construction that it is easy to understand why so many farmers throughout the world specify Fordson Super Major whenever they are considering a new machine.

53·7 B.H.P. AND ALL THE BIG PLUS FEATURES

★ 3½ litre Diesel Engine 53·7 B.H.P. at only 1,700 R.P.M.
★ Max. 47 H.P. at the P.T.O. at 1,700 engine R.P.M.
★ 42 H.P. at 540 R.P.M. at P.T.O. (only 1,470 engine R.P.M.).
★ Sustained-lift Hydraulics with Automatic Double Acting Top Link, Quadrtrol, Position Control and Dual Flow Control.
★ Big Drawbar pull in excess of 8,500 lb.
★ Powerful disc brakes, diff. lock.
★ Advanced safety and comfort features, including new optional 'Rest-O-Ride' seat.
★ Optional equipment includes Live P.T.O., Belt Pulley, Power Steering, Automatic Pick-Up Hitch etc.

Slogging power at low speeds is an outstanding feature of this 53·7 B.H.P. engine. This is vital under arduous conditions.

If it's BIG power you need from the Blue Team sit in the seat of the Fordson Super Major, press the starter and feel the extra surge of eager power from its increased power engine. Yes, here's the tractor with the engine that's designed to help you farm faster, easier, more economically. You'll find that the new 53·7 B.H.P. developed from this 3½ litre diesel is a match for every job on the farm and it's the engine built to stand up to your heaviest demands. Such features as heavy duty five bearing crankshaft giving reduced load on each bearing with corresponding reduction in wear, special five ring pistons, wet cylinder liners, forced feed lubrication, direct fuel injection, are typical of that EXTRA toughness built into this mighty power unit. Yes, here's the BIG 4 cylinder engine that can 'take it' and 'give it' — power governed by the inline Super Response Injection Pump ensuring instant response to changes in engine load and consequent smoother more profitable work rate.

Three furrow reversible ploughing, the sure quick way to cover all the field with no later disadvantage of ground undulations — this job needs the power of the Super Major.

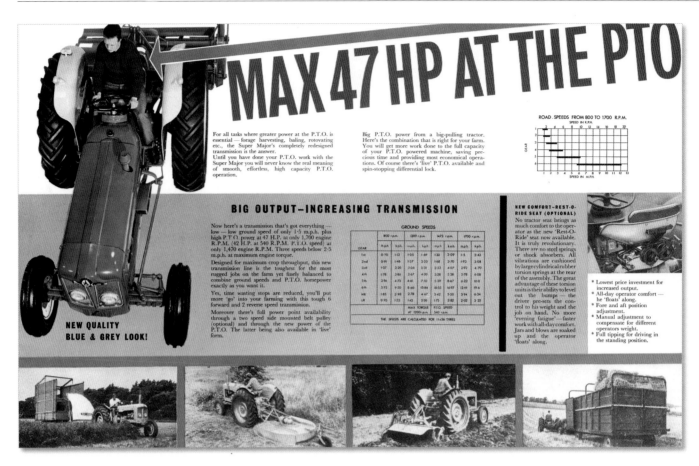

The 'New Performance' Super Major was fitted with a different ratio crown-wheel and pinion to give slower ground speeds for power take-off work. The hydraulics were also improved by a dual-flow control-valve that controlled both the rate of lift and lowering.

The styling of the 'New Performance' Super Dexta was unchanged apart from a new Fordson decal on the side of the bonnet. The man giving the tractor the thumbs-up on the cover of the brochure was Ford's demonstrator, Arthur Battelle.

The specification of the 'New Performance' Super Dexta included a new automatic pressure-relief valve similar to that fitted to the Super Major. This was located in the hydraulic top-cover and allowed a sustained lift under all operating conditions.

THE NEW SUPER DEXTA

New Fordson Super Dexta and FR TS81 two-furrow
reversible plough.

BRIEF SPECIFICATION

Engine 3-Cylinder Diesel BHP at 2,000 RPM	44·5
Length Overall	118⅜ in.
Width Overall (min. track)	64½ in.
Height Overall (steering wheel)	54.4 in.
Wheelbase (min. track)	72⅛ in.
Turning Circle (with brakes)	18 ft.
Ground Clearance (under axles)	21 in.
(under transmission)	12 in.
Weight	3,100 lb.
Belt speed (2,000 engine RPM)	3,000 ft./min.
CAPACITIES	
Fuel Tank	7 gallons
Engine Sump	12½ pints
Transmission	23 pints
Rear Axle and Power Lift	34 pints

The standard Dexta had been given a mechanically-governed Minimec pump in 1961. Except for the new colours (and cost-saving bonnet decals), nothing else was changed for the 'New Performance' version apart from the addition of an automatic relief valve in the hydraulics to bring it inline with the other tractors in the range.

PTO POWER

The Minimec injector pump fitted to the Super Dexta was up-rated slightly to boost the power to 44.5hp. This gave the tractor 34hp at the power take-off – ideal for operations such as rotary tillage.

FOWLER

The Fowler FD3 went into full production early in 1946 with a three-cylinder diesel engine and a six-speed transmission. The Fowler-Sanders engine, with a 4¼in bore and 6¼in stroke, gave 35hp at 1,250rpm. Steering was a conventional clutch-and-brake system.

The sheer amount of new tractors coming onto the British market in the period immediately after the Second World War can make it difficult to cover every model produced by each manufacturer. And nowhere does it get more confusing than with the machines produced by John Fowler & Co (Leeds) Ltd. It was a time of mixed fortunes for the business, which was going through several changes of ownership, and the company muddied the waters even further by producing a number of different crawlers with similar designations using both Arabic and Roman numerals.

Fowler's Steam Plough Works in Leeds, as the name suggests, had its roots in steam. The company was one of Britain's most celebrated engineering concerns with a long history dating back to the mid-nineteenth century. The founder, John Fowler, had been one of the pioneers of cable-ploughing with steam.

Fowler delivered its last set of steam ploughing tackle in 1933, by which time the company had already started to make the transition into a tractor manufacturer. It had already dabbled with motor ploughs and its diesel-powered rotary cultivators, the famous Fowler Gyrotillers, were enjoying limited success.

A pre-war line of agricultural crawlers, fitted with a high-speed diesel engine developed by Harry Cooper and later improved by Arthur Freeman-Sanders, showed great promise, but sales were disappointing. Crippled with financial debt, Fowler's board ended tractor production in 1938.

Fowler's board of directors was in disarray and it was looking as if the company would fold when the outbreak of war came to its rescue. In 1941 the business was compulsory purchased by the Ministry of Supply and the Steam Plough Works was given over to tank production.

Towards the end of the war, at the Ministry of Supply's instigation, the engineering team at Leeds began developing a new range of crawler tractors – the FD range with Fowler-Sanders diesel engines. In 1944 the government put the Fowler business up for sale and the company was bought the following year by Australian émigré, Arthur Howard. Howard's company, Rotary Hoes Ltd of Essex, was already well-known for its rotary cultivators and drainage machines.

Development of the Fowler crawler range continued under Howard's ownership with four models proposed: the FD1, FD2, FD3 and FD4. The FD2 was a Howard design for the horticultural sector, while the three-cylinder FD3, launched in late 1945,

FOWLER *FD3* DIESEL CRAWLER TRACTOR

"There's a future in farming – with Fowlers"

was a 35hp design aimed squarely at the agricultural market. The FD1 never appeared and production of the 54hp FD4 was only just getting underway when Rotary Hoes Ltd sold John Fowler & Co (Leeds) Ltd to Thomas W Ward Ltd of Sheffield for a not inconsiderable profit on 17 December 1946.

The Thomas W Ward Group already had a controlling interest in Marshall, Sons & Co Ltd. This Lincolnshire firm was another famous engineering concern with its roots in steam. Its Britannia Works at Gainsborough was home to the Marshall single-cylinder diesel wheeled tractor and a pooling of resources with Fowler had obvious benefits.

The Fowler FD3 crawler had been well received and some 700 were built before production ended in mid-1947. The Ward Group had been unable to secure the patents to the Fowler-Sanders engines, resulting in the abandonment of the FD range.

The FD3's replacement was the Fowler VF, powered by an engine from the Field Marshall wheeled tractor. Unveiled in July 1947 the single-cylinder VF seemed a poor replacement for the arguably more refined FD3, but it was competitively priced (at £1,050 it was less than half the price of the equivalent Caterpillar) and its simple design and unrivalled fuel economy drew in the customers. Upgraded into the VFA in 1953, it remained on the market until January 1957 and more than 6,000 were sold.

The premature demise of the FD range prompted the development of two more powerful crawler tractors: the Fowler Challenger l and the Challenger Mark ll. Both were powered by Marshall diesel engines of an unusual design – being two-cylinder two-stroke units with a Roots blower providing scavenging and charging of the cylinders.

The Challenger l was launched in 1951 and its ED5 engine developed 50hp. Plagued with high oil consumption and poor starting problems, the tractor was by no means a success although it remained on the market until November 1955. Powered by the 80hp ED8 engine, the Challenger Mark ll, which in Fowler's typically confusing way actually appeared a year earlier than the Challenger l, was even more of a disaster and was quickly abandoned.

During 1951 the Mark ll was replaced by the Challenger lll with a six-cylinder Meadows 6DC630 diesel engine. The change from Roman to Arabic designations saw the tractor become the Challenger 3 with a six-cylinder Leyland AU600 power unit offered as an alternative to the Meadows engine. Both engines were rated at 95hp.

An even larger machine, the Fowler Challenger 4 with a 150hp Meadows 6DJ970 engine, made its debut at the 1953 Royal Show. In 1956 the Chal-

lenger 2 (not to be confused with the Mark ll) with a 60hp six-cylinder Leyland AU350 engine was introduced to slot into the range below the Challenger 3.

A revamp of the Fowler range in 1958 saw the Challenger 2 become the Challenger 22 with more modern styling. Similar styling was applied to the Challenger 3, which adopted the 125hp Leyland AU680 engine to become the Challenger 33. The Challenger 4 was dropped.

The Challenger 22 remained in production until 1961 when the Challenger 33 became the last Fowler crawler on the market. After the Steam Plough Works closed in 1974, production was transferred to Gainsborough where the 33 continued as the Track-Marshall 140 – now with a 140hp version of the Leyland AU680 engine – until 1987.

The Fowler FD2 was a Howard design and most were sold with a Rotavator attachment for horticultural use. Its four-cylinder Fowler-Sanders diesel engine was rated at 25hp and steering was via a controlled differential.

Following trials, the VF crawler was unveiled as a Marshall-Fowler product at the Royal Show in July 1947. The Marshall name was never applied to the production tractors, which were only ever sold under the Fowler name.

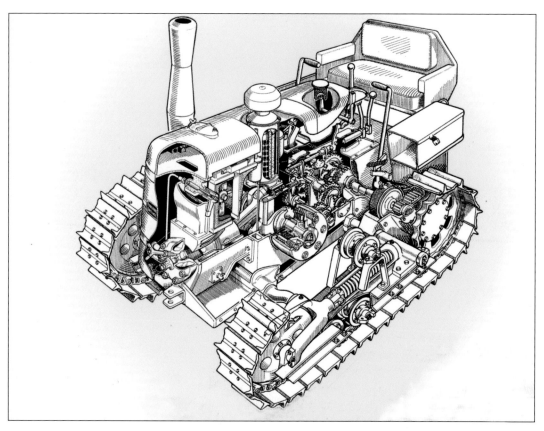

The Fowler VF was powered by Marshall's single-cylinder two-stroke diesel engine, which delivered 40hp at a leisurely 750rpm. The transmission gave six forward speeds and the steering was via a controlled differential.

One of the patented features of the Fowler VF was the track stabiliser – a cranked front axle that allowed the independent oscillation of each track for crossing uneven ground. The operator's platform was uncluttered, but the driver sat high up and was exposed to the elements.

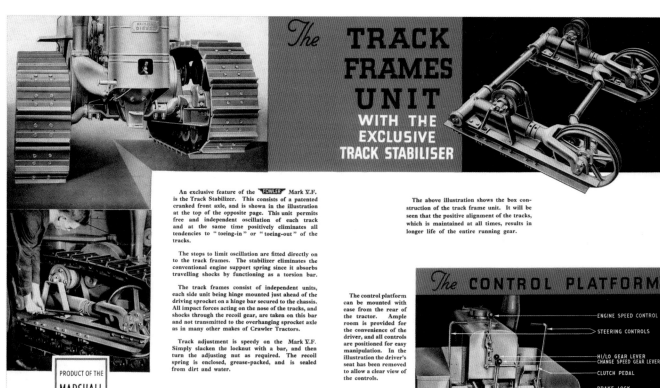

The
TRACK
FRAMES
UNIT
WITH THE
EXCLUSIVE
TRACK STABILISER

An exclusive feature of the FOWLER Mark V.F. is the Track Stabilizer. This consists of a patented cranked front axle, and is shown in the illustration at the top of the opposite page. This unit permits free and independent oscillation of each track and at the same time positively eliminates all tendencies to "toeing-in" or "toeing-out" of the tracks.

The stops to limit oscillation are fitted directly on to the track frames. The stabilizer eliminates the conventional engine support spring since it absorbs travelling shocks by functioning as a torsion bar.

The track frames consist of independent units, each side unit being hinge mounted just ahead of the driving sprocket on a hinge bar secured to the chassis. All impact forces acting on the nose of the tracks, and shocks through the recoil gear, are taken on this bar and not transmitted to the overhanging sprocket axle as in many other makes of Crawler Tractors.

Track adjustment is speedy on the Mark V.F. Simply slacken the locknut with a bar, and then turn the adjusting nut as required. The recoil spring is enclosed, grease-packed, and is sealed from dirt and water.

The above illustration shows the box construction of the track frame unit. It will be seen that the positive alignment of the tracks, which is maintained at all times, results in longer life of the entire running gear.

PRODUCT OF THE
MARSHALL
ORGANISATION

The CONTROL PLATFORM

The control platform can be mounted with ease from the rear of the tractor. Ample room is provided for the convenience of the driver, and all controls are positioned for easy manipulation. In the illustration the driver's seat has been removed to allow a clear view of the controls.

ENGINE SPEED CONTROL

STEERING CONTROLS

HI/LO GEAR LEVER
CHANGE SPEED GEAR LEVER

CLUTCH PEDAL

BRAKE LOCK

CLUTCH HAND LEVER

THE MARSHALL-FOWLER
MARK V.F DIESEL CRAWLER TRACTOR

A MARSHALL-FOWLER PRODUCT

CLIVE UPTTON

Competitively priced, the Fowler VF was able to match its competitors in terms of performance and was more frugal on fuel. The 'VF' designation should actually be read as '5F' and denoted that the tractor could handle five furrows.

The Fowler Mark VF is the Leading All-British Diesel Crawler

FOWLER

At the time of its launch there were few other British companies manufacturing crawlers and the VF was almost in a league of its own with a drawbar pull in excess of 10,000lb. However, once International, David Brown, County and Roadless started offering multi-cylinder machines, it became increasingly difficult to promote Fowler's simpler but cruder single-cylinder concept.

diesel power

FOWLER Mark VF

Diesel power was still a novelty in the late 1940s and early '50s and this was a big selling point for the VF. Many were exported with substantial sales to India. A total of 4,658 Fowler VF crawlers were built before the model was revamped in September 1952.

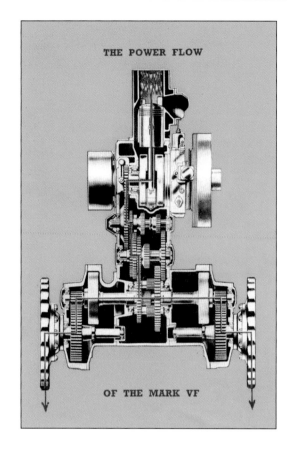

The Fowler VF's power-train couldn't have been simpler. Because the single-cylinder engine had a transverse crankshaft all the transmission shafts could be parallel to the final drives. The gears were all straight-cut and there was no need for any bevel gears or a crown-wheel and pinion.

The Fowler VF was also marketed as an angledozer with Bray hydraulic equipment. Blades were also offered by Blaw-Knox and Bomford. However, the stresses of heavy industrial work revealed a weakness in the final-drive casing, which was addressed with the introduction of the VFA model.

FOWLER MARK VFA
DIESEL CRAWLER TRACTOR
WITH MARSHALL SINGLE CYLINDER TWO-STROKE DIESEL ENGINE

The Fowler VFA, introduced in September 1952, incorporated a number of engine improvements introduced with the Field Marshall Series 3A wheeled tractor. At the same time changes were made to the transmission, tracks and running-gear with the final-drive assembly strengthened. In 1953 the 'Mid Brunswick Green' paint was changed to a new 'Chrome Orange' livery.

CHALLENGER I DIESEL CRAWLER TRACTOR

The Fowler Challenger l made its debut at the Smithfield Show in December 1951 with a price tag of £2,259. The tractor was powered by an unusual two-cylinder two-stroke diesel engine, which was matched to a six-speed transmission with two speeds in reverse. The early models were started by a 5hp Coventry Victor auxiliary petrol engine.

The Fowler Challenger Mark ll was rushed into production in 1950, but its two-cylinder two-stroke ED8 engine, delivering 80hp at just 825rpm, proved to be a complete disaster. The transmission gave six forward and four reverse speeds. Probably no more than a dozen were built.

The **FOWLER** LEEDS
Challenger MARK II
BRITISH DIESEL CRAWLER

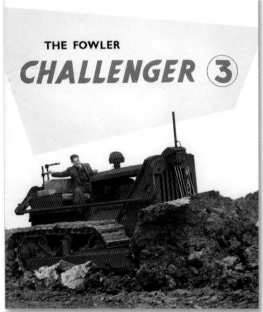

THE FOWLER **CHALLENGER 3**

The Fowler Challenger 3 replaced the Mark ll model in 1951. Both Meadows and Leyland six-cylinder diesel engines were offered and it proved to be a largely reliable and very successful model for the Marshall-Fowler organisation. Steering was by clutch-and-brake with the assemblies incorporated into a 'bevel box' with the crown-wheel.

To simplify maintenance all the Challenger 3's main assemblies were contained within a rigid hull that formed the backbone of the tractor. The gearbox was the same as fitted to the Mark ll. On the early Challenger 3s, a reduction-box had to be inserted in front of the gearbox because the Meadows power unit ran at nearly twice the speed of the ED8 engine.

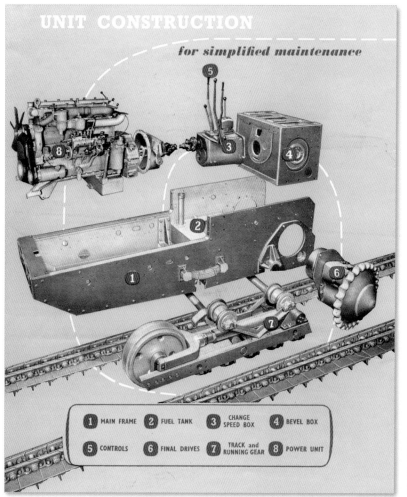

UNIT CONSTRUCTION
for simplified maintenance

| 1 MAIN FRAME | 2 FUEL TANK | 3 CHANGE SPEED BOX | 4 BEVEL BOX |
| 5 CONTROLS | 6 FINAL DRIVES | 7 TRACK and RUNNING GEAR | 8 POWER UNIT |

FOWLER CHALLENGER 3

The CHALLENGER 3

Designed and built entirely in Britain the Fowler Challenger 3 Diesel Crawler Tractor has proved itself in service in Britain and in many countries overseas.

THE CHALLENGER RANGE
The machines in the Challenger Range cover all requirements from 50-150 b.h.p. Already in production in addition to the 95 b.h.p. Challenger 3 are —
The 50 b.h.p. Challenger 1 with a new Marshall twin 2-stroke loop-scavenged Compression Ignition Oil Engine.
The 150 b.h.p. Challenger 4 with a Meadows Engine.

The six-cylinder Meadows 6DC630 power unit fitted to the Challenger 3 was arguably more refined than the optional Leyland power unit. Its 633 cu in (10,350cc) capacity gave 95hp at 1,500rpm. The running-gear for the tracks included five bottom rollers, two top rollers and a solid cast front-idler.

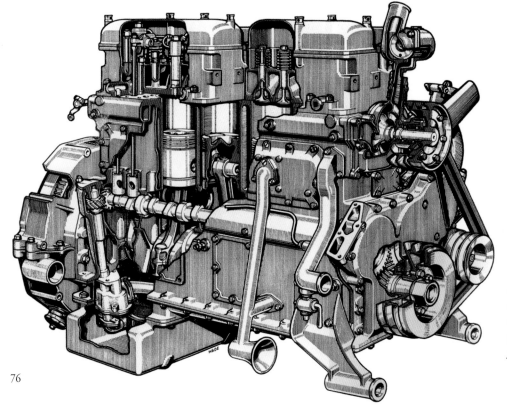

The Leyland AU600 power unit offered for the Challenger 3 was basically a standard six-cylinder lorry engine with a deep well sump to prevent oil starvation on steep gradients. It delivered 95hp at 1,550rpm from a capacity of 597cu in (9,790cc).

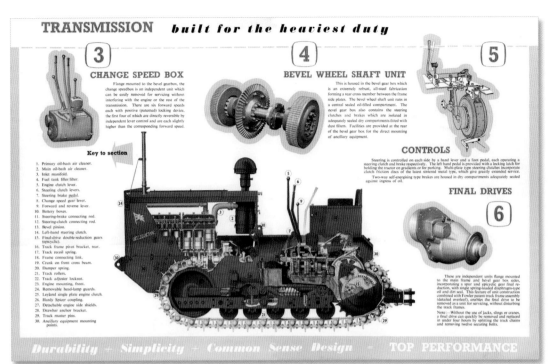

TRANSMISSION *built for the heaviest duty*

3

CHANGE SPEED BOX

Flange mounted on the bevel gearbox, the change speedbox is an independent unit which can be easily removed for servicing without interfering with the engine or rest of the transmission. There are six forward speeds each with positive (patented) locking device, the first four of which are directly reversible by independent lever control and are each slightly higher than the corresponding forward speed.

Key to section

1. Primary oil-bath air cleaner.
2. Main oil-bath air cleaner.
3. Inlet manifold.
4. Fuel tank filler/filter.
5. Engine clutch lever.
6. Steering clutch levers.
7. Steering brake pedal.
8. Change speed gear lever.
9. Forward and reverse lever.
10. Battery boxes.
11. Steering-brake connecting rod.
12. Steering-clutch connecting rod.
13. Bevel pinion.
14. Left-hand steering clutch.
15. Final-drive double-reduction gears (epicyclic).
16. Track frame pivot bracket, rear.
17. Track recoil spring.
18. Frame connecting link.
19. Crank on front cross beam.
20. Damper spring.
21. Track rollers.
22. Track adjuster locknut.
23. Engine mounting, front.
24. Removable hand-lamp guards.
25. Leyland single plate engine clutch.
26. Handy Spicer coupling.
27. Detachable engine side shields.
28. Drawbar anchor bracket.
29. Track master pins.
30. Ancillary equipment mounting points.

4

BEVEL WHEEL SHAFT UNIT

This is housed in the bevel gear box which is an extremely robust, all-steel fabrication forming a rear cross member between the frame side plates. The bevel wheel shaft unit runs in a central sealed oil-filled compartment. The bevel gear box also contains the steering clutches and brakes which are isolated in adequately sealed dry compartments fitted with dust filters. Facilities are provided at the rear of the bevel gear box for the direct mounting of ancillary equipment.

5

CONTROLS

Steering is controlled on each side by a hand lever and a foot pedal, each operating a steering clutch and brake respectively. The left hand pedal is provided with a locking latch for holding the tractor on gradients or for parking. Multi-plate type steering clutches incorporate clutch friction discs of the latest sintered metal type, which give greatly extended service.

Two-way self-energising type brakes are housed in dry compartments adequately sealed against ingress of oil.

FINAL DRIVES

6

These are independent units flange mounted to the main frame and bevel gear box sides, incorporating a spur and epicyclic gear final reduction, with single spring-loaded diaphragm-type oil and dirt seal. This feature of unit construction combined with Fowler patent track frame assembly (detailed overleaf), enables the final drive to be removed as a unit for servicing, without disturbing the track frames.

Note:—Without the use of jacks, slings or cranes, a final drive can quickly be removed and replaced in under four hours by splitting the track chains and removing twelve securing bolts.

Durability + Simplicity + Common Sense Design = TOP PERFORMANCE

The improved M2 version of the Fowler Challenger 3 had revised ratios in the gearbox that did away with the need for the reduction-box. The transmission was now driven directly from the engine clutch via a Cardan-shaft. This is the Leyland-powered version of the tractor.

THE FOWLER
CHALLENGER **4**

Fowler's mightiest machine, the Challenger 4, was in production from 1953-58. It was very much an overgrown version of the Challenger 3 with a 150hp Meadows engine driving a six forward, four reverse speed transmission. Aimed at the construction industry, it was an expensive machine at £6,950 and less than 140 were built.
.

The prototype Fowler Challenger 4 was started by a twin-cylinder Coventry Victor unit (seen behind the main engine). Later production models were offered with a 10hp Ford auxiliary engine or 24-volt electric starting.

The Challenger 4 was powered by a six-cylinder Meadows 6DJ970 diesel engine. Its output of 150hp at 1,500rpm was very conservative for a 970cu in (15,900cc) unit. The Meadows engine was a very sophisticated and intricately engineered power unit.

The Fowler Challenger 2 made its appearance in 1956 with a 60hp Leyland AU350 diesel engine providing the power. The price for the base machine was £2,450 and around 80 were sold during the two years that the tractor was in production. Several attachments including a bulldozer blade were offered.

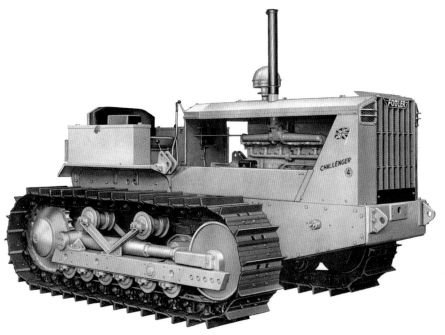

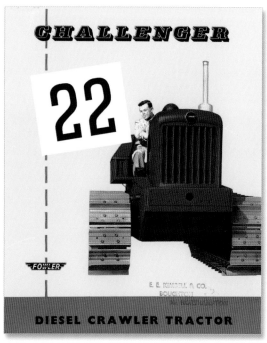

A production model Challenger 4 with 24-volt electric starting. The layout of the machine was much the same as other Fowler crawlers with the main components contained within a rigid hull. Six bottom rollers were fitted.

The Fowler Challenger 22 replaced the Challenger 2 in 1958 with a number of improvements including revised transmission ratios, 24-volt electrics and the fuel tank relocated to the rear of the seat.

FOWLER

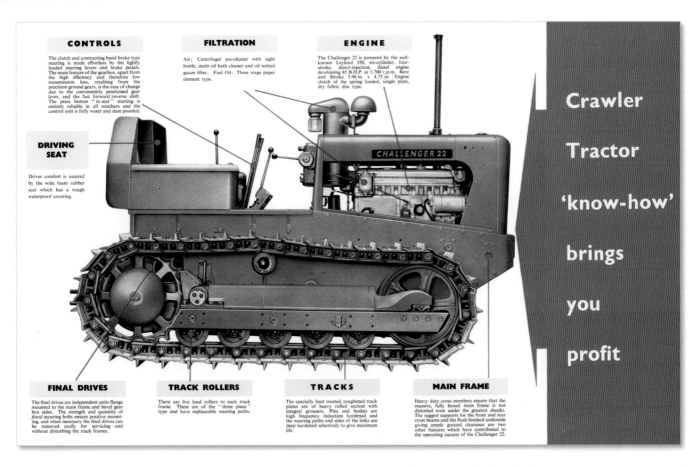

CONTROLS

The clutch and contracting band brake type steering is made effortless by the lightly loaded steering levers and brake pedals. The main feature of the gearbox, apart from the high efficiency and therefore low transmission loss, resulting from the precision ground gears, is the ease of change due to the conveniently positioned gear lever, and the fast forward/reverse shift. The press button "in seat" starting is entirely reliable in all weathers and the control unit is fully water and dust proofed.

DRIVING SEAT

Driver comfort is assured by the wide foam rubber seat which has a tough waterproof covering.

FILTRATION

Air; Centrifugal pre-cleaner with sight bottle, main oil bath cleaner and oil wetted gauze filter. Fuel Oil: Three stage paper element type.

ENGINE

The Challenger 22 is powered by the well-known Leyland 350, six-cylinder, four-stroke, direct-injection, diesel engine developing 65 B.H.P. at 1,700 r.p.m. Bore and Stroke 3.96 in. x 4.75 in. Engine clutch of the spring loaded, single plate, dry fabric disc type.

FINAL DRIVES

The final drives are independent units flange mounted to the main frame and bevel gear box sides. The strength and quantity of fitted securing bolts ensure positive mounting, and when necessary the final drives can be removed easily for servicing—and without disturbing the track frames.

TRACK ROLLERS

There are five load rollers to each track frame. These are of the "three piece" type and have replaceable wearing paths.

TRACKS

The specially heat treated, toughened track plates are of heavy rolled section with integral grousers. Pins and bushes are high frequency induction hardened and the wearing paths and sides of the links are deep hardened selectively to give maximum life.

MAIN FRAME

Heavy duty cross members ensure that the massive, fully boxed main frame is not distorted even under the greatest shocks. The rugged supports for the front and rear cross beams and the flush finished underside giving ample ground clearance are two other features which have contributed to the operating success of the Challenger 22.

Crawler Tractor 'know-how' brings you profit

The Challenger 22's six-cylinder Leyland engine ran at 1,700rpm, an increase of 100rpm over the Challenger 2, which upped the power to 65hp. The six-speed gearbox had shuttle reverse on the four lower speeds. At £2,950, it was an expensive machine for agricultural use, although a few were sold to larger farms.

If properly maintained the Fowler 33 proved to be a reasonably reliable machine that would give many hours of economic service. It was simple to repair and was offered with a comprehensive range of attachments. The colour was changed from orange to yellow at the 1965 Smithfield Show.

In 1958 the Challenger 3 morphed into the Fowler Challenger 33 with the adoption of the 125hp Leyland AU680 engine. No Meadows alternative was offered. Apart from the new styling, little else changed. The price for a base machine in 1960 was £5,975.

79

HOWARD

The Howard name is probably more synony-
mous with rotary cultivators than tractors,
but the concern did manufacture a lightweight crawler for a short time in the 1950s. The
machine was called the Platypus, and an explana-
tion for the choice of title was given in the tractor's
instruction book:

"Ornithorhynchus (Platypus to you and me) is
an unusual little fellow. Small yet very powerful for
his size, the Platypus is a tireless worker. He is as
much at home in the water as on the land. His
webbed feet can dig and handle soil as well as any
human-made tool. Add that Platypus comes from
two Greek words meaning 'flat-footed' and you
can easily understand why this name was chosen
for our crawler tractor."

The Platypus was also a mammal native to
Australia – the land of Arthur Clifford Howard's
birth in 1896. Howard was the son of an
Australian farmer from New South Wales. He
began experimenting with rotary cultivation while
serving an engineering apprenticeship in 1912.
Spending time in England on munitions work
during the First World War, he tried unsuccessfully
to interest British manufacturers in his concept of
rotary tillage.

Returning to Australia, Howard formed Austral
Auto-Cultivators Ltd in 1922 to manufacture
rotary hoes, rotary cultivators and pedestrian-
controlled tillers. He also built a small tractor in
1928. For a time Howard's products were manufactured under licence in the UK by J & F
Howard (no relation) of Bedford – the contract
being arranged by Essex farmer, Captain E N
Griffiths.

In 1938 Arthur Howard came to Britain and
entered into a partnership with Captain Griffiths
to establish Rotary Hoes Ltd at East Horndon in
Essex to build pedestrian-controlled and tractor-
mounted rotary cultivators. Production was
suspended during the Second World War, but
resumed in 1945 with a range of rotary cultivators
to suit most of the popular tractors of the time.
The company also manufactured drainage
machines based on Fordson tractor skid units.

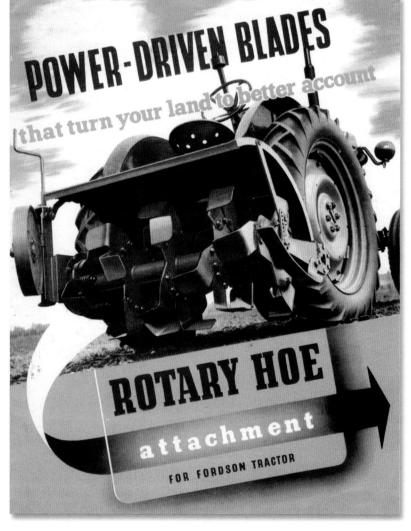

*The Rotary Hoe cultivator for the Fordson E27N Major was designed
to be an integral part of the tractor with a four-point attachment. The
drive gearbox bolted directly onto the rear of the Fordson
transmission. Similar rotary cultivators were later offered for
Ferguson, Nuffield, David Brown, County and International tractors.
Howard also developed a reduction gearbox for Fordson and Ferguson
tractors to make their gear ratios more suitable for the job.*

The early tractor-mounted Howard Rotary Hoe had a four-point attachment, but the E Type Rotavator, introduced in 1954, was suitable for a standard three-point linkage. Probably the best known of the company's products was its range of pedestrian-controlled rotary cultivators. Topping the range was the Howard Gem Rotavator that was first launched in 1940 and remained on the market for more than 50 years.

It was the success of the Rotavator ranges that financed Rotary Hoes Ltd's purchase of the Fowler concern and its Steam Plough Works at Leeds in 1945. The Fowler business was sold within just over a year, allegedly netting Howard a healthy £250,000 profit, which he used to finance his own tractor project.

Much of the layout of the Platypus crawlers was inherited from the Fowler FD2, including the controlled-differential steering and the tracks, which were of a pin-and-plate design with cast-steel links. Development began in 1950 and the project was overseen by Arthur Howard's son, John.

The Platypus '28', which was a narrow-gauge machine with an overall track-width of 39in, was launched in 1952. The tractor was offered with the choice of a Standard petrol engine or a Perkins P4(TA) diesel. The following year manufacture was moved to a new factory at Basildon, which operated under the name of the Platypus Tractor Company, and the '30' model was introduced. The Platypus '30' was available with alternative gauges and widths of track plates, but the only engine option was the Perkins P4(TA).

In 1954 work began on a more powerful version of the tractor, which was provisionally designated as the Platypus '50'. The '50' was an enlarged version of the '30' with a 51hp Perkins L4 engine mated to a two-ratio gearbox giving six forward speeds. This new model was released for production in July 1955 as the Howard Platypus PD4. At the same time the '30' model became the Platypus PD2.

Experiments had also been carried out with a 70hp version of the PD4 fitted with a six-cylinder Leyland engine to meet the requirements of Australian farmers who demanded more power. The Leyland-powered Platypus never went beyond the prototype stage, and the 70hp tractor was eventually fitted with a six-cylinder Perkins R6 diesel engine. This machine was launched in 1955 as the Platypus PD4 (R6), but only a handful were built.

Sales of the Platypus crawlers were never that great and less than 550 were built before production ceased in 1956. Many were exported with the main markets being Australia and New Zealand.

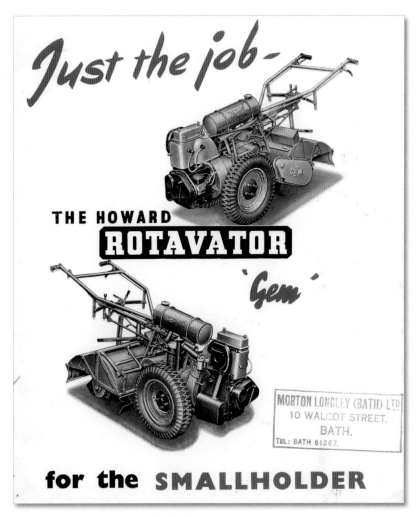

Just the job —

THE HOWARD

ROTAVATOR

'Gem'

MORTON LONGLEY (BATH) LTD
10 WALCOT STREET,
BATH.
TEL: BATH 61267.

for the SMALLHOLDER

Introduced in 1952, the Series IV version of the Howard Gem Rotavator was powered by the company's own 810cc air-cooled petrol engine rated at 9.8hp. The gearbox gave three forward speeds and a single reverse. A choice of rotor widths from 20-30in was available.

The Howard Platypus '28' crawler was launched in 1952 with a choice of a Standard petrol engine or a four-cylinder Perkins P4(TA) diesel unit. The '28' had a 31in gauge with 8in track-plates giving an overall width of 39in. The diesel version (shown) delivered 30hp at 1,600rpm and was priced at £1,280.

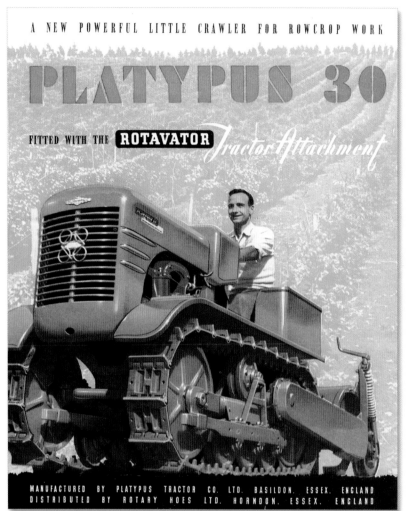

Introduced in 1953, the Platypus '30' was powered by an up-rated version of the Perkins P4(TA) diesel engine, which developed 39hp at 2,000rpm. Most were sold with either a 48in or 60in Howard Rotavator attachment, which was hitched to the tractor's hydraulic linkage.

The 'Bogmaster' was an extra-wide-gauge version of the Platypus '30' with 54in track centres. Track-plates of up to 32in in width could be fitted for working on peat bogs, forestry projects and rice cultivation. The tractor was priced at £1,500 and customers included peat extraction operations in Ireland and a palm oil estate in Malaya.

The Howard Platypus '30' had an epicyclic differential steering system and the gearbox gave six forward and two reverse speeds. The linkage was raised by a single hydraulic ram operated by a foot pedal to the right of the transmission. The track-frames pivoted on a cross-axle mounted in front of the drive sprockets.

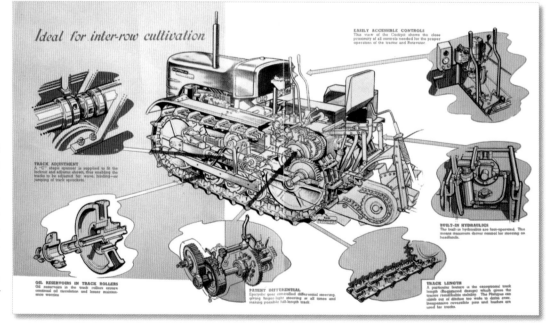

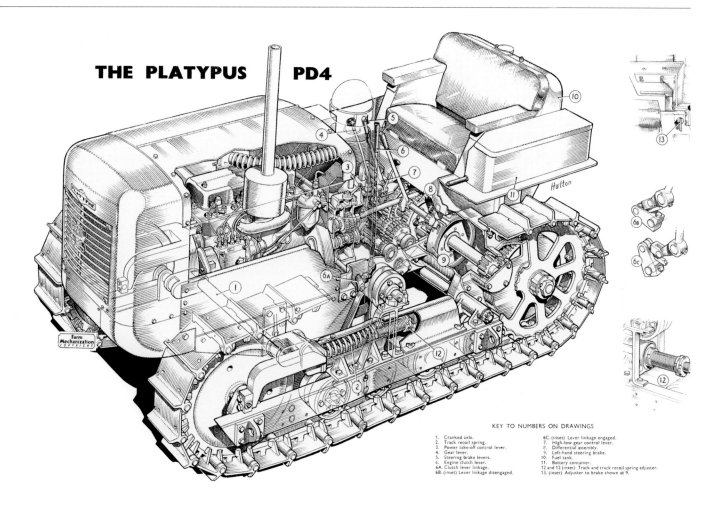

THE PLATYPUS PD4

KEY TO NUMBERS ON DRAWINGS

1. Cranked axle.
2. Track recoil spring.
3. Power take-off control lever.
4. Gear lever.
5. Steering brake levers.
6. Engine clutch lever.
6A. Clutch lever linkage.
6B. (inset) Lever linkage disengaged.

6C. (inset) Lever linkage engaged.
7. High-low gear control lever.
8. Differential assembly.
9. Left-hand steering brake.
10. Fuel tank.
11. Battery container.
12 and 12 (inset) Track and track recoil spring adjuster.
13. (inset) Adjuster to brake shown at 9.

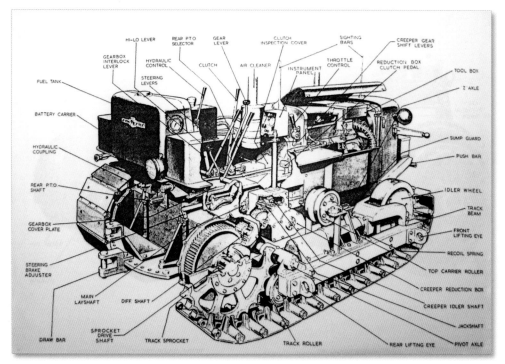

The Platypus '50', which appeared in July 1955, was a larger and more powerful crawler with a Perkins L4(TA) diesel engine rated at 51hp at 1,600rpm. The specification included differential steering, 14in clutch, two-speed power take-off and four bottom-rollers. The dual-range gearbox still gave six forward and two reverse speeds, but the ratios and change-sequence was altered. The fuel tank was also moved to the rear of the seat. The base machine cost £1,750.

Launched in 1955, the Platypus PD4 (R6) was a 70hp machine with a six-cylinder Perkins R6 diesel engine. The prototype (shown) had pin-and-plate tracks with the gear-selection levers for an optional creeper-box mounted on a pedestal to the right of the operator's platform. Probably no more than 13 were built before Howard ended tractor production in 1956.

INTERNATIONAL

The International Harvester Company of Great Britain was established in 1906 as an offshoot of the parent American concern, which had been formed just four years earlier from a merger of several harvester and reaper manufacturers, including McCormick and Deering. The British division operated out of offices and warehouses in London and distributed imported American International machinery, and later tractors, across the UK and Ireland.

By the 1930s International Harvester was the largest supplier of farm machinery in the UK. Its tractors, sometimes sold under the McCormick-Deering brand, had an enviable reputation for quality and reliability. Assembly depots for the imported equipment were established at Leith in Scotland, Dublin and Liverpool, but the company had no British manufacturing base.

The first step towards opening a British factory was made in 1938 when International acquired the Wheatley Hall site in the Yorkshire town of Doncaster. A manufacturing base in the UK was the vision of Arthur Neale, the chairman and managing director of the International Harvester Company of Great Britain. However war intervened and the fledgling factory was almost immediately requisitioned for munitions work. The plant was returned to International after the war and began making implement parts in 1946.

The first tractor to be built at Doncaster rolled off the line at 10am on 13 September 1949. This first British International was by no means a new

The first British International tractor, the Farmall M, went into production at Doncaster in 1949 using assemblies shipped from the USA. The proven four-cylinder petrol/TVO engine was a rugged and economical overhead-valve unit that gave 33hp at the drawbar. The gearbox gave five forward speeds and a single reverse.

design and was actually based on the American Farmall M, produced in the USA by the parent International Harvester Company of Chicago.

Early production at Doncaster was little more than an assembly operation using out-sourced components. Many of the assemblies, including the engine, were shipped from the American Farmall Works at Rock Island in Illinois. The opening of a new grey-iron foundry and an extension to the tractor manufacturing shop to house engine production at the Wheatley Hall site saw the tractor gradually become an all-British product, which was reflected in a change of designation to Farmall BM during 1951.

A further £2 million investment programme in the Doncaster operation saw the company introduce its first British diesel tractor, the Farmall BMD model, in December 1952. The years that followed saw the Doncaster-built four-cylinder spark-ignition and diesel engines fitted to a growing line of British International tractors.

A Product of our works at Doncaster, Yorkshire

The Farmall M tractor with adjustable wide front axle and pneumatic tyres

SINGLE FRONT WHEEL

Single front wheel attachment, with a 9.00 × 10 pneumatic tyre, is available for use in crops having narrow row spacing.

The M was designed as a rowcrop tractor with plenty of ground clearance for inter-row cultivations. The high driving position gave good visibility and the front axle could be adjusted for different row widths. The only visual difference between the British and American Farmall M was in the steering arrangement. Unlike the American tractors, which had the track-rod in front of the axle, the Doncaster-built machines had the rod positioned behind the axle mounting.

The British International Farmall M was also available as a tricycle tractor with a single front wheel attachment fitted with a 9.00 x 10 tyre for use in crops with narrow row spacing. The rear tread on both the three- and four-wheel models was altered by loosening the hubs and sliding the wheels in or out on the axle.

MᶜCORMICK INTERNATIONAL

FARMALL BM

The first all-British International engine was manufactured at Doncaster in February 1951. A greater reliance on in-house components following the opening of a new grey-iron foundry at the plant that same year saw the tractor re-designated as the Farmall BM.

Probably the most significant introduction of this period was the BTD-6 crawler of 1953, which meant that the range had now been extended to include tracklayers as well as wheeled tractors.

Before long, the International Harvester Company of Great Britain was faced with having to expand its manufacturing facilities to meet the demand for its products. In 1954 an additional factory was acquired at Idle, near Bradford in Yorkshire, to house production of a new small tractor. This new model, the B-250, was launched at the Smithfield Show in December 1955 as International's answer to the encroaching tide of 'grey Fergies'.

Around 30,000 B-250s were built, but the subsequent B-275, launched in 1958, took International to even dizzier heights with a production run of nearly 57,000 tractors with over 40-a-day rolling out of the Bradford plant. The workforce at Idle was doubled and production was stepped up to the point where the factory had the capability to turn out over 25,000 tractors per year.

Meanwhile, back at Doncaster, the earlier wheeled models had been superseded by the new B-450 diesel tractor in 1958. The same year, International took the opportunity to enlarge its crawler range by introducing the giant BTD-20 – a 14-ton monster powered by a six-cylinder Rolls-Royce diesel engine. A 60hp crawler, the BTD-8, was also

Mechanically the BM model was identical to its American counterpart and the British-built power unit had the same capacity at 247.7cu in. It was a powerful engine and it ensured that the tractor lived up to its 'Farmall' name as a true general-purpose machine. The design included an oil-bath air cleaner, a large oil filter and an adjustable heat control for the vaporiser incorporated into the intake manifold.

Outstanding
FARMALL BM
Points

This is the sturdy 4-cylinder engine with which the Farmall BM is equipped. Bore 3⅜ inches; stroke 5¼ inches.

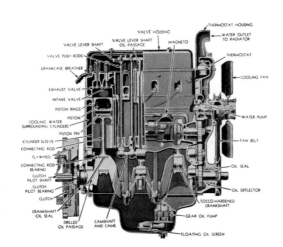

The large oil-type air cleaner assures clean air to Farmall BM engine. The cap, which the demonstrator is holding in his left hand, prevents chaff and other dirt from getting into the air-cleaner.

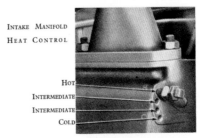

INTAKE MANIFOLD HEAT CONTROL

HOT
INTERMEDIATE
INTERMEDIATE
COLD

The oil filter on the Farmall BM is extra large, and is equipped with replaceable filtering elements. These make it possible to use the oil twice as long without draining and therefore saves the cost of replacing the elements many times over.

launched at the 1960 Royal Show.

Tractors were only part of the story and International also manufactured a full range of farm machinery including trailed and mounted ploughs, disc harrows, grain drills, fertiliser distributors, mowers, manure spreaders, a baler and a trailed combine. Much of the machinery was built at Doncaster, but the balers and other equipment were assembled in a satellite plant at Liverpool.

A draft-control hydraulic system was offered for the first time on a British International tractor in 1961 following the launch of the B-414 model at the Royal Show. The B-414, built at Idle, was later joined by the International B-614, which was introduced at the 1963 Smithfield Show. Unlike its smaller brother, the Doncaster-built B-614 didn't have draft-control hydraulics because it would have required a complete redesign of the rear transmission, which it had inherited from the B-450.

By the mid-1960s increased crawler production and an expanding line of construction machinery were putting pressure on the Doncaster facilities. In 1965 the assembly of the B-450 and B-614 was moved to a new satellite factory, the Carr Hill Works at nearby Balby. Several of the older International product lines, including the combine, were also cleared out to make way for the growing range of industrial equipment.

One tractor with both agricultural and industrial applications was the International BTD-5, which was introduced at the end of 1963. This little crawler was a joint product of the Bradford and Doncaster works. The Idle plant provided the engine and transmission, while Wheatley Hall manufactured the running gear and completed the final assembly.

In 1966 the B-414 was replaced by the 434 model, while the B-614 was superseded by the International 634 in 1968. The 634 had draft control using a unique torsion-bar system of lower-link sensing, but both it and the 434 fall outside the scope of this book. However, in a way, these two models were the last of the 'old guard' of International tractors.

The 1970s saw the phased introduction of a new worldwide range of tractors – new from the

The BMD's four-cylinder diesel engine, designated BD-264, was a direct-injection unit with a CAV injection pump. It featured renewable dry cylinder liners and full-pressure lubrication. It was based on the Farmall BM's spark-ignition unit with the bore increased to give a larger swept volume of 264cu in. Rated at 40hp, the BD-264 was a very steady running engine, governed to a maximum 1,450rpm.

International's first British diesel tractor, the Farmall BMD, joined the BM model in December 1952. The BMD had the same chassis and rowcrop configuration as its sister model, but the diesel engine gave it tremendous lugging power and the tractor would punch far above its weight, often putting larger and higher horsepower machines to shame. Despite its engine being a somewhat unrefined unit with a very pronounced diesel knock, particularly when cold, the diesel version quickly outsold its spark-ignition counterpart.

ground up with the emphasis on modern styling and driver comfort. The old British lines were swept away as the new models went into production at Wheatley Hall, Carr Hill and Bradford.

THE FARMALL BMD ENGINE
A great new Diesel

In designing this powerful new Diesel engine for the Farmall, International Harvester engineers were able to draw on the experience accumulated by the organization in nearly 50 years of tractor manufacture—20 years of which have included the production of a long series of internationally popular Diesels for agricultural work.

With a higher horsepower rating than the Farmall BM, the Farmall BMD engine is of the dry-sleeve type and has four cylinders. It affords the greatest possible economy, not only by using cheaper fuel, but less fuel ; consequently its higher initial cost, as compared with the BM engine, will be offset by higher performance and lower running costs.

The BMD starts as easily as a conventional petrol engine, being assisted by glow-plugs and a heavy Diesel-type starter motor. A prolonged, steady power stroke and smooth running are assured by the through type combustion chambers and single-aperture injectors, the latter having the characteristic advantage that they are less prone to gumming-up and blockage than the multi-spray type.

The all-important need for absolute cleanliness of fuel in a Diesel-powered unit is provided for by a filter which incorporates a water-trap and has replaceable elements. The water trap has a glass bowl so that the presence of water and other impurities may easily be detected.

The BMD's fuel injection pump has been selected for its accuracy and economy in delivery, and the centrifugal-type governor for its quick response to engine load variations.

The introduction of this new Diesel was planned before the first vaporizing oil engines were built at Doncaster and many of the components have been designed to be interchangeable.

You get instant and effortless control of implements with FARMALL THREE-POINT LINKAGE and LIFT-ALL HYDRAULIC SYSTEM

Designed specifically for fitting to Farmall BM and BMD tractors, the three-point linkage may be used in conjunction with many makes of mounted implement. Its use does not preclude the operation of a forward-mounted hydraulic power cylinder for other purposes, nor does its attachment interfere with the use of the drawbar for trailed implements.

A control for levelling purposes is fitted on the right-hand side, and the positions of the link arms are adjustable. The operating height of the link arms may also be varied on the control rod for the hydraulic pump, which is by the tractor driver's right hand.

The illustration shows how by well-planned leverage the mounting lends itself to utilizing the power of the Lift-All pump to the full.

THE FARMALL LIFT-ALL hydraulic unit can be easily and quickly fitted inside the clutch housing of Farmall BM or BMD tractors. The 2¼ in. diameter POWER CYLINDERS are supplied complete with hose and should be ordered separately from the hydraulic unit, which will accommodate and operate three cylinders at the same time. These are single-acting cylinders, using hydraulic pressure to lift; the weight of the implement returns the piston when lowering. A DELAYED LIFT VALVE and a DROP-RETARDING VALVE are available.

1. *Pump, Valves and Reservoir.*
2. 3. 4. *Cylinders.*
5. *Pump drive.*
6. *Delayed lift valve.*
7. *Oil filler.*
8. *Control Rod (extends to within reach of operator).*

(RIGHT) Schematic diagram of Lift-All system showing the control lever in neutral position C. Moving the lever to position D raises the implement. To lower front section independently of rear section the lever is moved from C to B. To lower rear section independently of front section the lever is moved from B to A. If it is desired to lower both the front and rear sections simultaneously the control lever is moved direct from neutral position C to position A. If the operator starts to lift the implement and then for any reason does not want to complete the lift, he can move the control lever to any of the other positions instantly.

The Farmall BM and BMD tractors could be fitted with International's optional 'Lift-All' hydraulic system, which incorporated both a basic three-point linkage arrangement and an auxiliary cylinder for mid-mounted implements. The system was powered by a gear-type pump located inside the clutch housing.

In July 1953 International launched a new British crawler tractor, the International BTD-6 powered by the 40hp BD-264 diesel engine as fitted to the BMD wheeled tractor. Based on the American International TD-6 tractor, the new tracklayer was ideal for 'top work' such as drilling or cultivating light land, but didn't really have enough weight for heavy-land ploughing. A petrol/TVO version of the crawler was also launched as the BT-6, but this was built in very limited numbers.

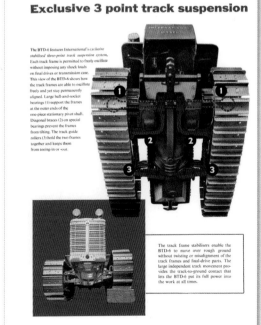

The BTD-6 had a fairly conventional layout with clutch-and-brake steering. The crawler's track frames pivoted on the sprocket shaft; the oscillation being controlled by a pattern of braces between the frames. The specification included a 17-gallon fuel tank, a single top-roller placed close to the drive sprocket and four bottom-rollers.

During 1953 the BMD model was upgraded into the more powerful Farmall Super BMD. It was fitted with the same BD-264 engine, but International's engineers had managed to coax an extra ten horses out of the diesel unit to give the revamped model a useful 50hp. The BM also evolved into the Farmall Super BM with the enlarged BC-264 engine.

The Super BWD-6 was launched at the 1954 Royal Show with a price tag of £735; the 'BWD' designation standing for British wheeled diesel tractor. The new British model was based on the American International W6 tractor and was a standard 'low-build' design for general-purpose work.

The Super BWD-6 shared its five-speed transmission with the Super BMD tractor and it had the same 50hp version of the BD-264 engine. The driving position was uncluttered and the tractor was fitted with independent brakes to assist turning. The model wasn't as popular as the Farmall version, but more than 2,500 rolled out of Doncaster during the first two years of production.

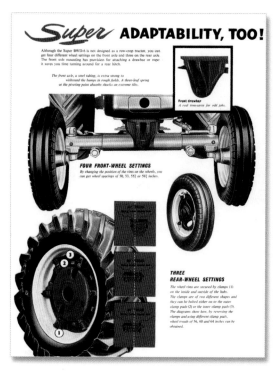

The Super BWD-6 didn't have the BMD's rowcrop facility, but changing the position of the wheel rims gave four different tread settings. The front axle, however, was not adjustable.

The Super BWD-6 could be fitted with an optional hydraulic lift powered by an engine-mounted pump. The gear-driven pump offered 'live' hydraulics and the rear linkage was operated by a double-acting ram. The massive torque of the low-revving BD-264 engine gave the tractor enough slogging power to handle three furrows with ease.

Introduced in 1955, the Super BW-6 was the petrol/TVO version of the BWD-6 tractor. It was fitted with the Super BM's spark-ignition BC-264 engine, but most customers opted for the diesel model. 'Paraffin' tractors were going out of fashion and just 280 were built.

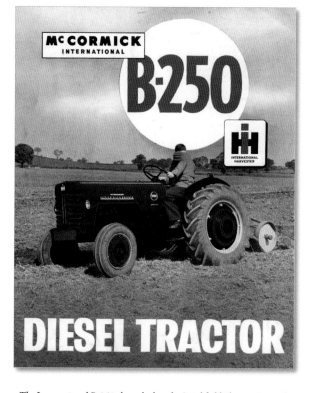

The International B-250, launched at the Smithfield Show in December 1955, was built in the old Jowett car factory at Idle near Bradford. International's answer to the Ferguson TE-20, it was a lively performer with several features that were unique for a tractor of its size. The B-250 was a particularly successful machine for the company and by 1957 it was being sold in 50 countries of the world and nearly 8,000 were exported from Bradford in 1957 alone.

PERFECT WEIGHT DISTRIBUTION

Nearly two-thirds of the B-250's weight is on the rear wheels, yet the tractor does not 'rear up'. As a result, the B-250 can do considerably heavier drawbar work before extra weight is needed.

1 **FUEL FILTER**—with replaceable cartridge element.
2 **AIR CLEANER**—Big-capacity oil-bath type with centrifugal pre-cleaner.
3 **BATTERY COMPARTMENT**—12-volt system. Batteries are two 6-volt in series, providing 76 amp. hr. capacity at 10 hr. discharge rate.
4 **INJECTOR SPILL-OFF PIPES**—These allow excess fuel, caused through pressure build-up, to return to fuel tank.
5 **HIGH PRESSURE, PINTLE TYPE INJECTION NOZZLES**—produce fine atomization of fuel for positive and complete combustion.
6 **COMBUSTION CHAMBER GLOW PLUGS**—ensure easy all-weather starting.
7 **INJECTION PUMP**—Pneumatic governor provides responsive fuel regulation.
8 **WATER TRAP**—with easily-removable glass bowl.
9 **STARTER MOTOR**—Heavy duty type, with manually-controlled engagement.
10 **CLUTCH**—Easy acting, easily adjustable, 10 inch, single dry plate, spring loaded.
11 **GENERATOR**—12-volt, shunt wound, 2-brush type.
12 **WATER PUMP**—The closed, pressurized cooling system has radiator by-pass with thermostatic control and safety valve filler cap.
13 **HYDRAULIC PUMP**—provides hydraulic pressure whenever the engine is running.
14 **FULL-FLOW OIL FILTER**—All the oil passes through this filter which has easily-replaceable 120-hour elements.
15 **OIL PUMP**—Camshaft driven, it ensures oil supply at 30/35 p.s.i. pressure to all parts of the engine.

Beneath the B-250's bonnet was a four-cylinder diesel engine – the Bradford-built BD-144 power unit developing 30hp. Like its Doncaster cousins, the power unit was indirect-injection with glow-plug starting and had a CAV in-line fuel pump with a pneumatic governor. An engine-mounted pump gave 'live' hydraulics.

Many of the B-250's features such as a five-speed gearbox, disc brakes and a differential lock were unusual on a small tractor in the 1950s. However, a single-stage clutch meant that the model didn't have 'live' power take-off. Twin drag-links simplified the job of adjusting the front axle to alter the tread width. The hydraulics had a basic system of depth control via a mechanical arrangement with a control screw that could be adjusted to limit the downward movement of the implement. It provided a degree of weight transference, but was not a true draft-control system.

During 1955, the International BTD-6 crawler was fitted with the 50hp version of the BD-264 power unit. Later models were offered with a choice of four- or five-roller track frames – the extended version exerting a ground pressure of just 4.7psi that was ideal for soft conditions.

The BTD-6 was probably the most successful British crawler tractor of all time. Over 10,000 had been built by 1960 and total production exceeded 20,000. It remained on the market until 1975, giving it the longest production run of any British-made tracklayer.

The success of the BTD-6 in both the agricultural and industrial sectors of the marketplace prompted International to enlarge its crawler range. A new heavyweight machine, the BTD-20, went into production at Doncaster in the summer of 1958. Although designed for industrial applications the new tracklayer, priced at £6,450, was also sold for agricultural use. The original machines were designated as the 200 series.

The BTD-20's transmission gave six speeds in both forward and reverse. The reverse speeds were 20 percent faster than the forward ratios to keep the idle return stroke of the production cycle as short as possible. The specification included box-section track frames, six-bottom and two-top rollers, multi-plate steering clutches and self-energising brakes. The rollers were specially-hardened and the track-chains were heat treated to reduce wear. The rear drive-sprockets were also reversible for extra life.

The BTD-20 was powered by a six-cylinder Rolls-Royce 'C' Range diesel engine developing 124hp. As would be expected, it was a high-quality unit with Simms equipment and the injectors directly cooled via copper-alloy sleeves swelled into the cylinder head. The engine had direct-injection and the displacement was a massive 743cu in (12,170cc).

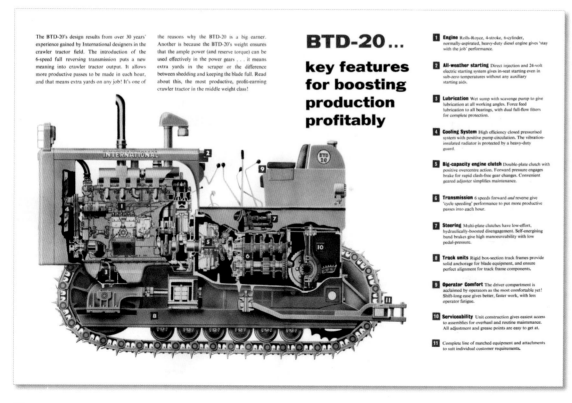

McCORMICK INTERNATIONAL
B-450
DIESEL TRACTOR

THE BEST IN USABLE POWER

The line of wheeled tractors at Doncaster was revamped in 1958 with the introduction of the B-450 model, which superseded both the Super BMD and Super BWD-6. The styling was slightly more modern, but much of the design could be traced back to the previous models. However, the 'live' hydraulics were much improved and the system had its own reservoir. An isolating valve diverted oil to externally-mounted equipment, while in the field a control valve with two-stage response boosted traction by weight transfer.

Reliable IH BD-264 indirect injection diesel engine
for
SMOOTH
ECONOMICAL
POWER

This robust, reliable IH engine gives you big power output with good fuel economy. It is built and equipped to outlast other engines and to require less maintenance, too. Key to its overall superiority is proved basic design and high quality production engineering methods.

OFFICIAL TESTS PROVE

53·5 BELT HORSEPOWER*

*STANDARD B-450 N.I.A.E. TEST NO. 213/BS

IH Serviceability is an Asset

The BD-264 replaceable piston and sleeve assembly is just one example of the engine's construction which saves you time and money on engine overhaul.

Heavy-Duty Forged Steel, Induction-Hardened Crankshaft gives Smooth Running with Long Journal and Bearing Life

The forged steel crankshaft is typical of the quality engineering in the BD-264 engine. As well as being dynamically balanced to give vibration-free performance, it is induction-hardened to provide hard wearing surfaces with maximum ductile core strength.

BRAKED AND STEERED FOR SAFE POSITIVE CONTROL

SELF-ENERGISING DISC BRAKES
BETTER, SAFER, LONGER-LASTING BRAKES

The B-450 disc brakes are immensely powerful, and once the braking surfaces are brought together they *apply themselves*—without grab or chatter. With tractor moving forwards *or backwards* you can make pivot turns, stop quickly, and hold the heaviest loads on gradients. Simple, adjustment is provided to maintain equalised braking on both wheels, while linings outlast those of conventional type brakes. Easy-to-reach brake pedals may be operated individually for tight turning or latched together to give uniform braking on both wheels for road work. A convenient latch is provided for parking.

How B-450 disc brakes work. When brake pedal is depressed, parallel plates (A) make a partial revolution in opposite directions and are forced apart by steel balls which operate in a conical track (B) bringing revolving brake linings (C) into contact with stationary braking surfaces (D). Brakes are self-energising—tractor movement forcing the plates farther apart, thus increasing braking action.

COMPLETE STEERING EASE TAKES THE FATIGUE OUT OF STEERING

New, easy-action, self-centring steering with inclined king pins gives particularly high leverage that reduces manual effort to a minimum, and makes the B-450 a joy to handle, particularly when turning on headlands and in confined spaces. This simple, robust steering system is designed for long life and will remain rock-steady even after years of hard work-a-day wear.

The B-450 was a direct descendant of Doncaster's earlier models. Many of the BMD and BWD-6 components were carried over into the new tractor, including the trusty BD-264 engine, which now boasted 55hp following a slight increase in engine speed to 1,500rpm.

The B-450 boasted a new, self-centring steering system with inclined king-pins, which made the tractor easy to handle with minimum effort, particularly when turning in confined spaces. Self-energising disc brakes also provided positive stopping power. Both the front axle and the rear wheels could be altered to provide different tread widths for rowcrop work. A differential lock was also part of the specification.

International's line of smaller tractors from Bradford was also revamped during 1958 with the launch of the B-275 model. The B-275 was essentially the same tractor as the B-250 with a number of significant improvements. Its BD-144-A version of the engine ran at 1,850rpm and developed 35hp through changes to the fuel system.

The B-275 had 'live' hydraulics provided by an engine-mounted Plessey pump. The hydraulic system was largely similar to that of the B-250, although a two-stage control valve was added in 1960.

The B-275 didn't immediately replace the B-250, which remained in production until 1961. Improvements brought in with the new model included changes to the steering layout with a single steering-arm and drag-link. An extra lever atop the gearbox denoted extra speeds – eight forward and two reverse – while a two-stage clutch gave 'live' power take-off.

An industrial version of the B-275 was introduced for municipal or ground-care work. Features included a dual-braking system, wide fenders and an automatic hitch. It was advertised as having a 'ten-speed' transmission, although this only equated to eight forward gears and two reverse. An industrial version of the B-250 was also offered.

The industrial B-275 tractor had much to recommend it with a dual-braking system, eight-speed gearbox, differential lock, a 'live' hydraulic system and constant-running power take-off all part of the standard specification. The B-275 also became the first British International tractor to be exported to the USA.

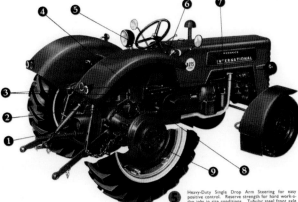

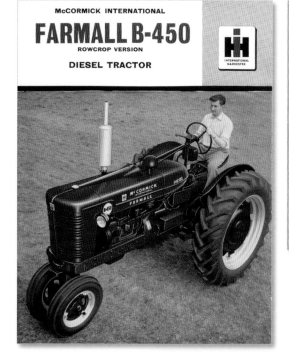

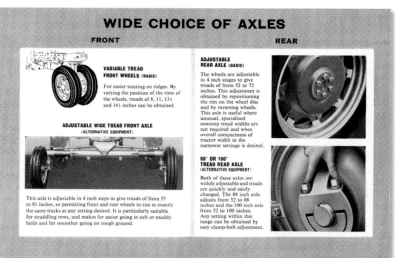

The B-450 Farmall was offered with a wide choice of wheel and axle equipment. It could be fitted with an adjustable wide-front axle or a pedestal for narrow-front variable-tread wheels. At the rear it could have sliding hubs on a bar-axle or a fixed axle for wheels with adjustable pan-centres.

Bowing to the demand from customers who still preferred the old Farmall layout, International introduced a second version of the B-450 at the 1959 Smithfield Show. This tractor was finished in the earlier rowcrop configuration with the high-clearance front axle. Known as the B-450 Farmall, it was priced at £780, which was actually £15 cheaper than the standard B-450.

Another new crawler, the BTD-8, was launched at the 1960 Royal Show. Designed to slot into the range between the BTD-6 and the BTD-20, this was a 60hp machine with a new BD-281 diesel engine..

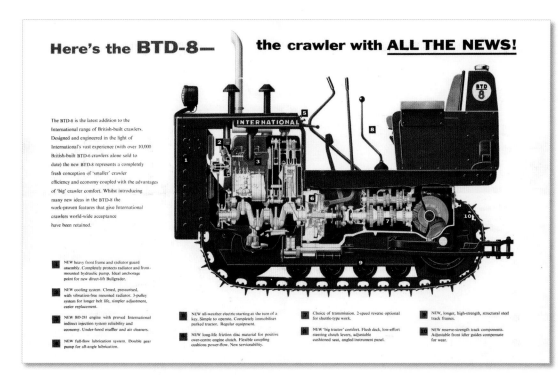

Here's the BTD-8— the crawler with ALL THE NEWS!

The BTD-8 is the latest addition to the International range of British-built crawlers. Designed and engineered in the light of International's vast experience (with over 10,000 British-built BTD-6 crawlers alone sold to date) the new BTD-8 represents a completely fresh conception of 'smaller' crawler efficiency and economy coupled with the advantages of 'big' crawler comfort. Whilst introducing many new ideas in the BTD-8 the work-proven features that give International crawlers world-wide acceptance have been retained.

1 NEW heavy front frame and radiator guard assembly. Completely protects radiator and front-mounted hydraulic pump. Ideal anchorage point for new direct-lift Bullgrader.

2 NEW cooling system. Closed, pressurised, with vibration-free mounted radiator. 3-pulley system for longer belt life, simpler adjustment, easier replacement.

3 NEW BD-281 engine with proved International indirect injection system reliability and economy. Under-hood muffler and air cleaners.

4 NEW full-flow lubrication system. Double gear pump for all-angle lubrication.

5 NEW all-weather electric starting at the turn of a key. Simple to operate. Completely immobilises parked tractor. Regular equipment.

6 NEW long-life friction disc material for positive over-centre engine clutch. Flexible coupling cushions power-flow. New serviceability.

7 Choice of transmission. 2-speed reverse optional for shuttle-type work.

8 NEW 'big tractor' comfort. Flush deck, low-effort steering clutch levers, adjustable cushioned seat, angled instrument panel.

9 NEW, longer, high-strength, structural steel track frames.

10 NEW reserve-strength track components. Adjustable front idler guides compensate for wear.

Features of the new BTD-8 included heavy-duty steering clutches with heat-resistant sintered-metal facings. There was a choice of transmissions: five forward and a single reverse, or four forward and two reverse. Standard running gear was four bottom-rollers and a single top-roller with 14in track plates, but extended frames with five bottom-rollers and two top-rollers were optional.

NEW BD-281 DIESEL ENGINE

Develops 60 h.p. at 1,600 r.p.m., with a maximum torque of 225 lb. ft. at 1,100 r.p.m. that hangs on as low as 950 r.p.m. This new engine gives power for new productivity and with new economy. The new weight of the BTD-8 makes full use of the engine's power and extra torque developed under overload.

- Proved International indirect injection system reliability and economy.
- Maintenance-free pintle-type nozzles remain carbon free.
- Sensitive centrifugal governor with inbuilt torque control device that boosts torque 10%, under overload.
- New heavy-duty components — crankcase, induction-hardened crankshaft, connecting rods.

Proved International injection system

The pintle-type nozzle's high injection pressure gives the required spray pattern to penetrate the swirling, highly compressed air in the combustion chamber for thorough fuel/air mixing. The nozzles require no regular servicing, as they do not become clogged-up or carbonised in service.

New all-weather starting covenience

The new BTD-8 is on the job at the turn of a key! The BD-281 glowplug system is reliable and simple to operate. Completely immobilises the parked tractor. Regular equipment.

The BTD-8's four-cylinder BD-281 diesel engine was an enlarged version of the proven BD-264 unit with the bore increased from 4in to 4⅛in to give a swept volume of 281cu in (4,600cc). Features included renewable dry cylinder liners, full-pressure lubrication and a CAV injection pump. Like the BD-264, the new engine had tremendous lugging power.

McCORMICK INTERNATIONAL

B-414 Diesel Tractor 40 b.h.p.

INTERNATIONAL HARVESTER

Launched at the Royal Show in 1961, the new International B-414 was the latest addition to the line of Bradford-built machines. The tractor, which cost around £700, had a more modern appearance with new bonnet panels, a new front grille and a 'de-luxe' adjustable seat.

NEW BD-154 40 h.p. diesel engine

GIVES PLUS POWER ☐ PLUS PERFORMANCE
ECONOMY ☐ LONG LIFE

There is big lugging power in International's own indirect diesel injection engine. Pre-combustion chamber design, plus 23:1 compression ratio gives complete fuel-air mixing for controlled and more efficient combustion, glowplugs are incorporated for certain all-weather starting. The BD-154, like all IH engines, has four cylinders to give more power at low, wear-saving engine speed. Economy in running costs comes from the combustion-tight seal provided by five ring pistons — the top one being chromed for long engine life.

Replaceable wet cylinder sleeves in a full-length water-jacket give greater heat dissipation. The **oil pump** ensures 'full-flow' pressure lubrication of filtered oil to all shell bearings and valve lever mechanisms. A floating gauze screen in the sump filters the oil, no matter what the tractor's working angle.

The **crankshaft** is built for a long, dependable life and is **dynamically balanced** for a vibration-free performance. **Cam faces** are 'chill'-hardened and ground for silent valve-lifting operation at all engine speeds. **Pintle-type nozzles** with their high operating pressure prevent carbon build-up. The **cooling system** is pressurised, with forced positive circulation by belt-driven pump and is thermostatically controlled. The **10½-gallon capacity fuel tank** means more hours' work without refuelling.

The B-414 had a new 40hp engine with a CAV rotary pump. This BD-154 power unit was based on the earlier Bradford-built engines with an increased bore giving a 154cu in capacity. Features included replaceable wet cylinder-liners and full-pressure lubrication.

The B-414 was the first British International tractor with full draft-control hydraulics. The new 'Vary Touch' system, operated by a quadrant to the right of the driver's seat, offered position control, draft control and response control with an isolating valve for external hydraulics. Accurate draft control was provided by top-link sensing.

VARY TOUCH for precision depth control and self-thinking, self-adjusting draft control

—YOU CHOOSE THE SETTING; VARY TOUCH DOES THE REST!

The new IH Vary Touch hydraulic system incorporates position control with an in-built variable hydraulic response control. In operation this means the implement is lowered always to the same selected depth; then Vary Touch automatically ensures constant draft on the implement. The rate at which Vary Touch works can be varied by the operator from his tractor seat. In addition to the dual action top link which, through compression and tension influences the response and action of the hydraulic system, Vary Touch incorporates all the up-to-the-minute refinements in implement control, including weight transfer to the rear of the tractor for maximum traction.

1 Position control gives infinite command over the working depth or height of implements, always returning them to the pre-set working position after having been lifted. An adjustable 'stop' prevents passing the desired pre-selected position.

2 Draft control automatically maintains constant draft on below-ground implements by compensating for varying ground conditions, resulting in a steady forward travel speed of the tractor.

3 Flow rate valve governs the lifting speed of the linkage action. SLOW RATE for any below ground implements. FAST RATE for above ground implements such as front-end loaders, tipping trailers. External hydraulic tappings are provided.

4 Engine-driven hydraulic pump provides full hydraulic power immediately the engine is started, completely independent of the transmission or engine clutch. The separate large oil reservoir provides ample capacity for all regular hydraulic equipment.

REVERSIBLE DUAL CATEGORY 3-POINT LINKAGE
This doubles the usefulness and versatility of the B-414, and is designed to give maximum work output with both Category 1 and Category 2 implements. The lower links are provided with two alternative front hitch pin points to enable the best performance to be gained under varying ground conditions.

IN-BUILT WEIGHT TRANSFER gives positive traction

Implement thrust transmitted through top link actuates the Vary Touch hydraulic system which automatically provides a constant tractor load. Some thrust continues to the front wheels, improving steering characteristics.

The Vary Touch hydraulic system, together with the superior design three-point linkage, transfers a proportion of the implement weight and resistance on to the rear wheels, increasing their traction.

5 P.T.O. SPEED COMBINATION

to choose from!

The B-414 offers the widest choice of p.t.o. speeds available today. There are *three* p.t.o. speeds to choose from—540 r.p.m., 745 r.p.m. and 1,000 r.p.m.; and *two* dual speed combinations—540 and 745 r.p.m. and 540 and 1,000 r.p.m. In fact, the B-414 can be ordered in no less than *six different ways!* All these p.t.o. speeds are obtained with the engine running at full governed engine r.p.m. This means full power for the job in hand.

1 **540 and 745 r.p.m. two-speed constant-running p.t.o.** The most practical p.t.o. speed combination on any tractor now available, covering virtually every power-driven implement now in use, changes from one speed to another at the touch of the lever.

2 **745 r.p.m. single-speed constant-running p.t.o.** This p.t.o. speed has been made available especially for use with high speed p.t.o. implements. The B-414 provides the 745 r.p.m. at full 2,000 engine r.p.m. Throttling back the engine to 1,440 r.p.m., the B.S.I. p.t.o. speed of 540.

3 **540 and 1,000 r.p.m. two-speed constant-running p.t.o.** This combination gives the B.S.I. recommended speed for the majority of today's implements—and tomorrow's, too!

4 **540 r.p.m. transmission p.t.o.** or

5 **540 r.p.m. single-speed constant-running p.t.o.**—gives the recommended B.S.I. p.t.o. speed at full engine power!

6 **No p.t.o.** The B-414 is available without this attachment to meet specialised applications. The exclusive choice of p.t.o. attachments allied with eight forward ground speeds gives this tractor unequalled versatility in power take-off applications.

Power for the constant-running p.t.o. comes from the second stage of the big-capacity dual clutch. In this way a gear change is made without interrupting the p.t.o. To stop the p.t.o., depress the clutch pedal to the full limit of travel. This pedal action does not interfere with hydraulic operation.

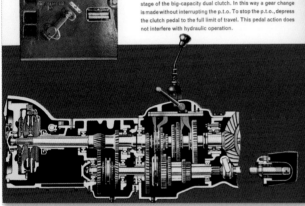

McCORMICK INTERNATIONAL
NEW B-614
62½H.P. DIESEL TRACTOR

INTERNATIONAL HARVESTER

Although the hydraulic system was new, many of the B-414's other features including the steering arrangement, eight-speed gearbox, differential lock and disc brakes were carried over from the B-275. The 'live' power take-off gave a choice of three speeds: 540, 745 and 1,000rpm. The tractor cost around £700.

The new B-614 model, which was introduced at the 1963 Smithfield Show, offered the International customer even greater performance. The grille, cowling and bonnet were styled to match the B-414, but unlike the smaller tractor, the B-614 didn't have draft-control hydraulics. The single-acting hydraulic system provided just lift, hold and lowering functions. Despite its lack of sophistication, the lift had a capacity of more than 1½ tons at the lower-link ends, and the tractor's pulling power was legendary.

NEW HARNESSED POWER for high-speed farming!

The new McCormick International B-614 tractor delivers big power for high-speed, high-production farming . . . power effectively harnessed through the gears, the axles, the p.t.o., the lift and the drawbar. This is the tractor for the big-acreage farmer and the man who farms heavy land. This is the tractor engineered to wield its dependable power with optimum efficiency . . . the tractor that matches its tremendous pulling power with the utmost stability. Get this *harnessed power* earning for you!

62½ HORSEPOWER

FOOT OPERATED **DIFF-LOCK**

Gets a grip on wheel slip

The B-614 was basically a B-450 with more modern styling and the BTD-8's more powerful BD-281 engine with the horses upped to 62½hp. The tractor also had a greater number of gears than the B-450 with a dual-range transmission giving eight-forward and two-reverse speeds. Another new feature was an independent power take-off, which was operated via a separate multi-plate clutch.

The BTD-20 crawler came in for an upgrade in 1963 when it was revamped into the 201 Series. The main improvement was the addition of a transmission oil pump, which circulated and filtered the gearbox oil following the failure of too many of the earlier transmissions through oil starvation. Hydraulic track adjusters and a dry-element air cleaner were also added to the specification list, and the power of the Rolls-Royce engine was boosted to 135hp.

Launched in late 1963, the 40hp BTD-5 was a joint product of the Bradford and Doncaster works. The Idle plant provided the engine, eight-speed gearbox and final-drives, while Wheatley Hall manufactured the running gear and completed the final assembly. The crawler had several novel features including an unusual track layout with the front idler being smaller than the drive sprocket. The single top roller was mounted just forward of the sprocket.

Unique for this size of crawler was the BTD-5's planetary steering system. Partial movement of the steering levers allowed gradual turns, while tight turns were achieved by pulling the levers right back. A built-in hydraulic lift with three-point linkage allowed the tractor to be used with mounted implements. The tractor was powered by the same BD-154 engine as fitted to the International 414 wheeled tractor.

LOYD

The son of a Berkshire magistrate, Vivian Graham Loyd served as a captain in the Royal Field Artillery during the First World War. In 1925, after a spell in the motor trade, he entered into a partnership with Captain Sir John Valentine Carden, an Irish Baronet and gifted engineer, to form Carden-Loyd Tractors Ltd. Operating from premises in Chiswick, the partnership developed a series of light armoured and amphibious military vehicles using Ford components.

The company's tracked carriers, or 'Tankettes', were so successful that Vickers-Armstrong bought the rights in 1928. Under Vickers's ownership, the design was developed into the 'Universal' or 'Bren-gun' carrier that saw widespread service during the Second World War.

Loyd, who lost his partner in 1935 after Carden was tragically killed in an air crash, continued to experiment with tracked vehicles. After the war he formed Vivian Loyd & Co Ltd and began converting military-surplus carriers into agricultural tractors from premises at

Camberley. The Ministry of Supply agreed to the release of materials and Loyd was offered the remaining stocks of carrier parts.

The first Loyd crawler made its appearance at a National Institute of Agricultural Engineering open day at Askham Bryan in October 1945. It was powered by a Ford V8 petrol engine, had differential steering and was fitted with carrier tracks. The tractor was cheap at just £350, but it drank fuel like it was going out of fashion and none of the four speeds offered by its military truck gearbox were much use for land work.

A more refined version of the crawler appeared in 1949 with its Ford V8 engine rated at 30hp. The carrier tracks now had extra shoes bolted on to increase grip and flotation and the price had risen to £495. That same year saw the launch of a diesel version – the Loyd DP Model fitted with a V4 Turner 4V95 engine, which also developed 30hp, but was a much more economical alternative. In 1950 the power of the Turner engine was upped to 40hp.

The most sophisticated tractor that Loyd produced was the Dragon, introduced at the 1950 Smithfield Show. The most notable feature of this new crawler was the option of heavy-duty tracks. These were made for Loyd by Fowler and were identical to those fitted to the Leeds company's current VF model. Fowler rollers, front idlers, track-chains and plates were used with Loyd's own track frames and sprockets. The 'light' carrier tracks were also offered as an alternative.

Two models of Dragon were offered with two different types of diesel engine. The D Model 1079 had the V4 Turner engine, while the D Model 1071 had an indirect-injection Dorman 4DS power unit of similar horsepower. Steering was by clutch-and-brake, and the drive from the engine was via a standard automotive clutch to a Ford four-speed truck gearbox.

Despite the track improvements, the Dragon was not robust enough for agricultural or industrial work. The final drives were particularly weak and it was not unknown for the casings to split in half. It was more expensive than a Fowler VF, but the sales remained just enough to keep the tractor in production until 1952 when the manufacture of Loyd crawlers at Camberley was brought to a close.

The Loyd DP, which appeared in March 1949, was powered by a V4 Turner 4V95 engine developing 30hp at 1,500rpm. The transmission and running gear were still based on carrier components, and extras included a power take-off, pulley, winch and 12-volt electric lighting. Extension arms, welded to the front of the track frames, were attached to a crossbeam that supported the front of the crawler.

The LOYD TRACTOR

THE NEW LOYD DIESEL

THIS tractor, which is powered by a 40 h.p. Diesel Engine, embodies the latest type of clutch and brake steering, and tracks which give a long working life. It will pull a five furrow plough in heavy soil and hilly country, and for plantation work overseas can pull a four tine grubber that has been put down to 12 ins. in virgin soil. It is an ideal motive power for Drainage, Land Reclamation and Afforestation Machinery, and can be fitted with a Bulldozer and Winches

PRINCIPAL FEATURES
- Diesel Engine developing 40 B.H.P.
- 32 Drawbar Horse-power
- Drawbar Pull 6,500 lb.
- Electric Starting
- Rubber Sealed, Lubricationless Balance Beam
- Clutch and Brake Steering
- Normal track centres 50 ins.
- Weight 7,200 lbs.

Royal Agricultural Show - Oxford - July 4/7
Be sure and visit STAND 48, BLOCK F, AVENUE I

VIVIAN LOYD & CO. LTD.

Factory:
BRIDGE ROAD, CAMBERLEY, SURREY, ENGLAND.
Telephone: Camberley 1813

Head Office and Export Dept.:
I, BALFOUR PLACE, LONDON, W.I. ENGLAND.
Telephone: REGent 4877
Cables: Baxaloyd, London

The Loyd Dragon was launched at the 1950 Smithfield Show. This D Model 1071 has the indirect-injection Dorman 4DS diesel engine and 'heavy-duty' Fowler tracks. The 'light' carrier tracks remained an option for £1,250 as opposed to £1,450 for the Dragon with Fowler tracks. The specification included a rear-mounted belt pulley.

Steering on the Dragon was by clutch-and-brake, and the track frames oscillated on a pivoted crossbeam beneath the radiator. The Ford four-speed truck gearbox gave speeds of 0.8mph in first, 1.8mph in second, 3.3mph in third and 5.5mph in fourth; reverse being 0.75mph. The result was one of the worst ranges of speeds possible for agricultural work.

A cutaway drawing of the Loyd Dragon with the Dorman engine: (1) decompressor lever; (2) oil filler and breather; (3) starter-fuse holders; (4) fuel filters; (5) air cleaner; (6) throttle lever; (7) steering levers; (8) gear lever; (9) engine-clutch lever; (10) left-hand steering-brake pedal; (11) battery; (12) fuel tank; (13) right-hand toolbox; (14) parking-brake latch; (15) spiral pinion and gear; (16) left-hand steering clutch and brake; (17) final-drive reduction gear; (18) sprocket hub; (19) transverse axle; (20) top idler; (21) Layrub coupling; (22) gearbox; (23) track-recoil spring; (24) adjustable front idler; (25) self-cleaning oil filter; (26) track-frame stabiliser; (27) balance-beam and pivot connection; and (27a) balance-beam fulcrum.

MARSHALL

The Lincolnshire firm of Marshall, Sons & Co Ltd was one of the few great British steam manufacturers that successfully made the transition from traction engines to tractors. The company had been building steam engines at its Britannia Works in Gainsborough for more than half a century when it introduced its first tractor in 1904. These early 'Colonial' tractors were designed for prairie farming and were exported to Canada, South America, Australia, Africa, India and Russia before the venture came to an end during the First World War.

During the 1920s, with steam in decline, the company again turned its attention to internal-combustion engines. Most of the tractors on the market at the time were developed to run on petrol or paraffin distillates. But Marshall liked to plough its own furrow and it began experimenting with two-stroke compression-ignition and semi-diesel designs, taking its inspiration from Lanz of Germany.

Lanz powered its tractors with a single-cylinder horizontal crude-oil engine, which was a semi-diesel requiring a 'hot bulb' in the cylinder head to be heated by a blow lamp for starting from cold. Marshall used a similar single-cylinder design, but developed the concept as two-stroke full-diesel that could be started instantly from cold. A de-compressor in the cylinder head allowed the engine to be started by hand on half compression; the starting being assisted by the insertion of a glowing ignition-paper into the combustion chamber.

The new Marshall diesel tractor, designated 15/30, made its appearance at the 1930 World Tractor Trials in

The Marshall Model M was an evolution of the earlier 12/20 model with minor improvements and a slight increase in power to 22hp at the belt. The tractor was in production from 1938-45 and approximately 1,000 were built. Later models were painted green with red wheels and the price was £375.

The Model M was marketed as an all-British diesel tractor, but wartime production was limited by Marshall's commitments to the War Office, which included naval, anti-aircraft and anti-tank guns, aero-engine components and midget submarines.

Oxfordshire. Diesel engines were still a relatively untried concept, but the advantages of the Marshall tractor – particularly in terms of fuel economy – soon became evident. In 1932 the 15/30 was replaced with the 18/30 before the company realised that the market required something lighter.

The 12/20 model was already under development when Marshall ran into financial difficulty in 1935. The company was rescued by Thomas W Ward of Sheffield, a business built on scrap iron, which bought a controlling interest in the Gainsborough firm. The 12/20 was launched in 1936, evolving into the Marshall Model M two years later.

Marshall went to war with numerous government

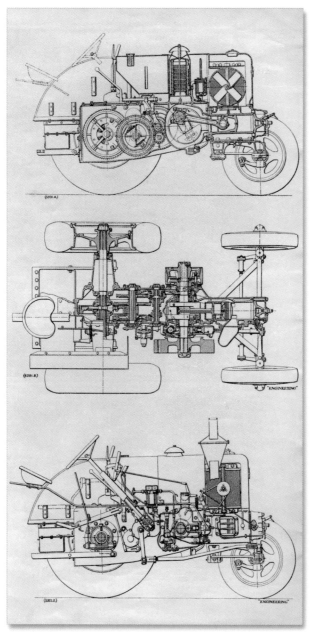

contracts that disrupted production of the Model M, but the tractor was built in limited numbers until June 1945 when it was replaced by the new Field Marshall. Produced in Mark 1 (general agricultural) and Mark 2 (Contractors) versions, the Field Marshall marked a new era in the company's fortunes with sales across the world.

Following a policy of continually upgrading its products, Marshall introduced the Field Marshall Series 2 in 1947 and the Series 3 in 1950. The Ward Group had brought Fowler into its fold at the end of 1946, and a pooling of resources with Marshall had resulted in the VF crawler. Several of the VF's features – including the six-speed gearbox – were incorporated into the Series 3, which was upgraded into the Series 3A in 1952. The 3A, which remained in production until 1956, was the last of the Marshall single-cylinder diesel tractors.

Marshall's first venture into multi-cylinder tractors was the MP4, which was developed in 1953 and fitted with a four-cylinder Meadows power unit. The MP4 never went beyond prototype stage, but the MP6, which was powered by a six-cylinder Leyland engine, was built in small numbers from 1954-56. Sales were hampered by transmission failures and the lack of a hydraulic lift. Less than 200 were made and most were exported.

The year 1956 marked a change of direction for the company with the launch of the new Track-Marshall, which was the replacement for the Fowler VFA crawler. Although the new tracklayer, powered by a Perkins L4 diesel engine, was built at Fowler's Steam Plough Works in Leeds it was very much a Marshall product with all the development work carried out at Gainsborough.

In 1959 the L4 engine was replaced by the new Perkins 4.270 power unit and the crawler became known as the Track-Marshall 55. The 55 was a particularly successful machine for the company; it remained in production until 1970 and helped Marshall capture some 60 percent of the UK agricultural crawler market.

A six-cylinder version of the crawler, the Track-Marshall 70 powered by a Perkins 6.354 engine, was added to the range in 1961. The 70 Type C with differential steering was joined by the 70 Type H, which had a hydraulically-operated clutch-and-brake steering system, in 1962. A new yellow livery was introduced in 1965 and both variants of the 70 remained in production until 1970 when a new range of Track-Marshall crawlers was launched with the eventual switchover in production from Leeds to Gainsborough beginning in late 1972.

The mechanical layout of the Marshall Model M was a simple arrangement with a single-cylinder horizontal engine driving a transverse three-speed gearbox. The two-stroke diesel engine had a 6½in by 9in stroke and ran at 700 rpm. The gearbox gave speeds of 2.2mph, 3.1mph and 5mph with 1.75mph in reverse. The weight of the tractor was 4,950lb.

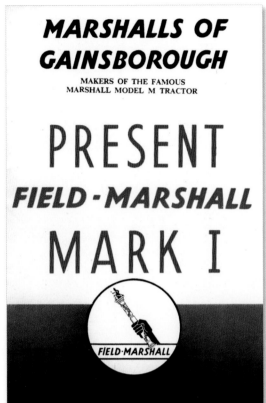

The development of the new Field Marshall tractor began in 1943 and the model was launched in June 1945. The Mark 1, which was the general agricultural version, sold for £550. Production continued until 1947 and more than 2,000 were built.

Resplendent in its 'Mid Brunswick Green' livery, the Field Marshall Mark 1 was a great improvement over the Model M with changes to the cylinder head, transmission and axles. The engine ran at 750rpm and developed 38hp. A cartridge-starting mechanism was provided for those customers who didn't want to start their tractor by hand.

Visually the Field Marshall Mark 1 had a much more modern appearance with its stylish tinwork and cigar-shaped exhaust silencer. The curved sheet-metal at the front hid an enlarged header-tank for the radiator, which increased the cooling capacity to 11 gallons. The raised driving position offered greater visibility for the operator – although the seat of a Field Marshall tractor was never the comfiest of places to be with the constant vibration from the single-cylinder engine!

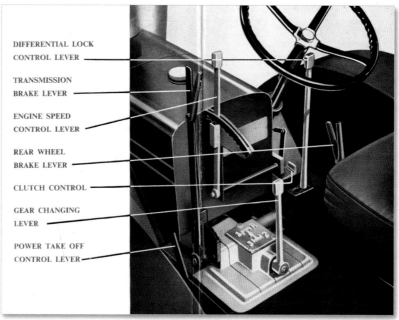

The Field Marshall Mark 2 was a special Contractors model with built-in winch, rear-wheel brakes, canvas canopy and lighting. Aimed at the threshing contractor, the tractor had a top speed of 9mph and cost £840. The winch, driven by an auxiliary gearbox, was mounted beneath the driver's platform.

The driver's platform of the Field Marshall Mark 2 Contractors model gave easy access to the controls. The clutch was operated by a hand lever. A differential lock was standard and power take-off was optional. The Contractors model had drum brakes on the rear wheels in addition to the standard transmission brake.

The Field Marshall Series 2 arrived in July 1947 with numerous improvements including independent brakes, a better cooling system, a larger-diameter clutch, a more comfortable seat and greater power. The engine modifications gave 40hp and the transmission was strengthened to cope with the extra power. The exhaust silencer, which was manufactured by Burgess, was also redesigned to reduce the echo.

The Field Marshall Mark 1 Series 2, priced at £625, was the general agricultural version of the tractor. The differential lock was deleted from the specification, but larger tyres (12.75 x 28 was standard) gave increased traction and four-furrows were well within the tractor's capacity under the right conditions. The Series 2 remained on the market until 1949 and around 7,000 were sold.

The Field Marshall Mark 2 Series 2 was the Contractors model with a heavy-duty Marshall winch. A light-duty Hesford winch was offered as alternative equipment. The tractor, priced at £870, was aimed at threshing contractors, but sales were also made to timber merchants and the industrial market.

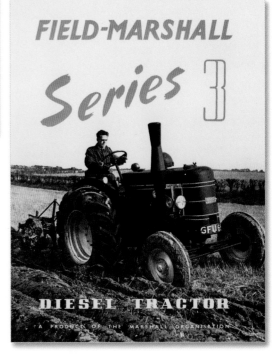

The Field Marshall Series 3 was launched in early 1950 following trials of pre-production models during 1949. The power was unchanged at 40hp and the engine dimensions still dated back to the Model M, but the cooling capacity was increased with a larger header-tank giving the tractor a bulkier appearance. Other new features included a centrally-mounted pto-shaft, dual fuel filters, a sturdier front axle, a stronger steering box and larger 14 x 30 tyres.

The most significant
improvement brought in with
the introduction of the Series 3
model was the change to a six-
speed gearbox. The extra ratios
were provided by high/low
pinions located either side of
the differential with the drive
to the rear axle via bull-gear
and pinion. To accommodate
the transmission changes, the
rotation of the engine was
changed to clockwise when
viewed from the pulley-side
of the tractor.

The Field Marshall Series 3 offered greater driver comfort
with the provision of an adjustable upholstered seat. The
throttle lever was relocated beneath the steering wheel and
the independent brakes were now foot-operated. The model
remained in production until 1952 and 3,205 were built.

The Field Marshall Series 3A was the final incarnation of
Gainsborough's single-cylinder diesel tractor. Unveiled in
September 1952, the 3A featured a number of small
improvements to enhance the engine performance. A pressurised
cooling system was introduced and the price rose to £845.

The Field Marshall Series 3A could be fitted with a heavy-duty winch, which was supplied with 75yds of steel cable and had an 11,000lb pull. Other options included a cab, electric lighting and an electric starting system. In July 1953 the colour of the tractor was changed to 'Chrome Orange'.

The Marshall MP4 heralded a change to multi-cylinder wheeled tractors. Development work on the new project began in 1953 and just two prototypes were released the following year. Both were powered by four-cylinder Meadows 4DC330 diesel engines rated at 65hp and the transmission gave six forward and two reverse speeds. No attempt was made to put the model into production and it is believed that the two prototypes were re-engineered into MP6 models.

Announced in December 1954, the Marshall MP6 was a six-cylinder tractor powered by a Leyland UE350 diesel engine mated to a six-speed transmission. The model went into full production in 1956 with a price tag of £1,450.

The Marshall MP6's six-cylinder Leyland AU350 diesel engine developed 70hp at 1,700rpm. The displacement was 351cu in (5752cc). The Leyland engine was probably chosen because similar units were already being supplied within the Ward Group to Fowler for its crawler range.

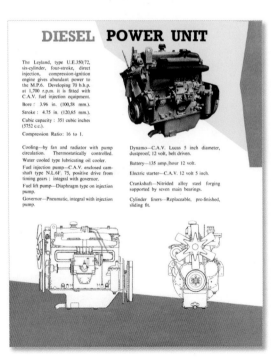

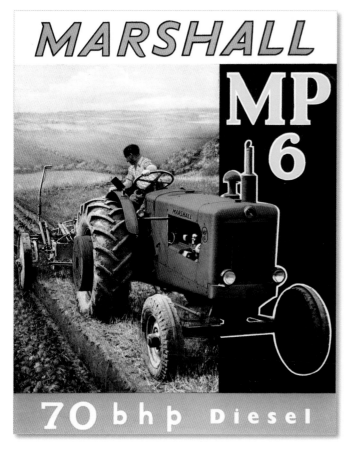

Aimed at the export market, particularly the sugar cane industry, the Marshall MP6 was designed for haulage or heavy cultivations. Early production was dogged by transmission failures and the lack of a hydraulic lift hampered sales. The tractor was expensive and just 197 were made before production ended in 1961.

The basic controls were grouped on the MP6's spacious control platform with pedals to operate the clutch and independent brakes. Power take-off was optional and the foam-rubber cushioned seat could be adjusted to suit the individual driver's needs.

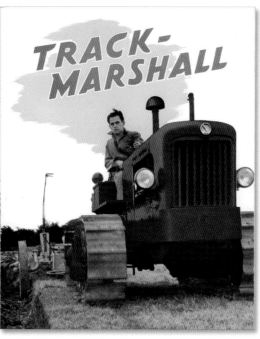

Introduced in 1956, the new Track-Marshall crawler was a joint Marshall-Fowler product with the development work carried out at Gainsborough and production centred at the Steam Plough Works in Leeds. The tractor was based on the Fowler VFA chassis using the proven differential steering system. The machine was priced at £1,445.

The Track-Marshall was powered by the four-cylinder, indirect-injection Perkins L4 diesel engine, delivering 48hp at 1,600rpm. Features included wet cylinder-liners and pressurised lubrication. A change from a pneumatic governor to a mechanically-controlled governor upped the power to 50hp on later tractors.

The Perkins L.4 diesel engine has been designed to give the tractor owner reliability, economy and push-button starting.

Quick starting long-life four stroke diesel engine

GENERAL PARTICULARS

48 b.h.p. at the rated engine speed of 1,600 r.p.m.

No. of cylinders	...	4
Bore ...	...	4¼ ins. (107,95 mm.)
Stroke ...	...	4¾ ins. (120,65 mm.)
Cubic Capacity	...	269.5 cu. ins. (4,42 litres)

NOTABLE DESIGN FEATURES

Combustion Chamber with fully machined chamber and throat incorporating the Perkins Patented system of combustion.

Wet Liners—pre-finished and easily replaceable.

Main and Big End Bearings—pre-finished and replaceable without the necessity of carrying out boring or scraping operations.

Overhead valves operated by push rods.

Timing Gear. Camshaft and fuel pump are gear driven from the crankshaft.

Hardened main and crankpin journals.

Oil pump is of the gear type, driven by spiral gears from the camshaft.

Lubrication—Lubricating oil is pressure fed through a large capacity full flow filter to Main and Big End Bearings.

Cold Starting—a 12 volt induction heater and a Priming Pump are provided as cold starting aids.

Starting equipment comprises a 12-volt 5 in. axial type starter with a belt driven dynamo.

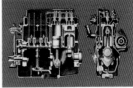

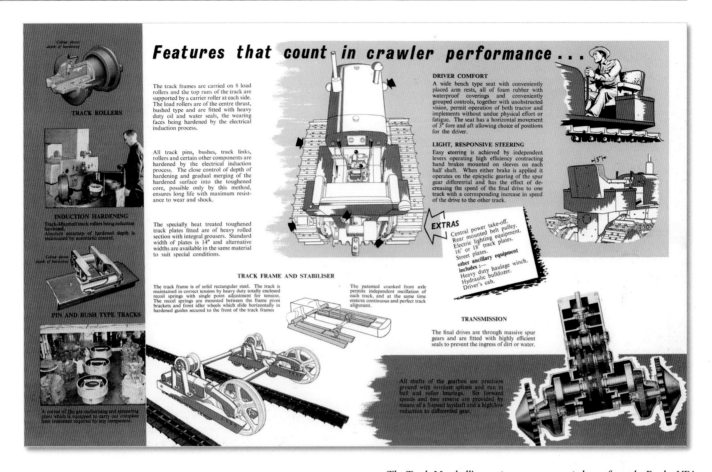

Features that count in crawler performance...

TRACK ROLLERS

The track frames are carried on 8 load rollers and the top runs of the track are supported by a carrier roller at each side. The load rollers are of the centre thrust, bushed type and are fitted with heavy duty oil and water seals, the wearing faces being hardened by the electrical induction process.

All track pins, bushes, track links, rollers and certain other components are hardened by the electrical induction process. The close control of depth of hardening and gradual merging of the hardened surface into the toughened core, possible only by this method, ensures long life with maximum resistance to wear and shock.

INDUCTION HARDENING

Track-Marshall track rollers being induction hardened. Absolute accuracy of hardened depth is maintained by automatic control.

PIN AND BUSH TYPE TRACKS

A corner of the gas-carburising and tempering plant which is equipped to carry out complete heat treatment required by any component.

The specially heat treated toughened track plates fitted are of heavy rolled section with integral grousers. Standard width of plates is 14" and alternative widths are available in the same material to suit special conditions.

TRACK FRAME AND STABILISER

The track frame is of solid rectangular steel. The track is maintained in correct tension by heavy duty totally enclosed recoil springs with single point adjustment for tension. The recoil springs are mounted between the frame pivot brackets and front idler wheels which slide horizontally in hardened guides secured to the front of the track frames.

The patented cranked front axle permits independent oscillation of each track, and at the same time ensures continuous and perfect track alignment.

DRIVER COMFORT

A wide bench type seat with conveniently placed arm rests, all of foam rubber with waterproof coverings and conveniently grouped controls, together with unobstructed vision, permit operation of both tractor and implements without undue physical effort or fatigue. The seat has a horizontal movement of 3" fore and aft allowing choice of positions for the driver.

LIGHT, RESPONSIVE STEERING

Easy steering is achieved by independent levers operating high efficiency contracting band brakes mounted on sleeves on each half shaft. When either brake is applied it operates on the epicyclic gearing of the spur gear differential and has the effect of decreasing the speed of the final drive to one track with a corresponding increase in speed of the drive to the other track.

EXTRAS

Central power take-off.
Rear mounted belt pulley.
Electric lighting equipment.
16" or 18" track plates.
Street plates.
other ancillary equipment
includes :—
Heavy duty haulage winch.
Hydraulic bulldozer.
Driver's cab.

TRANSMISSION

The final drives are through massive spur gears and are fitted with highly efficient seals to prevent the ingress of dirt or water.

All shafts of the gearbox are precision ground with involute splines and run in ball and roller bearings. Six forward speeds and two reverse are provided by means of a 3-speed layshaft and a high/low reduction to differential gear.

The Track-Marshall's running gear was carried over from the Fowler VFA with a number of improvements including track-frames constructed from solid rectangular steel instead of channel. Four bottom-rollers were standard and the transmission gave six forward and two reverse speeds.

COMPLETE PROTECTION ...
ALL ROUND VISION

TRACK-MARSHALL TRACTOR
with ALL-WEATHER STEEL CAB

The Track-Marshall was available with a large range of equipment for agricultural and industrial use including a bulldozer attachment, hydraulic control, toolbar, ripper, lighting equipment, power take-off, pulley and winch. The 'All-Weather' steel cab provided welcome protection from the usual British wind and rain! This is the 50hp version of the tractor.

TRACK-MARSHALL
DIESEL CRAWLER TRACTOR
with 55 b.h.p. diesel engine

From 1959 the Track-Marshall crawler was fitted with the Perkins 4.270 engine. This direct-injection unit gave 55hp at 1,800rpm. The cubic capacity was the same as the earlier L4 engine.

The change to the more powerful Perkins 4.270 engine in 1959 led to a redesignation of the crawler as the Track-Marshall 55 model for both agriculture and industry. The industrial model, priced at £1,810, had five bottom-rollers and could be supplied with a variety of equipment including a bulldozer, angledozer, scraper, side-boom crane or hydraulic backhoe.

The standard agricultural version of the Track-Marshall 55 had four bottom-rollers. The combination of the lively Perkins 4.270 engine mated to a six-speed transmission made it an ideal ploughing tractor. The differential steering system was largely reliable, although the crawler could sometimes be difficult to steer under load on bulldozing operations.

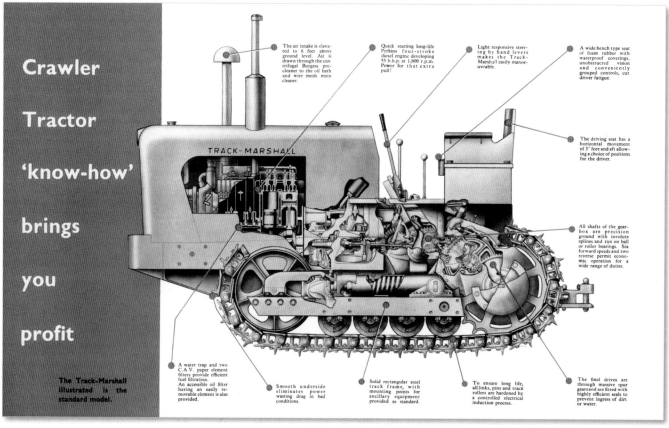

Crawler Tractor 'know-how' brings you profit

The Track-Marshall illustrated is the standard model.

The air intake is elevated to 6 feet above ground level. Air is drawn through the centrifugal Burgess pre-cleaner to the oil bath and wire mesh main cleaner.

Quick starting long-life Perkins four-stroke diesel engine developing 55 b.h.p. at 1,800 r.p.m. Power for that extra pull!

Light responsive steering by hand levers makes the Track-Marshall easily manoeuvrable.

A wide bench type seat of foam rubber with waterproof coverings, unobstructed vision and conveniently grouped controls, cut driver fatigue.

The driving seat has a horizontal movement of 3" fore and aft allowing a choice of positions for the driver.

All shafts of the gearbox are precision ground with involute splines and run on ball or roller bearings. Six forward speeds and two reverse permit economic operation for a wide range of duties.

A water trap and two C.A.V. paper element filters provide efficient fuel filtration. An accessible oil filter having an easily removable element is also provided.

Smooth underside eliminates power wasting drag in bad conditions.

Solid rectangular steel track frame, with mounting points for ancillary equipment provided as standard.

To ensure long life, all links, pins and track rollers are hardened by a controlled electrical induction process.

The final drives are through massive spur gears and are fitted with highly efficient seals to prevent ingress of dirt or water.

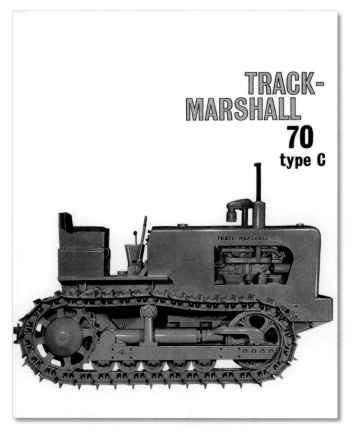

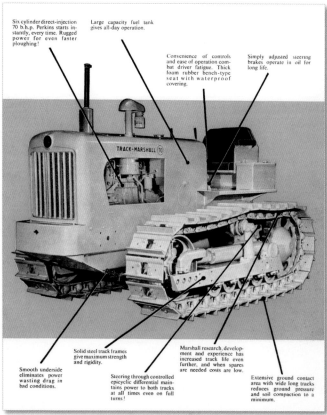

Six cylinder direct-injection 70 b.h.p. Perkins starts instantly, every time. Rugged power for even faster ploughing!

Large capacity fuel tank gives all-day operation.

Convenience of controls and ease of operation combat driver fatigue. Thick foam rubber bench-type seat with waterproof covering.

Simply adjusted steering brakes operate in oil for long life.

Smooth underside eliminates power wasting drag in bad conditions.

Solid steel track frames give maximum strength and rigidity.

Steering through controlled epicyclic differential maintains power to both tracks at all times even on full turns!

Marshall research, development and experience has increased track life even further, and when spares are needed costs are low.

Extensive ground contact area with wide long tracks reduces ground pressure and soil compaction to a minimum.

The six-cylinder Track-Marshall 70 arrived in 1961 with a Perkins 6.354 engine providing the muscle and was an instant success. The differential steering, as fitted to the Type C, had its limitations in a machine of this size, but it was inexpensive horsepower at £2,350 and the tractor gave few problems. Around 1,400 were built.

The Track-Marshall 70 was more than just an up-rated 55 and much was changed or strengthened to cope with the extra power – the Perkins 6.354 delivering 70hp at 1,700 rpm. Early tractors had a five forward and single reverse gearbox, but a shuttle change was introduced in July 1964 providing five forward and three reverse speeds. Hydraulic track-adjusters were also added to the specification early the same year.

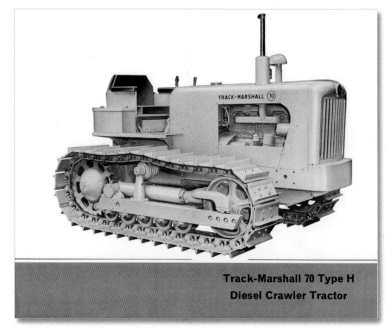

**Track-Marshall 70 Type H
Diesel Crawler Tractor**

The Track-Marshall 70 Type H arrived in 1962 offering clutch-and-brake steering as an alternative to the Type C's differential steering system. Controlled by hand levers, the multi-plate steering clutches and brakes were hydraulically-operated and self-adjusting. However, as the steering pump was driven from the gearbox, the tractor had to be in gear and moving before anything would happen. Just 450 Type H models were made.

MASSEY FERGUSON

Massey Ferguson has become one of the most recognised names in the industry, but as far as the datelines covered by this book are concerned it was a latecomer to the party. The seeds that led to the formation of the organisation were set in 1954 when Harry Ferguson's tractor and farm machinery business was merged with the Canadian Massey-Harris Company to form Massey-Harris-Ferguson.

Behind the scenes things were not so rosy: the MHF merger had not gone as smoothly as expected and the logistics of running two separate product lines was putting a financial strain on the company, which made a $4.7 million loss in 1957. A rationalisation of the manufacturing, sales and service divisions was desperately required if the company was to return to profitability.

In December 1957 the MHF board sanctioned the renaming of the company as Massey Ferguson Ltd. There would be one line of distributors and dealers and one line of MF badged products identified by the new triple-triangle symbol that had been

introduced a month earlier. The new corporate identity decreed that tractors would be painted red and grey. All mounted and Ferguson System equipment would remain grey, while trailed implements and combines would be red.

The Ferguson FE-35 tractor was re-launched at the 1957 Smithfield Show as the MF 35 in the new corporate livery. It was joined by the new Massey Ferguson 65, based on the North American Ferguson F-40 and fitted with a 50hp Perkins A4.192 diesel engine. The MF 35's engines were still supplied by the Standard Motor Company, but unfortunately its 23C power unit was by no means the best diesel on the market.

Aware of the 23C's shortcomings and not wanting to be held to ransom by the Standard Motor Company, which also controlled its Banner Lane manufacturing facilities, Massey Ferguson went shopping for a new engine supplier. It had the spare cash: its 1958 turnover of over $440 million left it with a pre-tax profit of nearly $22 million.

Almost £4.5 million was spent on acquiring F Perkins Ltd of Peterborough, which was brought into the MF fold in January 1959. Digging deep into its reserves, Massey also managed to buy out Standard's tractor manufacturing interests after some stiff negotiating for £11.8 million the following July.

Now fully in control of its own destiny, Massey Ferguson introduced the MF 35 with the 40hp Perkins A3.152 diesel engine at the 1959 Smithfield Show. Standard's four-cylinder petrol and TVO engines remained an option, but the lively three-cylinder Perkins motor allowed Massey Ferguson to justifiably claim that the MF 35 was 'the World's finest light tractor'.

In November 1960 it was the Massey Ferguson

The Ferguson FE-35 tractor was re-launched at the 1957 Smithfield Show as the Massey Ferguson 35 in the new corporate red and grey livery. Beneath the paint nothing had changed and it was still offered with petrol, TVO, lamp oil and diesel engine options, all supplied by the Standard Motor Company. Early MF 35s were no more than repainted FE-35s, still wearing the Ferguson badge on the front of the bonnet, but this was quickly replaced by the triple-triangle emblem.

65 tractor's turn for a revamp. The MF 65 Mark ll offered minor styling changes and the differential lock, previously optional, was now standard. A change to a Perkins A4.203 engine ramped up the power to 56.8hp. When the tractor was tested by the National Institute of Agricultural Engineering at Silsoe it recorded 58.3hp, so Massey was able to up its advertised power without making any changes to the engine!

The three-cylinder 35, originally advertised as a 37hp machine, was now shown as having 39.6hp. This was because Massey Ferguson originally quoted its belt horsepower figure rather than its true brake horsepower – an anomaly that has sometimes led to the misconception that there was a later power increase, which was not the case. From May 1962 the MF 35 was offered with optional differential lock and PAVT rear wheels.

In August 1962 Massey Ferguson introduced its new Multi-Power transmission as an option on the MF 65. This turned the 6 x 2 gearbox (six forward and two reverse) into a 12 x 4 transmission with the change between ratios in each gear being made by the flick of a switch.

December 1962 saw the launch of the ultimate MF 35 tractor – the 35X model. This was only available with an up-rated version of the A3.152 diesel engine, which delivered 44.5hp through modifications to the fuel system and an increase in the engine speed. The 35X was also available with Multi-Power.

Production of the MF 35 and 65 models at Banner Lane peaked at 375 tractors per day. But greater things were to come with the arrival of the 100 Series 'Red Giants' at the end of 1964. The 100 Series, which included the 135, 165 and 175 from Banner Lane, was shipped to 140 different countries and on some days as many as 16 tractors an hour were rolling off the assembly line. This new range inherited the MF 35 and 65's lineage (the MF 135 was basically a 35X with new tinwork), but was part of a new era of tractors that is outside the scope of this book.

Today, Massey Ferguson is part of the global AGCO corporation, which itself was born out of a management buyout of the North American Allis-Chalmers farm equipment division. Banner Lane built its last tractor on Christmas Eve 2002, and European MF production is now centred at Beauvais in France.

The Massey Ferguson 35 industrial tractor was offered with a dual-braking system, horn, mirror and handbrake to meet the legal requirements for haulage or municipal work on a public road. Semi- or full-industrial versions were available with the option of a sprung-hitch, full-width mudguards and industrial tyres.

4 main features which provide **selectivity** and **flexibility** in tractor design and implement control

HYDRAULIC SYSTEM

The Ferguson hydraulic system is *built in* to the Massey-Ferguson 35 tractor—it is not added as an afterthought or "extra". The unique double quadrant offers *finger-tip* control of front, mid and rear mounted implements.

POWER TAKE-OFF

When you sit at the controls of your powerful '35' you get the choice of two different power take-off drives; select a drive that's in ratio to the engine *or* to the ground speed—and you have a P.T.O. drive to suit a host of jobs !

DUAL CLUTCH

The '35' De Luxe is fitted with a Dual Clutch which makes your "Engine Speed" P.T.O. *live*—that means a running P.T.O. (even though the tractor is stationary) for mechanically propelled attachments. Further, this unique Dual Clutch ensures a constant running hydraulic pump —a boon for loaders.

SIX-SPEED GEARBOX

An amazing range of speeds can be obtained from the Massey-Ferguson 35 ! There are no less than six forward and two reverse gears—a gear and a speed for every job. Creep as slow as 0·3 m.p.h. or speed up to 14 m.p.h. for fast jobs !

Within one design are incorporated the most advanced use of hydraulics, great engine power, a wide range of speeds, improved design and a score of other features—a basis for the most economical system of farm mechanisation !

MORE POWER AND MORE EXCLUSIVE NEW FEATURES

MASSEY-FERGUSON 35

The Massey Ferguson 35 had the same features as the FE-35 including the Ferguson hydraulic system, six-speed gearbox and two-speed power take-off. Like the FE-35 it was available in two levels of trim with the De-Luxe model offering 'live' power take-off and hydraulics, a footrest assembly, tractormeter and a cushioned foam seat.

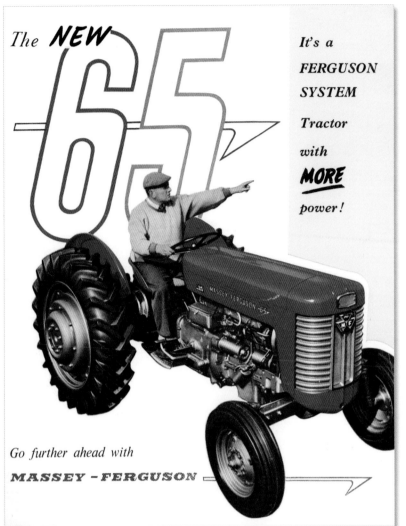

The *NEW* 65

It's a FERGUSON SYSTEM Tractor with **MORE** power!

Go further ahead with
MASSEY - FERGUSON

The Massey Ferguson 65 was a completely new model launched alongside the red/grey MF 35 at the 1957 Smithfield Show. The tractor had similar styling to the 35 model and inherited the Ferguson hydraulic system. Other features included a six-speed gearbox, two-speed power take-off and two-stage clutch giving 'live' hydraulics and pto.

the famous FERGUSON SYSTEM . . . . .

The Ferguson System is now truly established as an essential for those who practice really economical farm mechanisation . . . . . now the Ferguson System has the added punch of the powerful '65' . . . . . now you have two grades of tractor power—'35' and '65'—allied to one common line of implements!

The Ferguson Hydraulic System has been still further improved in the '65' but many of the established features in the popular '35' and famous '20' are still the same . . . . traction without built-in weight . . . . . draft control, overload release, three-point linkage, front-end stability, simple finger-tip control . . . . . features that have been proved and trusted in well over 1,000,000 Ferguson System tractors!

The most revolutionary advance the Ferguson System has made with the introduction of the '65' is the provision for even greater earning power per tractor unit . . . . now you can attach many of your existing Massey-Ferguson implements and Category 2 implements to your new '65'—in due course all existing Massey-Ferguson implements will be made to fit the '65'.

A completely new top link, variable in length from 24" to 30", has alternative connection points on the tractor. The strengthened lower links with pivoting and interchangeable ball-ends are but a few of many features which put the pioneers of tractor hydraulics even further ahead.

Greatly increased HYDRAULIC lift . . . . . .

A constant running, positive, four cylinder scotch-yoke piston pump of **57% greater displacement than the original** '20' is incorporated in the '65'. The pump takes oil from the rear axle and transmission oil sump, through the control valve and at a full engine speed is capable of delivering almost 4 gallons per minute. Oil pressure is limited by a safety valve to a maximum of 2,800 p.s.i. while the minimum blow-off pressure is 2,300 p.s.i.

Constant Gap overload release is a new feature for the Ferguson System—it provides safety protection to light draft implements and does not function in heavy working conditions until a sudden increased shock load is received.

The Massey Ferguson 65's hydraulic system was a development of that fitted to the 35 with a dual quadrant operating draft, position and response control. The system was supplied by a four-cylinder horizontally-opposed piston-type pump capable of delivering 4 gallons per minute.

NEW High-Power Engine

The new '65' is specifically a 4/5 furrow tractor with a difference—its powerful 50.5 h.p. *diesel engine* is married to the Ferguson System! This means that the power of the engine is utilised, according to the job in hand, in the most economical way possible.

Powering the Massey Ferguson 65 was a four-cylinder Perkins A4.192 diesel engine delivering 50.5hp at 2,000rpm. The engine had replaceable dry liners and its 3½in bore by 5in stroke gave a displacement of 192cu in (3,146cc). A CAV rotary injection-pump was fitted.

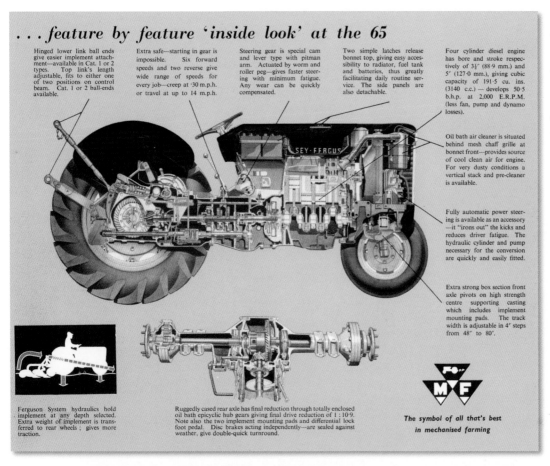

...feature by feature 'inside look' at the 65

Hinged lower link ball ends give easier implement attachment—available in Cat. 1 or 2 types. Top link's length adjustable, fits to either one of two positions on control beam. Cat. 1 or 2 ball-ends available.

Extra safe—starting in gear is impossible. Six forward speeds and two reverse give wide range of speeds for every job—creep at ·30 m.p.h. or travel at up to 14 m.p.h.

Steering gear is special cam and lever type with pitman arm. Actuated by worm and roller peg—gives faster steering with minimum fatigue. Any wear can be quickly compensated.

Two simple latches release bonnet top, giving easy accessibility to radiator, fuel tank and batteries, thus greatly facilitating daily routine service. The side panels are also detachable.

Four cylinder diesel engine has bore and stroke respectively of 3½" (88·9 mm.) and 5" (127·0 mm.), giving cubic capacity of 191·5 cu. ins. (3140 c.c.) — develops 50·5 b.h.p. at 2,000 E.R.P.M. (less fan, pump and dynamo losses).

Oil bath air cleaner is situated behind mesh chaff grille at bonnet front—provides source of cool clean air for engine. For very dusty conditions a vertical stack and pre-cleaner is available.

Fully automatic power steering is available as an accessory —it "irons out" the kicks and reduces driver fatigue. The hydraulic cylinder and pump necessary for the conversion are quickly and easily fitted.

Extra strong box section front axle pivots on high strength centre supporting casting which includes implement mounting pads. The track width is adjustable in 4" steps from 48" to 80".

Ferguson System hydraulics hold implement at any depth selected. Extra weight of implement is transferred to rear wheels ; gives more traction.

Ruggedly cased rear axle has final reduction through totally enclosed oil bath epicyclic hub gears giving final drive reduction of 1 : 10·9. Note also the two implement mounting pads and differential lock foot pedal. Disc brakes acting independently—are sealed against weather, give double-quick turnround.

The symbol of all that's best in mechanised farming

Copied from the North American Ferguson F-40, the MF 65's layout was a compact package with no unnecessary weight. The rear axle was ruggedly constructed with the final drive via epicyclic hub-gears. Features included Goodyear 'Ausco' double-disc brakes that could be operated together or independently to assist steering. The steering-box was a new design and the six-speed gearbox gave speeds from 1.31 to 14.43 mph. Differential lock was optional and the two-speed power take-off ran at ground-speed or 540rpm.

The finest 50 h.p. class tractor . . . the M-F 65

The MF 65 had Ferguson ancestry, but it was a leap in a new direction for the company with a considerable move up the horsepower ladder. It was the first time that the Ferguson System had been incorporated into a tractor in the 50hp class – and it proved to be exactly what the market wanted. The 65 was designed to be used with all the existing Ferguson implements, allowing the company to boast: 'Be wise and standardise with Massey Ferguson'.

The MASSEY-FERGUSON

Power, Performance, Pedigree

65

No other tractor in the 50 h.p. class can match the magnificent performance of the Massey-Ferguson 65, because it is the only tractor in this class with the extra **working** power of the Ferguson System.

The 65 has a drawbar pull of nearly 8,000 lbs.—almost twice its own weight. With this alone it could take the heaviest implement through the toughest going. But the 65 does more! It makes full use of every pound of implement working weight to provide extra soil-gripping traction on the tractor rear wheels.

Yet with all its rugged power the 65 costs less to own and operate. Only the Ferguson System makes it possible to build in immense power and strength without fuel-consuming excess weight.

Test it for toughness and ease of handling in **your** fields. Ask your Massey-Ferguson Dealer for a demonstration.

- Ferguson System — Automatic 2-way draught control ensures unsurpassed accuracy and implement depth control.
- Ferguson System — Two control levers giving you the most advanced tractor hydraulics in the World—no other system can give you every one of the 65's hydraulic control features working together.
- Ferguson System — Automatic overload release protects all draught implements.
- Disc Brakes—Sealed from dust, dirt, weather : give double-quick turn round.
- Differential Lock—Combats wheel slip on bad ground.
- Power Steering — Minimises Operator fatigue, ensures accuracy.
- P.T.O.—Either proportional engine speed or ground speed p.t.o.
- Dual Clutch — Heavy duty hydraulic pump, Epicyclic reduction and many other brilliant features.

Massey Ferguson claimed that the MF 65 had the best power-to-weight ratio in the 50hp sector. The tractor was a willing performer, but its sales were always overshadowed by the Fordson Super Major, which remained the market leader in its class.

The Massey Ferguson 35 was offered with even more options from December 1959. The four-cylinder Standard petrol, TVO and lamp oil engines were still on the table, but the old 23C diesel had been replaced by a new three-cylinder Perkins unit. Other options included vineyard and high-clearance versions of the tractor.

FAMOUS, ECONOMICAL A3.152 ENGINE

The A3.152 Diesel Engine has proved the absolute master of all farm jobs. Giving over 39 b.h.p. for heavy work, it produces immense torque at low speeds. This means that the engine "hangs on" to the load, pulling you through tough spots where less effective units fail. Years of experience plus the finest manufacturing methods give you exactly what you want — an engine that gets **all** the sheer pull out of every drop of fuel !

The A3.152 bristles with advanced features. A mechanical governor gives highly sensitive speed control. Twin filters keep fuel perfectly clean, even on the dustiest field. The rigid steel crankshaft, on four bearings, is carefully balanced for smooth running. With these come timing *gears*, for constant accuracy, a big 90 amp-hour 12-volt battery and a new self-ventilated heavy duty clutch. The A3.152 is ready for years of hard, slogging work !

"... Consider the advantages of the new '35' Mr. Farmer"

Although advertised as a 37hp unit, the MF 35's new Perkins A3.152 engine actually delivered 39.6hp. It was a superb free-revving power unit, one of the best that Perkins ever built with loads of torque while miserly on fuel. The displacement was 152cu in (2,500cc).

The Massey Ferguson 35 with the three-cylinder Perkins motor was a tractor transformed. The lively A3.152 engine offered more torque, greater economy, easier starting and lower maintenance costs. The new power unit better suited the gearbox ratios and made greater use of the six-speed transmission. The arrival of the new engine coincided with the fitment of a new self-ventilating heavy-duty clutch.

NOW *gives you more power per pound!"*

Here's a great combination of torque and horsepower

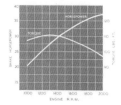

Torque gives your tractor its drawbar pull; horsepower its speed of working. The '35' has an extra margin of both, giving greater pulling power and economic use of the higher gears and more effective use of the '35's' excellent gear ratios. Note that with the 35's new engine, maximum torque is available at low engine speeds—where you need it.

MASSEY-FERGUSON 65 MARK II TRACTOR

New more powerful engine and extra standard features

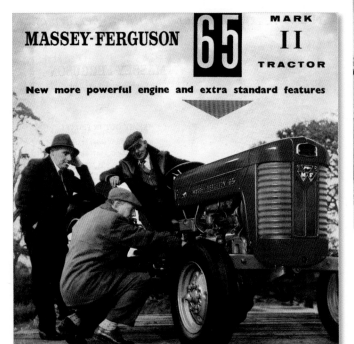

MF MASSEY-FERGUSON — PACE-SETTERS IN FARM MECHANISATION

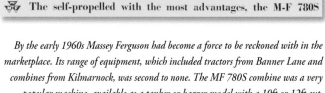

MF The self-propelled with the most advantages, the M-F 780S

By the early 1960s Massey Ferguson had become a force to be reckoned with in the marketplace. Its range of equipment, which included tractors from Banner Lane and combines from Kilmarnock, was second to none. The MF 780S combine was a very popular machine, available as a tanker or bagger model with a 10ft or 12ft cut.

The Massey Ferguson 65 Mark ll was introduced in November 1960 with a new Perkins A4.203 engine rated at 56.8hp. The A4.203 was a derivative of the 65's earlier A4.192 power unit with the bore increased to 3.6in to give a swept volume of 203cu in (3,330cc). As well as the power increase, torque was also up and the 65 Mark ll was a much livelier performer. The styling was also revamped and the differential lock was now standard.

MASSEY-FERGUSON

The World's
Best-Selling Tractor

35

TRACTOR

NOW
WITH
DIFF-LOCK

Massey-Ferguson Farms with the Farmer

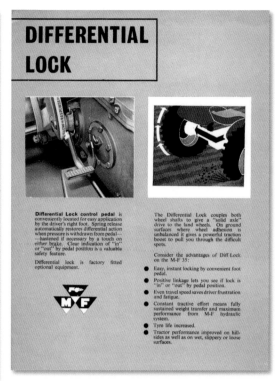

DIFFERENTIAL
LOCK

Differential Lock control pedal is conveniently located for easy application by the driver's right foot. Spring release automatically restores differential action when pressure is withdrawn from pedal——hastened if necessary by a touch on either brake. Clear indication of "in" or "out" by pedal position is a valuable safety feature.

Differential lock is factory fitted optional equipment.

The Differential Lock couples both wheel shafts to give a "solid axle" drive to the land wheels. On ground surfaces where wheel adhesion is unbalanced it gives a powerful traction boost to pull you through the difficult spots.

Consider the advantages of Diff Lock on the M-F 35:

● Easy, instant locking by convenient foot pedal.

● Positive linkage lets you see if lock is "in" or "out" by pedal position.

● Even travel speed saves driver frustration and fatigue.

● Constant tractive effort means fully sustained weight transfer and maximum performance from M-F hydraulic system.

● Tyre life increased.

● Tractor performance improved on hillsides as well as on wet, slippery or loose surfaces.

Differential lock, an option on the MF 35, was being offered by most manufacturers by the early 1960s. A pedal locked both axle-shafts together to provide a solid drive, which prevented wheel-spin in slippery conditions. The lock disengaged automatically when the pressure was released from the pedal for turning on the headland.

The Massey Ferguson 35 was quickly becoming one of the most popular British tractors on the market and more than a quarter of a million had been sold to over 140 countries by 1962. From the May of that year the model was offered with optional differential lock and PAVT rear wheels. The PAVT (power-adjusted variable-tread) wheels allowed quick and easy alteration of the track-width from 48in to 64in.

From August 1962 the MF 65 was available with the optional Multi-Power transmission. Multi-Power doubled-up the transmission speeds by the addition of a pair of high-ratio gears. These constant-mesh gears were actuated by a hydraulic clutch via a dog-toothed coupling. A selector-valve unit allowed the changes between the ranges to be made at the flick of a switch.

Change
on the
go-
at the flick
of a switch!

HIGH
MULTI-POWER
LOW

MASSEY-FERGUSON
65
with
MULTI-POWER

Multi-Power turned the MF 65's six-speed gearbox into a 12 x 4 transmission. The high/low ratios provided an overlap in each gear with an instantaneous on-the-move change being made by the flick of a switch. The only disadvantage of the system was that there was no engine-braking in low Multi-Power, which could be a problem when working on slopes.

With nearly 60hp on tap and the option of Multi-Power transmission, the Massey Ferguson 65 was now the tractor to beat. With 12 forward speeds it had a ratio for nearly every job. 'Live' and two-speed power take-off increased the tractor's versatility even further. No doubt the Fordson salesmen were quaking in their boots, except that the Super Major was still cheaper at £745 compared to £838 for the MF 65 – and even then Multi-Power was another £60 extra.

The Massey Ferguson 35X, launched in December 1962, was the ultimate 35 model with all the bells and whistles including the option of a Multi-Power transmission. The tractor was powered by an up-rated version of the Perkins A3.152 diesel engine, which had been tweaked to deliver 44.5hp. Yours for £752 with all the options!

MASSEY-HARRIS

Introduced in 1948, the Massey-Harris 744PD was originally developed for the British government's East African Groundnut Scheme. This venture was abandoned in 1950. The failure being due to the vast scale of the undertaking and an attempt to rush operations, compounded by a lack of foresight, administrative muddle and logistical difficulties.

Although a Canadian concern, Massey-Harris enjoyed a long relationship with British agriculture. The company had a small operation in the Trafford Park area of Manchester with warehouses and offices on Barton Dock Road. This facility had been established in 1919 to handle the importation of M-H implements into the UK.

A number of Massey-Harris tractors, built in the USA at the company's Racine factory in Wisconsin, arrived in the UK during the 1930s and '40s. After the Second World War the company's Trafford park premises expanded to handle the assembly and part manufacture of several Massey implements, but there were initially no plans to build a British tractor.

That all changed with the launch of the government's ambitious, but ultimately misguided East African Groundnut Scheme. This venture to turn millions of acres of barren scrubland in Tanganyika into productive arable land growing groundnuts was conceived in 1946. The scheme relied on intensive mechanisation with much of the equipment being supplied by Massey-Harris.

Tanganyika was in a sterling area and the British government, being desperately short of dollars through debts arising from the Second World War, wanted to stimulate home production of the necessary equipment. Consequently, Massey-Harris initiated a project for the part manufacture and assembly of tractors in the UK.

The plan was to build a British version of the American Massey-Harris 44K tractors using transmissions and rear axles imported from Racine with the other components manufactured or purchased in England. The six-cylinder Perkins P6(TA) diesel was chosen as the power unit, and this engine was found to fit the 44K tractor chassis without the need for major modifications.

Two prototype tractors, designated 744PD, were assembled at Manchester in early 1948. Following trials, a further batch of 150 machines were completed at Barton Dock Road for shipment to Tanganyika. There was little room for expansion at Trafford Park and it was obvious that large manufacturing facilities were required before full production could get underway.

Following discussions with the Board of Trade, the British government stepped in and offered both financial assistance and a new factory at Kilmarnock in Ayrshire through a governmental agency, Scottish Industrial Estates Ltd. Tractor manufacture was transferred to Kilmarnock during 1949, but it was never much more than an assembly operation with many of the components being bought in from outside suppliers.

Production was fully underway by November 1949 at a rate of around 200 tractors per month with around 80 percent being exported. Transmis-

FROM THE PLOUGHLANDS OF ENGLAND TO ...

... THE JUNGLES OF AFRICA

The Massey-Harris No. 744 Tractor tames the rough terrain of Africa as easily as it turns the rich soil of the English Counties. Standard, half-track and rowcrop models are hard at work under the varying climatic conditions of five continents. Some of the features contributing to the success of this all-adaptable tractor are the powerful 42 h.p. Diesel-engine with its specially designed transmission, the gear box comprising five forward speeds and reverse, instant push button starting and, of course, the economy resulting from reliability and low fuel consumption.

BUILT BY MASSEY-HARRIS LIMITED, MANCHESTER, GREAT BRITAIN—ASSOCIATED COMPANIES AND AGENCIES IN SEVENTY-TWO COUNTRIES

sions were still imported from Racine, but an arrangement was made with Beans Industries to have the units manufactured at Tipton in Staffordshire; the phased changeover beginning in early 1950. Tractors built at Kilmarnock using the British transmissions were renamed the 744D as opposed to the 744PD.

Unfortunately the groundnut scheme was abandoned during 1950 and the 744D tractor had lost its intended market. Sales on the home market were disappointing, mainly due to the tractor's expensive retail price. Export was its only saviour and just 68 of the total 5,225 Massey 744D tractors built during 1952 were sold in the UK.

The inability of the 744D to penetrate the British market was not because of any inherent design failures; the tractor marrying the enviable reputation of the Perkins P6 engine with solid Massey-Harris engineering. It simply wasn't competitive on price and the volume of sales was never enough to warrant the investment needed at Kilmarnock to move production from an assembly operation to full-scale manufacturing.

During 1953 production fell to meagre 2,546.

Meanwhile, an improved but cheaper version of the tractor was being developed by Kilmarnock engineer, Pat Mulholland. This new model, the Massey-Harris 745, was powered by a four-cylinder Perkins L4 diesel engine rated at 45hp.

The Massey-Harris 745 tractor went into production at Kilmarnock as a replacement for 744D in 1954. At the time of the launch, the tractor came under the umbrella of the newly-merged Massey-Harris-Ferguson organisation. Four versions were produced including the 'Standard', 'General-Purpose' and rowcrop 'High-Arch' models.

Following the formation of Massey Ferguson, the Massey-Harris 745 continued to be sold alongside the MF 35 and 65 models. But why would you buy a 745 for £735 when you could have the superior MF 65 for £10 less? The 745S model with a different steering arrangement was introduced in 1957, but by now most of the sales were for export. Some of the last tractors had a channel-iron chassis frame and production ended in 1959 with Kilmarnock becoming the home of Massey Ferguson combine production.

MASSEY-HARRIS *modern farm machinery*

The Massey-Harris 744PD was officially launched in Britain at the 1949 Royal Show. However, sales on the home market were disappointing, mainly due to the cost of the tractor: £854 10s in standard form or £925 as a rowcrop model.

P6(TA) TRACTOR TYPE DIESEL ENGINE
FOR MASSEY HARRIS 744PD TRACTORS

Perkins DIESEL ENGINES FOR ALL TYPES OF POWER APPLICATIONS
Inclusive of Belt Drives, Commercial Vehicles, Compressors, Cranes, Excavators, Generating Sets,
Locomotives, Marine Craft, Passenger Vehicles, Pumping Sets, Rail Cars, Road Graders and
Rollers, Tractors, Welding Sets, Winches, Etc.

The 'High-Arch' rowcrop version of the Massey-Harris 744D had a shorter frame and a bar-type rear axle. This version was priced at £925 compared to £854 10s for the standard model.

The engine chosen for the 744PD tractor was the six-cylinder Perkins P6(TA) diesel engine, which developed 42hp at 1,350rpm. It was a proven power unit with a 3½in bore and a 5in stroke giving a displacement of 288.6cu in (4,730cc).

The Massey-Harris 744PD was based on the American 44K tractor using transmissions and rear axles imported from Racine. The six-cylinder Perkins engine, which sat in a cast-iron hull, was connected to the five-speed transmission via a flexible coupling. The specification included a foot-operated Borg & Beck single-plate clutch.

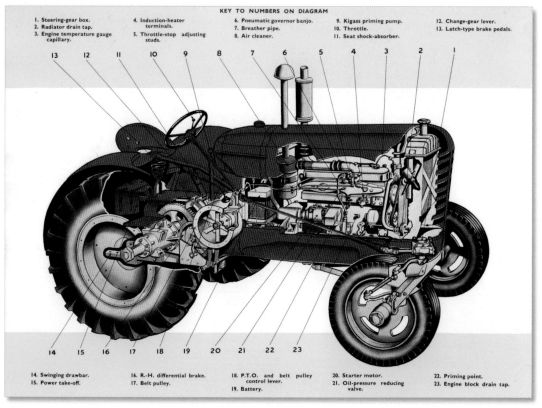

KEY TO NUMBERS ON DIAGRAM

1. Steering-gear box.
2. Radiator drain tap.
3. Engine temperature gauge capillary.
4. Induction-heater terminals.
5. Throttle-stop adjusting studs.
6. Pneumatic governor banjo.
7. Breather pipe.
8. Air cleaner.
9. Kigass priming pump.
10. Throttle.
11. Seat shock-absorber.
12. Change-gear lever.
13. Latch-type brake pedals.

14. Swinging drawbar.
15. Power take-off.
16. R.-H. differential brake.
17. Belt pulley.
18. P.T.O. and belt pulley control lever.
19. Battery.
20. Starter motor.
21. Oil-pressure reducing valve.
22. Priming point.
23. Engine block drain tap.

Every "744 P.D." has a starter that really starts. No matter the conditions, a simple push on the button and you have ample power to do your bidding. For conditions of extreme cold, an electric heating element for use in conjunction with the priming pump enables the starter fully to perform its duties. A small boy can start the engine.

PRECISION-BUILT DIFFERENTIAL
Strong precision-built differential. The differential is built with an extra margin of strength to exacting precision limits. The rear axle is built 2½ inches in diameter and made from quality alloy heat treated steel. Timken bearings are used in the axle sleeves.

The 744PD model offered a high level of specification, but was expensive because many of the components were produced by outside suppliers who accounted for 95 percent of the tractor's manufacturing cost. Power take-off was standard, but no hydraulic linkage was offered until August 1953 – an omission that undoubtedly didn't help sales in Britain.

Read the specification and you will appreciate why you must choose the Model 744 P.D. for your next tractor.

SPECIFICATION

Engine—Perkins P.6 Diesel; 6 cylinders; 3½" bore; 5" stroke; 288·6 cu. in. displacement.

Engine Speed—1,350 r.p.m.

Crankshaft—Forged from Chrome-Molybdenum Steel, heat treated, bearing surfaces hardened. Crankshaft mounted in seven bearings with steel shell liners, lined with lead bronze, and forged steel caps.

Connecting Rods—Highest quality steel, of aero specification, forged H section. Lead-bronze-lined steel shells fitted to big end bearings.

Pistons—Flat topped with fully floating gudgeon pins.

Piston Rings—Five per piston. Three compression and two scraper rings. One scraper ring above and below the gudgeon pin.

Timing Gear—The crankshaft and fuel pump shaft are driven by triple roller chains, with automatic tensioner. Automatically variable combustion timing to suit Perkins Combustion System at all speeds.

Cylinder Head—One-piece chromium iron casting head detachable, as a complete unit with tappets, rocker gear, inlet and exhaust valves and atomizers, leaving timing undisturbed. No masks or deflectors are fitted.

Injection Equipment—C.A.V. fuel injection pump and atomizers, with two-hole nozzles. Idling speed can be adjusted.

Lubrication—High pressure forced feed throughout by rotary slow speed pump, capable of maintaining 60 lbs. per sq. in. pressure. Two filters are fitted.

Cooling System—Tubular radiator water pump and large diameter six-blade fan provides ample cooling capacity.

Crankcase Ventilating System—High efficiency ventilation to the crankcase assures minimum of sludging.

Air Cleaner—Oil flush type.

Starter, Heater Switch—A heater is provided, used in conjunction with a fuel priming device; enables easy starting under extremely cold temperature conditions.

Transmission—Selective sliding gear type. Five speeds and reverse. All gears carburized and hardened. First reduction through spur gears; second through spiral bevels; final (3rd) reduction through spur gears.

Speeds:
	Standard Model 12·75 × 28 Tyres	Row Crop Model 11·00 × 36 Tyres
High	12·00	13·82
4th	5·56	6·46
3rd	4·35	4·97
2nd	3·28	3·86
Low	2·19	2·48
Reverse	2·85	3·45

Clutch—Borg and Beck 12 R.D. single plate, with ball thrust release bearing, foot operated.

Belt Pulley—13½" dia. × 6" face. 863 r.p.m. 3,051 feet per min.

Drawbar—Swinging or fixed, with lateral and vertical adjustment.

Brakes—Individual rear wheel brakes permit pivoting either rear wheel, or may be locked together for master brake control.

Wheels and Tyre Equipment—
	Standard Model	Row Crop Model
Front Rubber	6·00 × 19	6·00 × 16
Rear Rubber	12·75 × 28	11·00 × 36

Cast iron wheel centres, front-rear. Steel disc wheel centres, front-rear. Wheel weights fitted as standard equipment.

Wheel Base—Standard Model 89"; Row Crop Model 89¼".

Tread—Standard 55½"; Row Crop 52" to 88".

Power Take Off—1½" × 6B—SAE spline. 534 r.p.m. at 1,350 r.p.m. engine speed. Standard equipment.

Combined Power Take Off and Power Lift—Foot operated. Standard equipment on Row Crop Model.

Lighting Equipment—Can be supplied against special order.

Instrument Panel—Carries ammeter, oil pressure and water temperature gauges.

FIVE-SPEED TRANSMISSION
The "744 P.D." transmission is sturdily built all the way through to ensure long lasting, dependable operation. It is sliding gear type, with first, second, third and final reduction gears spur type, second reduction spiral bevel gears. All gears are case hardened steel and are cut accurately on high precision gear-cutting machines. The transmission has been carefully engineered to provide a wide selection of speeds to meet the requirement of every field job. The right speed to do the work with the utmost saving of time and fuel. Quiet running and oil bath lubricated. Individual brakes are mounted on the differential pinions for easy turning.

Page 3

This prototype 'pedestal' version of the 744D, which has the narrow-front axle and the bar-type rear axle, is thought to be the first tractor to be fitted with the B-type transmission manufactured by Beans Industries and the first to appear in this 'rowcrop twin' configuration.

A phased changeover from American to British transmissions, manufactured by Beans Industries of Tipton in Staffordshire, began in early 1950. The American units were known as the A-type transmissions, while those made by Beans became the B-type transmissions. Tractors built at Kilmarnock using the British transmissions became known as the 744D as opposed to the 744PD.

The Massey-Harris 745 tractor went into production at Kilmarnock in 1954. This new model was powered by a four-cylinder Perkins L4 diesel engine rated at 45hp. The transmission gave five forward speeds and a single reverse.

The Massey-Harris 745S arrived in 1957 with an improved steering box that replaced the earlier worm-and-sector arrangement. Later tractors had a channel-iron frame and production ended in 1959.

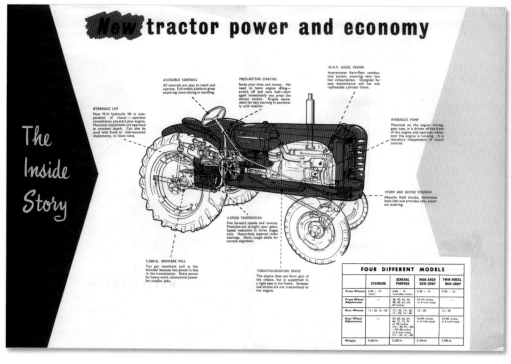

The Massey-Harris 745 was very similar in layout to the previous 744D model. Power take-off was optional and customers could also specify a hydraulic lift. This was a bolt-on unit and was developed in conjunction with Adrolic Engineering of Coatbridge in Scotland. It was powered by an engine-mounted pump, which was driven from the camshaft gear, and came complete with British Standard three-point linkage.

MATBRO

atbro's origins can be traced back to 1946 when Horace and Leonard Mathew formed H & L Mathew Ltd as a trading company; buying and selling ex-WD equipment, predominately batteries, generators and compressors sourced from the many war-surplus auctions held after the Second World War. The brothers operated from premises at Sandy Lane North in Wallington, Surrey, and relied on a second-hand Clark forklift truck to move their equipment.

The American Clark forklift quickly proved inadequate for the job. Its small wheels meant that it lacked both ground-clearance and traction, and it was continually getting stuck in the un-metalled yard. This prompted Len, who had a gift for engineering, to develop his own forklift based on a Fordson E27N Major skid unit. This experimental machine quickly proved its worth and Leonard persuaded his brother that they should consider putting it into production.

The production forklift, which was launched in 1950, proved to be the catalyst that propelled the business into manufacturing. A line of forklifts was followed by loaders and backhoes, all produced under the Matbro name. The manufacturing subsidiary was eventually incorporated as a separate company, Matbro Ltd, operating out of a new factory at Horley.

At about this time Len Mathew, together with his chief engineer George Chapman, began developing a centre-pivot steer design for a loading shovel. The principle was that the front and rear drive units were connected by vertical pivot-points for steering, but also pivoted in the horizontal axis to allow the axles to follow the contours of the ground.

The advantages of the system were that it nullified any 'wind-up' between the axles on a four-wheel drive machine and did away with the need for complicated and expensive drive-steer axles. The axles were also capable of carrying greater loads, the turning circle was reduced and the design was simpler with less power loss through complex joints. The centre-pivot steer principle was patented worldwide in 1957 and the first machine to incorporate the system, the Matbro Mastiff loading shovel based on Fordson Power Major components, appeared in 1958.

The loading shovel also provided the basis for the agricultural Mastiff tractor, which had two Fordson Super Major rear-axle/transmission units providing the front and rear drive units with the differential reversed in the front unit. A six-cylinder Ford 590E industrial engine, optimistically rated at 100hp, provided the power source. A standard Fordson gearbox gave the tractor six forward speeds.

The machine was steered by a double-acting hydraulic ram with the centre pivoting on tapered roller-bearings. The rear-mounted Fordson three-point linkage was strengthened by the addition of an assister ram and the system was powered by a crankshaft-driven pump. Hydraulically-operated differential locks were provided on both axles, and a single brake pedal operated a disc-brake on the propeller-shaft. Ballast was provided by a front-mounted weight beneath the engine and two side panniers just forward of the rear axle.

Following trials in Lincolnshire, the tractor was

THE **MATBRO** SERIES V RANGE OF YARD TYPE FORKLIFT TRUCKS

FOR HEAVY DUTY/ROUGH GROUND/OUTDOOR — OPERATION

Models	Capacity
Y60	6,000 lbs.
Y70	7,000 lbs.
Y80	8,000 lbs.
Y100	10,000 lbs.
Y120	12,000 lbs.
Y150	15,000 lbs.

ALL AT 24 INCH LOAD CENTRE

Forklifts had been the core of Matbro's business since 1950. By the 1960s its product range included many different forklift trucks and rough-terrain forklifts, as well as loading shovels, a dumper, scraper and other specialised materials handlers.

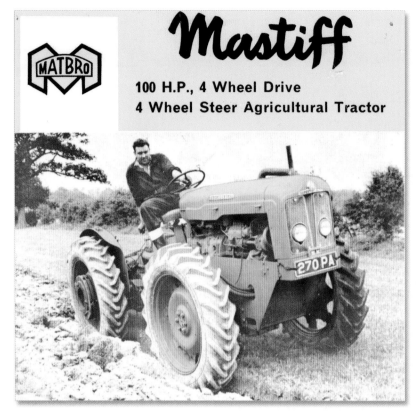

MATBRO

Mastiff

100 H.P., 4 Wheel Drive
4 Wheel Steer Agricultural Tractor

Matbro's pivot-steer agricultural tractor was launched as the Mastiff 6/100 MT with a price tag of £2,500 (less 17½ percent to the dealer). It was introduced to the public at a demonstration held in September 1962 with the tractor turning in wheat stubble on medium loam with a five-furrow Ransomes TS78 plough.

the Suffolk Ford dealers, Mann Egerton of Ipswich, to a local farming estate in March 1963. The tractor was ahead of its time, and prospective customers were reluctant to commit to such a novel design and sales were slow. High development costs also meant that the Mastiff was more expensive than its rival machines.

A total of just 20 tractors were built, six of which were exported with sales to Israel, Sweden and Denmark, before a halt was called to production in August 1964. Matbro developed a Mark ll version, based on a Ford 5000, in 1967, but only one was ever made.

The company failed to recoup its development costs on the tractor, but the Mastiff loading shovel proved to be a profitable venture. Furthermore, a $1 million agreement concluded with Caterpillar, International and Allis-Chalmers in 1962, allowing these American concerns to use Matbro's patented centre-pivot steer system on their loading shovels, more than compensated for any losses incurred with the project.

From the mid-1960s onwards, Matbro concentrated all of its efforts into materials handlers and loading shovels. In 1973, it acquired the rival firm of W E Bray and continued to trade as Matbro-Bray into the 1990s.

launched in 1962 as the Matbro Mastiff 6/100 MT. Production was at Matbro's recently-opened Frome factory in Somerset.

Sales were aimed at arable farmers operating heavy crawler tractors in the fens. The first Mastiff was sold by

The Matbro Mastiff tractor was constructed from two Fordson Super Major rear-axle/transmission units, which provided the front and rear drive units with the differential reversed in the front unit. The input shafts of the two assemblies were joined by a propeller-shaft with a universal joint at the pivot point. A six-cylinder Ford 590E industrial engine, mated to a normal Fordson six-speed gearbox, was mounted above the front drive unit. A five-section Reynolds chain inside a transfer case transmitted the drive from the gearbox to the propeller-shaft.

MINNEAPOLIS-MOLINE

Few people will recognise Minneapolis-Moline as a British tractor manufacturer, but the American firm established a satellite operation in the UK after the Second World War to build just one model of tractor with two engine options.

Minneapolis-Moline tractors and equipment from Minnesota had been imported into the UK since 1938 by Sale Tilney. This London commodity importer with roots in the food industry had been formed in 1933 by two partners with military backgrounds, George S Sale and Robert A G Tilney.

The tractors and equipment were imported into the UK through Chiswick, Millwall or London Docks until sustained German bombing during the Second World War forced the company to seek a safer refuge for its MM operation at Winnersh in Berkshire. In May 1941 Sale Tilney also opened a distribution depot at Essendine in Rutland, leasing premises from Eastern

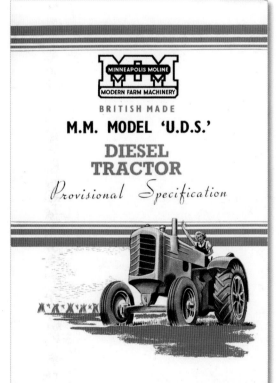

The provisional specification of the Minneapolis-Moline UDS was released in July 1946. A prototype was sent to the National Institute of Agricultural Engineering at Askham Bryan for testing, recording a 7,500lb pull ploughing five 12in furrows at a depth of 10in for over 12 hours.

Farm Implements, the MM distributor for East Anglia and the East Midlands.

Following the introduction of the post-war import restrictions, Robert Tilney and his sales manager, G R Greene, travelled to the USA to discuss proposals for the establishment of a British MM subsidiary. As a result of the meeting, Minneapolis-Moline (England) Ltd was formed with effect from 1 April 1946 with George Sale as chairman.

Minneapolis-Moline (England) Ltd took over Sale Tilney's premises at Winnersh and the freehold or leasehold of other properties. It also acquired the land and buildings at Essendine from Eastern Farm Implements. The company immediately announced a manufacturing programme for British combines and 'high-powered diesel wheel tractors'.

In July 1946 the company unveiled its English-made JV combine, which would be produced at Dowlais on the outskirts of Merthyr Tydfil. At the same time provisional specifications of a proposed tractor were released, detailing that it would be based on an American UTS transmission fitted with a British-built diesel engine supplied by W H Dorman & Co Ltd of Stafford. The engine chosen was Dorman's four-cylinder 4DWD power unit, rated at 46hp.

A Dorman engine was sent to MM's Lake Street facility in Minneapolis for evaluation, while back in the UK Sale Tilney hastily cobbled together a prototype for testing. Following a successful evaluation, a batch of 250 engines was shipped from Stafford and assembly began at Essendine using a similar number of UTS transmissions imported from the USA.

The shipments to Essendine began in September 1946 – the project being given Ministry of Agriculture & Fisheries priority to aid food production. Records suggest that the last Dorman engine was supplied in December 1948.

The Dorman-powered tractor was launched as the Minneapolis-Moline UDS with a price of £1,050. The transmission gave five forward speeds and was a standard UTS unit apart from the addition of Girling independent brakes. Power take-off and a belt pulley were standard equipment. Additional equipment included electric lighting, steel wheels, wheel weights,

The British-built Minneapolis-Moline diesel tractor was launched in September 1946. Two versions were offered with Dorman or Meadows engines, and both were advertised in this brochure under the UDS designation. The engine installations at Essendine were overseen by an American, P J Venables, who was seconded from the parent company in the USA.

strakes and a winch.

The alternative engine supplier for the British Minneapolis-Moline tractor was Henry Meadows Ltd of Wolverhampton. The four-cylinder Meadows diesel produced 65hp and was arguably a better and more refined power unit. It was also the more expensive alternative and pushed the price of the UDS to £1,200.

The Meadows-powered tractor used the UTI transmission with single-pedal (not independent) Bendix brakes. No doubt this heavy-duty industrial tractor transmission was specified to cope with the extra power. Both the Dorman and the Meadows versions were advertised in the same brochure under the UDS designation. However, the parts books distinguished between the UDS (Dorman) and UDM (Meadows) variants and the latter tractor is now usually referred to as the Minneapolis-Moline UDM, although this designation was never official.

Another, much larger batch of 500 transmissions was shipped from the USA in 1948. It seems unlikely that all of these were fitted with Meadows engines, and some may have had the Dorman engine installed. The records are inconclusive.

The British Minneapolis-Moline tractors from Essendine were exported to Australia, Argentina, Turkey and South Africa among other territories. The UDS/UDM was priced too high for the home market so UK sales were disappointing. Production ended in 1949 after Minneapolis-Moline (England) Ltd went into receivership and the Essendine factory was sold to Allis-Chalmers.

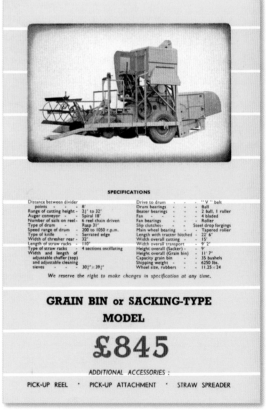

One of the combines manufactured by Minneapolis-Moline at its factory in South Wales was this British-built G8 model, which was based on the American G4. Priced at £845, the machine was offered with either a 28hp Meadows engine or a Ford V8 power unit. Sadly, the combine didn't live up to expectations and suffered from stress fractures in the mainframe.

POWERFUL · ECONOMICAL

The Minneapolis-Moline UDS tractors were assembled at Essendine using five-speed transmissions imported from the parent company's Lake Street facility in Minneapolis. The Meadows-powered version (shown) was fitted with the heavy-duty UTI industrial transmission, which had single-pedal Bendix brakes. A 24-volt electrical system was employed with four 6-volt Tungstone batteries to ensure good starting properties. Power take-off and a belt pulley were standard equipment, and the extras included electric lighting, steel wheels, wheel weights, strakes and a winch.

The version of the tractor with the Meadows engine, which was retrospectively known as the UDM model, was priced at £1,200. The four-cylinder Meadows 4DC420 diesel was a 421cu in (6,902cc) power unit developing 65hp at 1,275rpm. The engine had aluminium-alloy pistons, renewable cylinder liners and CAV fuel-injection and electrical equipment.

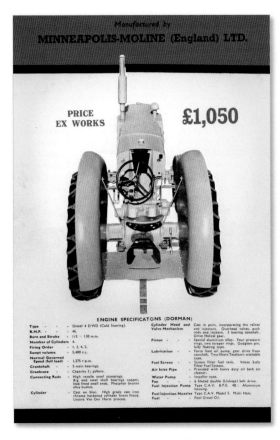

PRICE EX WORKS £1,050

The Dorman-powered version of the UDS was priced at £1,050. The four-cylinder 4DWD engine was a 329cu in (5,400cc) unit giving 46hp at 1,275rpm. It had an open combustion chamber and employed CAV/Bosch fuel-injection equipment. The build was noted as having a steel flywheel housing, an all-speed governor, special nickel-alloy pistons, cast-iron chrome-hardened liners and a 'David Brown type' cooling fan. This version of the tractor had Girling independent steering brakes.

PRICE EX WORKS £1,200

NEWMAN

Details of the prototype Kendall-Beaumont tractor were released in May 1945. Its power unit was a three-cylinder radial engine with poppet-type valves and the cylinders arranged at 120 degrees. The combustion heads were hemispherical and each contained two overhead valves and provided a compression ratio of 6.9:1. The 66mm bore and 58mm stroke gave a displacement of 595cc. The three-speed gearbox gave a top speed of 6mph.

The Newman must be unique in the annals of British tractor history in that the original design was developed by a sitting member of parliament. Denis Kendall, standing as an independent, served as the MP for Grantham in Lincolnshire from 1942-50.

Born in Halifax in 1903, William Denis Kendall was a most colourful character. He ran away to sea at the age of 14, managed a waterfront cabaret in Shanghai and worked as a steeplejack the USA before training as an engineer at a car plant in Philadelphia. In 1933 he travelled to Paris and became head of production at André Citroën's Quai de Javel factory, overseeing the introduction of the Traction Avant car.

Kendall returned to Britain in 1938 to set up an armaments business in Grantham, trading as the British Manufacturing & Research Company. Interestingly, he also seems to have come to the attention of the British security services amid speculation over alleged illegal arms dealing and his association with leading right-wing extremists.

In 1944 Kendall developed a three-cylinder radial petrol engine and announced proposals to build a

£200 'people's car' and £100 tractor using this unusual power unit, which had poppet-type valves, hemispherical combustion chambers and cylinders arranged at 120 degrees. The following year he formed Grantham Productions Ltd to manufacture both the car and the tractor.

The details of the prototype Kendall-Beaumont tractor were announced in May 1945. It was a three-wheel machine with a 6hp version of the radial engine driving a three-speed gearbox. Trials revealed the machine to be underpowered; experiments were carried out with a supercharged 7hp version of the radial power unit before it was replaced by a twin-cylinder 8hp Douglas petrol engine.

Production was established at Grantham at a surplus wartime factory on Springfield Road, which had been assigned to Kendall by the government. The tractor and car venture was reputedly financed by an Indian maharajah, but it wasn't enough to keep the company afloat and Grantham Productions Ltd ran into financial difficulty during 1947.

In March 1948 the business was acquired by Newman Industries, electrical and mechanical engineers from Yate near Bristol. The government reassigned the Springfield Road factory to Newman, and the plant was refurbished with new equipment for increased tractor production.

The tractor was reintroduced in two models: the Newman AN3 and AN4. Both were three-wheel machines of similar design to the Kendall with a three forward and single reverse gearbox. The power unit was now a flat-twin air-cooled Coventry-Victor petrol engine; 803cc for the 10¾hp AN3 model and 907cc for the 12hp AN4. The list of optional extras included a mid- or rear-mounted toolbar with hydraulic or manual lift, belt pulley and power take-off. Prices for the AN3 started at £240, while the AN4 cost from £250.

A third model, the Newman WD2, was added to the range in 1949. The three-wheel layout was similar to the petrol models, but the power came from a single-cylinder Coventry Victor diesel engine. This 10hp unit had a displacement of 567cc. It was water-cooled with long copper tubes connecting to

the radiator at the front of the tractor. The WD2 was slightly dearer at £330 for the basic model.

Development had already begun on a four-wheel model, which was eventually launched as the Newman E1 with an Enfield flat-twin diesel engine developing 14hp. This was replaced by the E2 model, which had a 12hp twin-cylinder Petter diesel engine, in 1951.

The E2 was the final incarnation of the Newman tractor. It had a four-speed gearbox, a Borg & Beck clutch and independent brakes. Options included a belt pulley, power take-off and hydraulic linkage. The E2 was listed until 1953 when Newman pulled out of the tractor market to concentrate on its electrical products. The organisation didn't completely forsake the agricultural scene and in 1971 it acquired F W Wheatley Trailers of Peterborough.

The Newman AN3 model developed 10¾hp from an 803cc Coventry-Victor flat-twin air-cooled petrol engine. Both the bore and stroke were 80mm. The gearbox gave forward speeds of 1.75mph, 3.5mph and 10.25mph with 1.15mph in reverse. Independent brakes were standard, and power take-off and hydraulic lift were optional.

The Newman WD2 diesel tractor was introduced in 1949. Its single-cylinder Coventry-Victor water-cooled engine developed 10hp at 1,900cc. An 85mm bore by 100mm stroke gave a displacement of 557cc. The three-speed gearbox, driving through a Borg & Beck clutch, gave a top speed of 8.85mph. Newman tractors were ideal for rowcrop work with good ground-clearance and the rear wheel-track adjustable from 42in to 72in.

The Kendall design was relaunched in 1948 as the Newman 'Light Tractor'. Two versions were available with the AN4 model being powered by a horizontally-opposed twin-cylinder Coventry-Victor air-cooled petrol engine with a 907cc displacement. The engine, which had an 85mm bore by 80mm stroke, developed 12hp at 2,200rpm.

NUFFIELD

The Nuffield tractor was a product of the Nuffield Organisation, which was an umbrella company under which the car divisions of Morris, MG, Riley and Wolseley operated. The tractor project was instigated at the suggestion of Lord Nuffield (formerly William Morris) and development began under the auspices of Nuffield Mechanizations Ltd. Much of the original concept of the Nuffield tractor was the work of a former David Brown engineer, Dr Henry Merritt.

From the outset two themes were followed: universal application (from which the tractor eventually took its name) and simplicity. Rather than designing for one specialised market, the aim was to create a basic unit that was adaptable to as many applications or territories as possible. The policy was to allow the farmer to tailor the tractor to his exact needs without having to purchase any unwanted equipment.

The project was initiated with government approval in early 1945. The development work was carried out in the Wolseley Works at Ward End in Birmingham. The first prototype was running by June 1945 and a further 11 prototypes were built during the year. Material shortages led to a temporary abandonment of the Nuffield programme in early 1947, but development resumed in September ready for the tractor's eventual launch in November 1948.

Painted in a striking 'Poppy Orange' livery, the

Advance details of the prototype Nuffield 'Universal' tractor were released in July 1946. At least 12 prototypes were built for testing between May 1946 and March 1947, but material shortages led to a temporary abandonment of the project and it would be September 1947 before the development work resumed.

tractor was known as the Nuffield 'Universal'. It was powered by a four-cylinder side-valve Morris Commercial truck engine modified to burn TVO. Both tricycle M3 and four-wheel M4 models were offered. Petrol (PM3/4) and Perkins diesel (DM3/4) tractors followed in 1950.

In 1952 the Nuffield Organisation merged with Austin to form the British Motor Corporation (BMC), which gave the tractor division access to even greater resources. The Perkins engine fitted to the DM3/4 models of the Nuffield 'Universal' was replaced by a 39hp BMC diesel in May 1954.

The Nuffield line became a two-model range in 1957 with the launch of the 37hp 'Universal Three' tractor, which was powered by a three-cylinder BMC diesel engine in a smaller mainframe. At the same time, the four-cylinder model was upgraded to 4DM specification as the 'Universal Four'. In November 1958 the 'Universal Four' was up-rated to 56hp.

Up until now all the Nuffield tractors had been built at Ward End. In 1961 a new factory opened at Bathgate in West Lothian and there began a phased transfer of tractor production from the Midlands to Scotland. The same year saw the introduction of the new 3/42 and 4/60 models featuring hydraulic depth control with top-link sensing. Power was also increased with the 3/42 delivering 42hp and the 4/60 rated at 60hp.

The new models brought depth control to the Nuffield range, but they also blemished the marque's reputation for outstanding reliability. The draft function combined with the extra power overloaded the single-pump hydraulic system when the tractor was working hard. The increased flow led to the hydraulics overheating, breaking down the structure of the oil and leading to pump failure.

The engineers solved the problem by using a Dowty two-stage pump and modifying the main valve assembly. This system operated at the same pressure (2,000psi), but reduced the rate of oil flow in the circuit. An added bonus was that the two hydraulic levers could now be used to operate a double-acting ram. The new 'dual-flow' hydraulic system was introduced on the 10/42 and 10/60

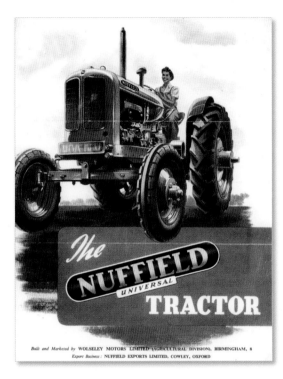

Launched in November 1948, the production model Nuffield 'Universal' was powered by a four-cylinder side-valve engine rated at 38hp. Designated ETA, the engine was developed from a proven power unit that had been used in Morris Commercial military trucks. One of the unique features of the engine design was that the main carburettor was for TVO operation only and there was an auxiliary 'starter' carburettor for starting up on petrol. The engine was mated to a five-speed gearbox and there were provisions for a hydraulic lift, power take-off and belt pulley. The four-wheel tractor was known as the M4 model.

The Nuffield 'Universal' M3 was the tricycle version of the tractor with a single front wheel carried in an inverted U-shaped fork. The axle arrangement was designed so that the tractor could be converted into a four-wheeler within half an hour. The rear hubs clamped to the axle shaft and could be adjusted for rowcrop work.

The Nuffield 'Universal' had a strong cast-iron mainframe forming a rigid backbone to the tractor. The basic unit was made up from seven main sub-assemblies: the mainframe, engine, clutch unit, steering box, transmission and two final-reduction units. The hydraulic lift assembly was an optional bolt-on unit, as were the power take-off and braking system. Most of the sub-assemblies could be removed or replaced without disturbing the adjoining units for ease of maintenance.

models, launched in October 1964.

The 10/42 and 10/60 models were heralded as the first of a new generation of Nuffield tractors. In essence they were the last of the old generation with a lot of new features. Most significant was a new 10-speed gearbox, which gave the revised models their '10' designation.

Teething problems with the new Bathgate factory meant that its workmanship often left something to be desired. It was the beginning of a malady of factory inefficiency that would eventually affect all BMC and subsequent British Leyland production.

The 10/42 and 10/60 models should have been the crowning glory of the Nuffield 'Universal' line, but the manufacturing defects shook customer confidence. The subsequent 3/45 and 4/65 models of 1967 brought several improvements, but the Nuffield name for quality was tarnished forever and was finally swept away in 1969 when the range was replaced with a new line of blue Leyland tractors.

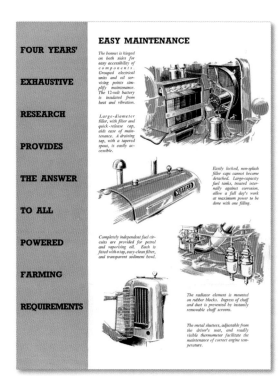

EASY MAINTENANCE

The bonnet is hinged on both sides for easy accessibility of components. Grouped electrical units and oil servicing points simplify maintenance. The 12-volt battery is insulated from heat and vibration.

Large-diameter filler, with filter and quick-release cap, aids ease of maintenance. A draining tap, with a tapered spout, is easily accessible.

Easily locked, non-splash filler caps cannot become detached. Large-capacity fuel tanks, treated internally against corrosion, allow a full day's work at maximum power to be done with one filling.

Completely independent fuel circuits are provided for petrol and vaporising oil. Each is fitted with a tap, easy-clean filter, and transparent sediment bowl.

The radiator element is mounted on rubber blocks. Ingress of chaff and dust is prevented by instantly removable chaff screens.

The metal shutters, adjustable from the driver's seat, and readily visible thermometer facilitate the maintenance of correct engine temperature.

The Nuffield 'Universal' tractor was designed with ease of maintenance in mind. The idea was to make the machine as 'user-friendly' as possible with easy accessibility of all the main components and service points.

The versatility of the Nuffield tractor was reflected in its name – 'Universal'. The aim was to create a basic unit that was adaptable to as many applications or territories as possible. The axles were adjustable and optional wheel configurations were offered so that the farmer could tailor the tractor to his exact needs. Comfort and safety were other important aspects of the design.

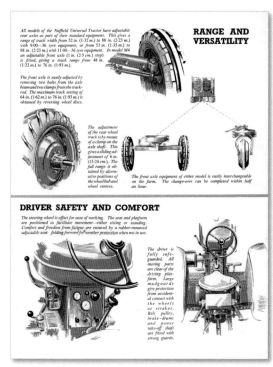

RANGE AND VERSATILITY

All models of the Nuffield Universal Tractor have adjustable rear axles as part of their standard equipment. This gives a range of track width from 52 in. (1·32 m.) to 88 in. (2·23 m.) with 9·00—36 tyre equipment, or from 53 in. (1·35 m.) to 88 in. (2·23 m.) with 11·00—36 tyre equipment. In model M4 an adjustable front axle (1 in. (2·5 cm.) step) is fitted, giving a track range from 48 in. (1·22 m.) to 76 in. (1·93 m.).

The front axle is easily adjusted by removing two bolts from the axle beam and two clamps from the track-rod. The maximum track setting of 64 in. (1·62 m.) to 76 in. (1·93 m.) is obtained by reversing wheel discs.

The adjustment of the rear wheel track is by means of a clamp on the axle shaft. This gives a sliding adjustment of 6 in. (15·24 cm.). The full range is obtained by alternative positions of the wheel/hub and wheel centres.

The front axle equipment of either model is easily interchangeable on the farm. The change-over can be completed within half an hour.

DRIVER SAFETY AND COMFORT

The steering wheel is offset for ease of working. The seat and platform are positioned to facilitate movement—either sitting or standing. Comfort and freedom from fatigue are ensured by a rubber-mounted adjustable seat folding forward for weather protection when not in use.

The driver is fully safeguarded. All moving parts are clear of the driving platform. Large mudguards give protection from accidental contact with the wheels or strakes. Belt pulley, brake-drums and power take-off shaft are fitted with strong guards.

CONCESSIONARIA ESCLUSIVA PER L'ITALIA:
DITTA VITTORIO CANTATORE
VIA SALUZZO, 64 **TORINO** TELEFONO 62.965

Diesel versions of the Nuffield 'Universal' tractor went into production in May 1950. The power came from a Perkins P4(TA) engine and the diesel versions were identified as DM3 (three-wheel) and DM4 (four-wheel) models. Exports had begun in 1949 and the Nuffield tractor was eventually sold in 75 different countries. This leaflet was issued by the Italian concessionaire, Vittorio Cantatore.

The four-cylinder Perkins P4(TA) had a 3½in bore by 5in stroke giving a displacement of 192cu in (3,150cc). Installed in the Nuffield tractor, it developed 38hp at 2,000rpm. The fuel system utilised a CAV inline injection pump with a pneumatic governor.

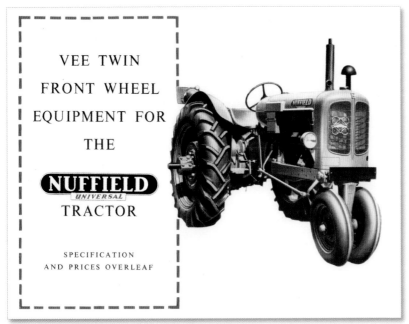

VEE TWIN
FRONT WHEEL
EQUIPMENT FOR
THE

NUFFIELD
UNIVERSAL
TRACTOR

SPECIFICATION
AND PRICES OVERLEAF

Introduced in 1950, the version of the Nuffield 'Universal' tractor with the narrow-front axle and pedestal for vee-twin wheel equipment was almost unseen in Britain and almost all must have been supplied for export. This is the diesel model with the Perkins P4 engine.

Nuffield 'Universal' was given a new four-cylinder BMC diesel engine in May 1954. It was still identified as a DM3 (three-wheel) or DM4 (four-wheel) model, but the tricycle version soon disappeared. The new diesel eclipsed the petrol/TVO variants, which were quietly dropped as the demand fell away.

A petrol version of the Nuffield Universal (PM3 and PM4 models with engines prefixed ETB) was released August 1950. Further engineering changes in March 1953 saw the spark-ignition power units replaced with the modified ETC (TVO) and ETD (petrol) engines with a higher compression ratio and more power. At the same time, the bolt threads on the tractor were changed from BSF to Unified.

PUBLICATION No. H. & E. 5614

NUFFIELD
UNIVERSAL

the tractor
that powers
all farm work
and reduces
costs

137

The four-cylinder BMC diesel engine fitted to the Nuffield 'Universal' was a de-rated version of the Austin and Morris truck engine developing 39hp at 2,000rpm. Designated OEA/2, it had a 95mm bore by 120mm stroke giving a displacement of 3.4 litres (208cu in). An OEA/2B version of the engine with a double clutch was offered from 1956 giving the option of 'live' power take-off.

The Nuffield 'Universal' with the BMC diesel engine adhered to the same layout as the earlier models and the salient points were unaltered. Features included an 11in clutch, a five-speed gearbox and a 12-volt electrical system with twin batteries for starting.

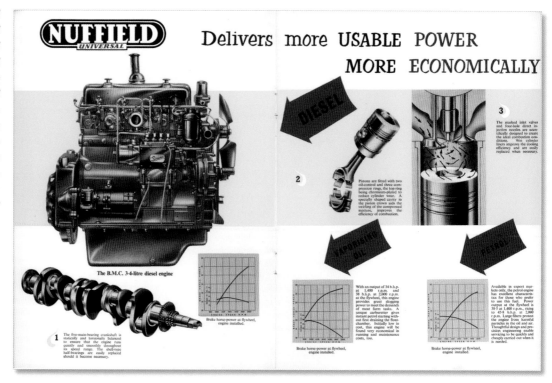

NUFFIELD UNIVERSAL

Delivers more USABLE POWER MORE ECONOMICALLY

DIESEL

VAPORISING OIL

PETROL

The B.M.C. 3·4-litre diesel engine

1 The five-main-bearing crankshaft is statically and torsionally balanced to ensure that the engine runs quietly and smoothly throughout its speed range. The shell-type half-bearings are easily replaced should it become necessary.

2 Pistons are fitted with two oil-control and three compression rings, the top ring being chromium-plated to reduce cylinder wear. A specially shaped cavity in the piston crown aids the swirling of the compressed mixture, improves the efficiency of combustion.

3 The masked inlet valves and four-hole direct injection nozzles are scientifically designed to create the ideal combustion conditions. Wet cylinder liners improve the cooling efficiency and are easily replaced when necessary.

With an output of 34 b.b.p. at 1,400 r.p.m. and 38 b.h.p. at 2,000 r.p.m. at the flywheel, this engine provides great slogging power to meet the demands of most farm tasks. A unique carburetter gives instant petrol starting without first draining the float-chamber. Initially low in cost, this engine will be found very economical in running and maintenance costs, too.

Available in export markets only, the petrol engine has excellent characteristics for those who prefer to use this fuel. Power output at the flywheel is 38·5 at 1,400 r.p.m., rising to 45·8 b.h.p. at 2,000 r.p.m. Large filters protect the engine from harmful particles in the oil and air. Thoughtful design and precision engineering enable servicing to be quickly and cheaply carried out when it is needed.

Brake horse-power at flywheel, engine installed.

Brake horse-power at flywheel, engine installed.

Brake horse-power at flywheel, engine installed.

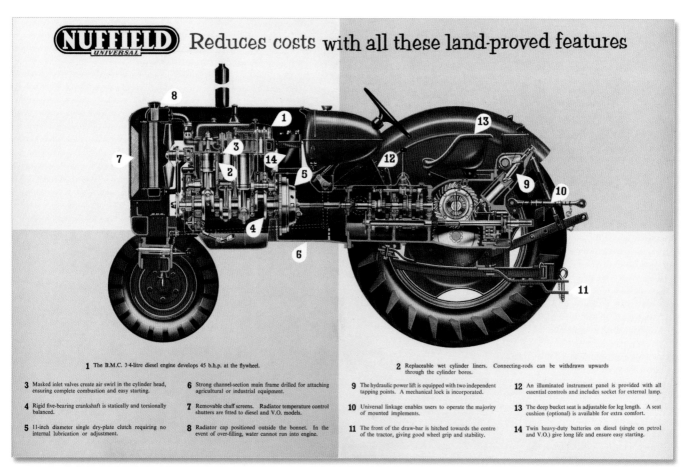

NUFFIELD UNIVERSAL

Reduces costs with all these land-proved features

1 The B.M.C. 3·4-litre diesel engine develops 45 b.h.p. at the flywheel.

2 Replaceable wet cylinder liners. Connecting-rods can be withdrawn upwards through the cylinder bores.

3 Masked inlet valves create air swirl in the cylinder head, ensuring complete combustion and easy starting.

4 Rigid five-bearing crankshaft is statically and torsionally balanced.

5 11-inch diameter single dry-plate clutch requiring no internal lubrication or adjustment.

6 Strong channel-section main frame drilled for attaching agricultural or industrial equipment.

7 Removable chaff screens. Radiator temperature control shutters are fitted to diesel and V.O. models.

8 Radiator cap positioned outside the bonnet. In the event of over-filling, water cannot run into engine.

9 The hydraulic power lift is equipped with two independent tapping points. A mechanical lock is incorporated.

10 Universal linkage enables users to operate the majority of mounted implements.

11 The front of the draw-bar is hitched towards the centre of the tractor, giving good wheel grip and stability.

12 An illuminated instrument panel is provided with all essential controls and includes socket for external lamp.

13 The deep bucket seat is adjustable for leg length. A seat cushion (optional) is available for extra comfort.

14 Twin heavy-duty batteries on diesel (single on petrol and V.O.) give long life and ensure easy starting.

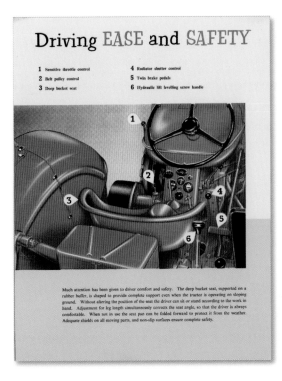

Much attention was given to driver comfort and safety, and the Nuffield 'Universal' was probably one of the first tractors to have its controls and driving position ergonomically designed. It was certainly a comfortable place to be and the steering was much lighter than on many of the competitors' machines.

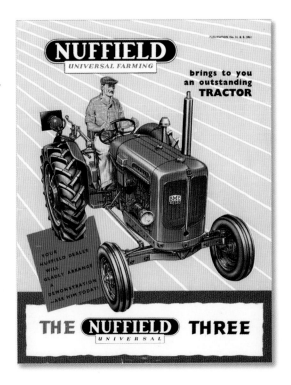

The three-cylinder Nuffield 'Universal Three' tractor, identified as the 3DL model, was introduced in 1957. The model was targeted at the Massey Ferguson 35 and Fordson Dexta, but was a much heavier machine.

The Nuffield 'Universal Three' was powered by the BMC OEC/2 (OEC/2B with the double clutch) diesel engine. This 2.55-litre (155cu in) unit developed 37hp at 2,000rpm. Features included a four-bearing crankshaft and a Simms inline injection pump with a pneumatic governor.

The Nuffield 'Universal Three' tractor shared many of its components with the four-cylinder model, but had a smaller mainframe to accommodate the three-cylinder engine. Smaller wheel equipment (10 x 28 rear tyres as opposed to 11 x 36 on the DM4 model) was fitted, but much of the specification, including the five-speed transmission, was the same as its bigger brother.

At the same time as the 'Universal Three' was launched, the four-cylinder model was given a facelift as the Nuffield 'Universal Four'. This up-rated model gained a bit more power and was designated 4DM.

The introduction of the 'Universal Four' brought in no major changes to the layout of the four-cylinder tractor. From November 1958 the model gained the tweaked OEA2/D (OEA/2E with the double clutch) engine giving 56hp. A differential lock was offered for both the three-cylinder and four-cylinder tractors from July 1959.

The Nuffield 3/42 and 4/60 models were introduced in 1961. The new tractors boasted extra power and featured hydraulic depth control with top-link sensing. Production had now moved to the new Bathgate factory in Scotland.

The hydraulic system fitted to the 3/42 and 4/60 tractors incorporated depth control with top-link sensing and a new valve unit connected to a control lever on the right-hand side of the hydraulic housing. The system was also now independent offering 'live' hydraulics for the first time on a Nuffield tractor.

The Nuffield 4/60 had a new OEE version of the four-cylinder BMC diesel engine with an increased (100mm rather than 95mm) bore delivering 60hp. The standard 4/60 with non-independent power take-off had the OEE/2 engine while 'De Luxe' 4/60 had the double-clutch OEE/3 power unit. Some of the 4/60s extra power came from a new inline Simms Minimec fuel-injection pump with mechanical governing. The tractor's transmission was also strengthened to cope with the additional horses.

The three-cylinder Nuffield 3/42 still had the old pneumatically-governed inline Simms pump and was little different to the 'Universal Three' apart from the hydraulic changes and a slight increase in power to 42hp.

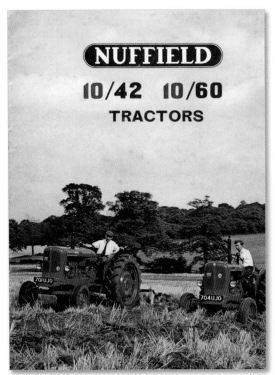

The Nuffield 10/42 and 10/60 tractors, launched in October 1964, featured a new 'dual-flow' hydraulic system and a new 10-speed and two reverse transmission. The hydraulic changes were made to address problems with the previous models.

The four-cylinder Nuffield 10/60 had the modified gearbox and hydraulic system, but the power was unchanged. Both it and the 10/42 model also featured new self-energising disc brakes, a new drawbar and a restyled instrument panel.

The Nuffield 10/42's three-cylinder engine was brought up to the specification of the four-cylinder model with a Minimec pump and the bore increased to 100mm. This gave it a displacement of 2.8 litres and it was identified by an OEG designation.

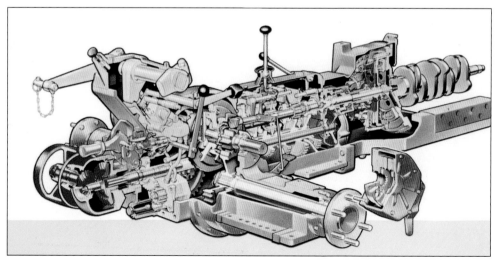

The 10/42 and 10/60's new 10-speed gearbox was basically the old five-speed box with an extended lay-shaft and a splitter-gear on the main drive-shaft to double-up the gears. The splitter-gear was carried on a sliding sleeve that was splined onto the main drive-shaft. It was engaged by a high/low selection lever to the left of the primary gear lever.

RANSOMES

The Ipswich firm of Ransomes, Sims & Jefferies was one of Britain's longest established implement makers with a history dating back to the end of the eighteenth century. In 1785 Robert Ransome patented a process for tempering cast-iron plough shares, founding a business that became famous worldwide.

Ploughs remained the mainstay of Ransomes' business, but the company's product range was both wide and diverse. It dabbled with tractors as early as 1903 after it acquired a design patented by the motor industry pioneer, Frederick R Simms, but just one was built. Later ventures with an oil tractor, a motor plough and a 'Colonial' tractor were all over by the late 1920s.

Ransomes returned to the tractor business in the early 1930s after it asked Roadless Traction Ltd to develop a small rubber-tracked crawler for horticultural use. Initiated in 1932, the project was designated MG for 'market garden' – the area of use at which the tractor was targeted.

The first prototype was a pedestrian-controlled machine with the driver walking behind. During trials the tractor proved to have insufficient traction and the design was shelved. In October 1933 plans were drawn up for a second design, MG2, with the idea of sitting the driver on the tractor to add weight and therefore improve the adhesion of the tracks.

A prototype was built and tested in 1934 and pre-production models were sent to Ransomes for trials the following year. The tractor went into production at Ransomes' Orwell Works in Ipswich in 1936 and was demonstrated to the public for the first time on 29 April of that year.

Priced at £135, the Ransomes MG2 'motor garden cultivator' was powered by a single-cylinder Sturmey Archer Model T petrol engine developing 6hp. It was a proven air-cooled unit that was also fitted to Ransomes' larger lawn mowers. The tractor had a centrifugal clutch, and the simple transmission gave a single forward and reverse speed of 2mph. Steering was by two hand levers operating contracting brake bands.

The Second World War saw Ransomes embark on a massive wartime production run producing armaments and munitions for the War Office – everything from tank tracks to gun carriages. But the company also had to meet the vital requirements of agriculture, manufacturing ploughs in their thousands to bring even more land into arable production. Despite these heavy demands the needs of horticulture were not forgotten and some 1,200 MG crawlers were assembled in the Engine Works at the Orwell factory.

The MG2 was replaced by the new Ransomes MG5 model in 1948. One can only assume that MG3 and MG4 became victims of the exigencies of war and never left the drawing board. Most significantly, the MG5 had a new engine – Ransomes own 600cc single-cylinder unit. The tractor was priced at £250 and the wide range of optional equipment included a TVO conversion kit, power take-off and a bolt-on hydraulic lift assembly.

The Ransomes MG6 was launched at the 1953 Smithfield Show. The 600cc engine was unchanged,

The Ransomes MG2 crawler remained in production until 1948 and some 3,000 were built. Later models were fitted with an improved Sturmey Archer TD single-cylinder air-cooled engine with a dry sump.

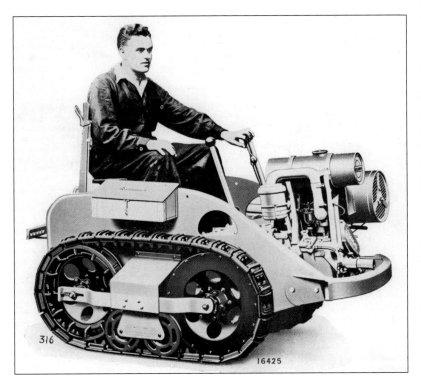

143

GENERAL DESCRIPTION

In the design of Ransomes' MG.5 all the experience gained with the popular MG.2 model has been utilised to provide a still better all-purpose tractor.

The attractive features of the previous model have been maintained but the design is new throughout to achieve the highest performance at the lowest running cost.

As with the larger types of tractors, the driver RIDES WHILE HE WORKS.

It is an ALL-PURPOSE tractor, since it has ample power for the heavy work of ploughing, cultivating and harrowing, yet for inter-row cultivation it is sensitive to control for work requiring the greatest accuracy.

The MG.5, with its wide range of implements, is therefore a complete answer to the mechanisation of holdings up to 25 acres, while on larger acreages it has been found ideally suitable for inter-row cultivation.

but was advertised as being capable of running on petrol or TVO and was rated at 7hp. The major change was a new transmission giving three forward and one reverse speeds. A hydraulic lift and power take-off were optional.

The MG6 and the previous MG5 model were particularly successful products for Ransomes and around 5,000 of each were built. An optional 8½hp Drayton two-stroke diesel engine was offered for the MG6 from 1956 when the ITW (Industrial Tractor Wheeled) and ITC (Industrial Tractor Crawler) derivatives were introduced. The ITW was a skid-steered machine on rubber tyres with the front wheels chain-driven from the rear axle. WR4 dumper and WR8 loader versions were later made by the trailer manufacturer, Whitlock Bros Ltd of Great Yeldham in Essex.

The Ransomes MG40 replaced the MG6 in 1960. The new model inherited the MG6's centrifugal clutch and gearbox, but the choice of engines included Ransomes' own 8hp side-valve petrol/TVO unit or a Drayton Type 34R two-stroke overhead-valve diesel rated at 10hp. The MG40 also brought in a new green and red colour scheme.

By the early 1960s demand for the little 'market garden' tractor was falling away in the face of competition from cheaper horticultural machinery imported from Japan. The MG40 was dropped in 1966 when the 30-year production run of the Ransomes crawler came to an end. Total production of all the MG models was about 15,000.

Announced in 1948, the Ransomes MG5 had the company's own 600cc single-cylinder petrol engine. This air-cooled side-valve unit had a dry-sump with a pressurised lubrication system. It drove via a centrifugal clutch to the single-speed gearbox, which gave forward and reverse speeds of 2¼mph. Fuel consumption was 3-4½ pints of petrol per hour.

The mechanical layout of the Ransomes MG5 was largely similar to that of the previous MG2 model. It was marketed with a full range of Ransomes implements and equipment including a toolbar and tandem disc harrows. A Ransomes TS42A self-lift trailing plough was specially developed for the crawler.

Launched in 1953 the MG6 crawler was still fitted with Ransomes own single-cylinder air-cooled petrol engine. It was a 7hp side-valve unit with an Amal carburettor and a Wico magneto. As before, steering was by two hand levers operating contracting brake bands.

The Ransomes MG6 was a very popular machine and around 5,000 were built. Its three-speed gearbox gave speeds of 1⅛mph, 2¼mph and 4mph. The centrifugal clutch engaged automatically once the engine speed increased above 500rpm.

145

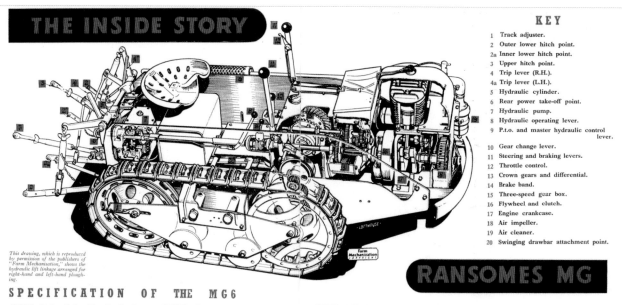

THE INSIDE STORY

KEY

1 Track adjuster.
2 Outer lower hitch point.
2a Inner lower hitch point.
3 Upper hitch point.
4 Trip lever (R.H.).
4a Trip lever (L.H.).
5 Hydraulic cylinder.
6 Rear power take-off point.
7 Hydraulic pump.
8 Hydraulic operating lever.
9 P.t.o. and master hydraulic control lever.
10 Gear change lever.
11 Steering and braking levers.
12 Throttle control.
13 Crown gears and differential.
14 Brake band.
15 Three-speed gear box.
16 Flywheel and clutch.
17 Engine crankcase.
18 Air impeller.
19 Air cleaner.
20 Swinging drawbar attachment point.

RANSOMES MG

SPECIFICATION OF THE MG6

ENGINE. Single cylinder, side valve 4-stroke. Bore, 86.84 mm. Stroke, 101 mm. Capacity, 600 c.c. B.h.p., 7. Petrol or V.O. equipment.

LUBRICATION by plunger pump; oil filter incorporated in crankcase.

COOLING by high speed impeller fan.

IGNITION. Wico magneto with impulse coupling.

CARBURETTOR. Amal single lever type with choke.

FUEL PUMP. Diaphragm type with integral filter.

AIR CLEANER. Oil bath type.

CHASSIS. All-steel welded. Ground clearance 13¼-in. with drawbar removed.

CLUTCH. Automatic centrifugal type controlled by engine speed.

GEARBOX. Three forward and reverse speeds. Speeds at 2,000 r.p.m.: 1st, 1¼ m.p.h. 2nd, 2¼ m.p.h. 3rd, 4 m.p.h.

DRAWBAR PULL. 1st, 900 lbs.; 2nd, 800 lbs. 3rd gear, 450 lb.

MAIN DRIVE. From gearbox to differential thence to final drive sprockets by gear wheels.

TRACKS. Rubber jointed type requiring no lubrication. Width, 6-in. Tracks can be set at 2-ft. 4¼-in.; 2-ft. 7¼-in.; and 2-ft. 10¼-in. centres. Ground pressure 5 lb./sq. in.

TRACK SPROCKETS. Dished steel plate construction with hardened rollers to form sprocket drive for tracks. Reversible on hub.

STEERING AND BRAKING. By hand levers operating contracting brake bands.

DRAWBAR. Swinging drawbar adjustable laterally and vertically. Floating drawbar (for hand lift equipment), adjustable vertically.

DIMENSIONS. Height, 3-ft. 4½-in.; Width, 3-ft. 2-in.; Length, 6-ft. 8½-in.

WEIGHT. (Basic tractor), 13 cwts.

OPTIONAL EQUIPMENT.

POWER TAKE-OFF. Speed, 700 r.p.m. at engine speed of 2,000 r.p.m. Will transmit on stationary work 4 h.p.

HYDRAULIC POWER LIFT. Gear type pump driven by p.t.o. shaft, feeding oil at 500 lb. sq. in. into cylinder on back plate of tractor.

Hydraulic lift and power take-off were optional on the MG6 crawler. The drive for the power take-off, which was taken from the three-speed gearbox, also powered the gear-type hydraulic pump at the rear of the tractor. The pump delivered oil at 500psi to the hydraulic cylinder that operated the linkage. The power take-off ran at 700rpm. The driver sat above the fuel tank for optimum weight distribution.

Ransomes MC 40 TRACTOR

RENOWNED FOR ....

SIMPLE OPERATION & MANOEUVRABILITY, STABILITY, VERSATILITY AND FUEL ECONOMY

THE SMALL TRACTOR WITH THE BIG PULL

The Ransomes MG40 arrived in 1960 with a choice of power units: Ransomes' own 8hp side-valve engine for running on petrol or TVO or a Drayton Type 34R two-stroke overhead-valve diesel rated at 10hp. Both engines had wet-sump lubrication and the fuel consumption of the diesel unit was 3 pints per hour.

NEW LOOK BONNET AND WINGS

These are available as optional extras and whilst enhancing the appearance of the machine, they serve a functional purpose in streamlining the engine and track-gear thus preventing damage to overhanging foliage.

Ideally suited for general use when working in soft fruit orchards and vineyards.

The bonnet being hinged at the front of the machine allows easy access to the power unit for general maintenance.

This small, compact—yet powerful tractor, built by Ransomes Sims and Jefferies Ltd. to precise engineering limits and backed by 150 years of manufacturing experience in the field of Agricultural Machinery is one of the most versatile units in its class, meeting all the requirements of the Horticulturalist, Fruitgrower, Market and Landscape Gardener, etc.

EASY TO DRIVE

No foot controls—automatic clutch controlled by engine speed. Finger-tip pressure only is required to operate the steering mechanism which gives the tractor positive and extreme manoeuvrability.

PROVED IN PRACTICE

The above illustration shows the "de luxe" version of the MG 40 fitted with bonnet and side wing extensions.

The MG40 was available as a 'de-luxe' version with an enclosed bonnet and side-wing extensions for working in vineyards and orchards. Later models were fitted with a two-stroke Sachs diesel engine. The Roadless rubber-jointed tracks, which had been a feature of all the MG models since 1936, were strengthened for the MG40.

ROADLESS

Roadless Traction Ltd was one of those anachronistic concerns that only Britain could produce. Steeped in the past, it was more interested in mechanical endeavour than monetary gain.

The company was founded in 1919 to exploit patents held by a group of British Army officers involved in tank development during the First World War. Its founder and managing director, Lieutenant-Colonel Philip Johnson, was fascinated with technology.

He served with the Royal Engineers' Steam Road Transport Company during the Boer War and later rose to become superintendent of the government's Department of Tank Design & Experiment.

As would be expected, many of Roadless's early developments involved tracks. The company's tracked conversions were applied to just about every vehicle imaginable – from a wheelbarrow to a steam roller. Its later 'elastic-girder' rubber-jointed tracks, designed for low-maintenance and silent-running, were fitted to a variety of different makes of tractors during the 1930s.

Roadless, operating from a former nunnery in Hounslow in Middlesex, initially shied away from full-scale manufacturing, preferring to licence its products to other companies to engineer machines on their behalf. Two significant projects were the development of the Bristol tractor and the Ransomes MG crawler.

All that changed after the Second World War, during which Roadless constructed half-track conversions of Fordson and Case tractors for the RAF's grass airfields. In 1945 the company developed a new type of 'driven girder' or DG half-track, which was designed to lock in a predetermined curve equal to a wheel of 20ft in diameter. The half-tracks, manufactured at Hounslow, were offered as a conversion for a number of different models of tractor, but the company enjoyed significant sales of the DG4 version of the tracks for the Fordson E27N Major and, to a lesser extent, the Massey-Harris 744PD.

Despite the success of its DG half-tracks, Roadless didn't completely abandon its earlier rubber-jointed full-track designs. A derivative of the 'elastic-girder' tracks were fitted to a Fordson E27N Major skid unit to provide a new crawler tractor, which was released as the Roadless Full Track Model E in July 1950. This was the first time that Roadless had marketed a complete tractor under its own name rather than just a conversion kit.

The Model E crawler only sold in limited numbers and it is thought that no more than 25 were built.

Two Tractors in One Two Tractors in One

Roadless Fordson Major
on test with a 6 furrow plough Photo by courtesy of N.I.A.E.

Two Tractors in One

- *Utilise all the power the engine provides*
- *Ensure maximum fuel economy at all times*
- *Girder track guarantees maximum adhesion*
- *And makes you independent of the weather*

All Fordsons can be fitted with D.G. Equipment

ROADLESS TRACTION LIMITED,
HOUNSLOW, MIDDLESEX, ENGLAND
Registered users of the Trade Mark FORDSON.

The Roadless DG4 half-track conversion for the Fordson E27N Major was introduced in September 1945. The conversion kit was sold as a Ford approved attachment, but wasn't cheap at £175, which was about three-quarters the cost of the tractor.

The DG4 half-track arrangement for the Fordson E27N Major was a relatively simple conversion requiring no modification of the tractor. The drive sprockets were fitted in place of the rear wheels, and the axle carrying the rear idlers was mounted on a bracket bolted to the rear transmission. Note how the profile of the track in contact with the ground curved in the same arc as a large wheel for increased traction and low rolling-resistance.

Roadless claimed that the half-tracks could be fitted or removed without the need for any special equipment. The literature stated that the Fordson could be turned back into a wheeled tractor in as little as two to four hours. It was not always that easy in a mud-soaked farmyard and few owners could be bothered to go through the rigmarole of removing the tracks.

Roadless enjoyed greater success with a subsequent full-track conversion, which was based on the new Fordson E1A Major. The new crawler was launched as the Roadless J17 at the 1953 Smithfield Show.

Roadless also redeveloped its DG4 half-track conversion to suit the E1A Major. In 1953, the DG4 tracks were superseded by the improved DG15 tracks, but sales of tracked conversions – both half- and full-track – were beginning to dwindle by the mid-1950s and the company began to explore other avenues.

Other Roadless products developed at this time

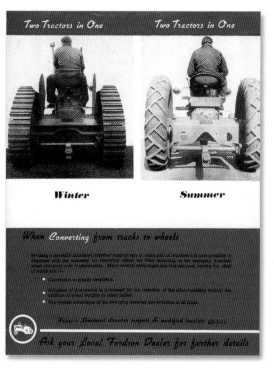

included high-clearance front axles for Fordson tractors and a tricycle conversion of the Diesel Major. The rowcrop tricycle conversion was developed on behalf of the Ford Motor Company for the North American market.

The tracked conversions continued into the early 1960s, but the outcome of a visit that Philip Johnson made to Italy in the 1950s had meanwhile propelled the company into a completely new direction. During his trip, Johnson met with Dr Segre-Amar, the founder of Selene of Turin. Selene had developed a four-wheel drive conversion for tractors using ex-US Army war-surplus axles.

After further negotiations, Selene agreed to licence its four-wheel drive system to Roadless. Johnson was given exclusive rights to manufacture the conversion for Fordson tractors and sell it in the UK, the British Commonwealth and certain other countries of the world. The Roadless conversion, based on the Fordson Diesel Major, was launched at the 1955 Smithfield Show and went into full production the following year.

The four-wheel drive conversion was marketed as the Manual-Roadless Fordson Major and was available as either a conversion kit or a complete tractor. The front axle was sourced from an ex-US military GMC truck with the drive provided by a transfer box sandwiched between the tractor's gearbox and rear transmission. It was an instant success with sales for agricultural, industrial and logging applications.

After the Fordson Diesel Major was superseded by the Power Major, the Manuel-Roadless conversion was fitted to the new model as well as the later Super Major. A similar four-wheel drive conversion, using a Dodge truck axle, was offered from 1959 for the Fordson Dexta and subsequent Super Dexta tractors.

By the early 1960s it was becoming evident that the market wanted something more powerful. Roadless responded by strengthening and modifying a four-wheel drive Super Major to take a six-cylinder Ford 590E engine. Following trials in 1962, this 76hp machine was launched the following year as the Roadless Ploughmaster 6/4. Other projects included four-wheel drive conversions of the B-450 and B-614 tractors for International Harvester and a high-clearance Land Rover for the Forestry Commission.

The year 1965 marked the beginning of a new era for Roadless – and the end of an old one after Philip Johnson passed away, aged 88, in November. The tracked conversions had been swept away and the company was now working on fresh designs of four-wheel drive models based on the new range of Ford tractors flowing out of Basildon. Four-wheel drive tractors remained the core of Roadless's business until the company ceased trading in 1983.

Probably the second most popular application
for the Roadless DG half-track was a conversion
for the Massey-Harris 744D tractor. The
conversion, using DG4A tracks, was introduced
in 1951 and the kit cost £245.

The Roadless Full Track Model E crawler, based on the Fordson
E27N Major skid unit, was launched in July 1950. The tractor,
which used the company's E3B 'elastic-girder' rubber-jointed
tracks, cost £850 for the petrol/TVO model or £1,150 for a
diesel version fitted with the Perkins P6 engine.

The arrival of the Fordson E1A Major in November 1951 saw
the DG4 half-track conversion modified to suit the new
tractor. Improved DG15 tracks for the Major were introduced
in 1953. Roadless claimed in its advertising that a complete
Fordson Diesel Major on Roadless half-tracks was the 'cheapest
40hp crawler in the world' with a total cost of £766 5s.

ROADLESS J17 FULL TRACK

The Fordson Major fitted with Roadless J17 full track equipment
gives an increased drawbar pull and is capable of handling up to
6-furrow ploughs easily and economically. The J17 is fitted with
rubber jointed tracks which mean that a high proportion of the
shock loads never reach the tractor's transmission system, but are
absorbed by the rubber joints. Rubber blocks in compression make
the track elastic in operation and endow it with a high resistance to
abrasion.

This type of track construction ensures long life, silent operation
and reduces driver fatigue.

Introduced in 1953, the Roadless J17 crawler was based on
the Fordson Diesel Major. The tractor used the new J-type
rubber-jointed track, which had been scaled-up from the
tracks fitted to the Ransomes MG crawlers.

The Roadless J17 remained in production until the early 1960s with the very last machines being based on the 'New Performance' Super Major. Like the early County crawlers, the J17 was steered via internal-expanding shoe-type clutches assisted by external-contracting brake bands.

Following a request from its North American customers, the Ford Motor Company asked Roadless to develop a tricycle version of the Fordson Diesel Major for rowcrop work. The conversion involved developing a new narrow-front axle and pedestal for twin wheels with a modified steering arrangement. The tricycle model was unveiled at the 1954 Smithfield Show and the first batch of tractors was assembled at Hounslow the following year. Most were exported with the bulk of the machines going to the USA; just one was sold in Britain.

Roadless moved into the four-wheel drive market in 1955 with the launch of its Manuel-Roadless conversion for the Fordson Diesel Major. The conversion was fitted to the Fordson Power Major from 1958 with production at Hounslow peaking at around 65 complete tractors or kits per month by the early 1960s.

The Manuel-Roadless conversion used modified ex-military axles sourced from war-surplus GMC trucks. The drive to the front axle was via a propeller-shaft taken from a transfer box sandwiched between the tractor's gearbox and rear transmission. The propeller-shaft was fitted with a torque-limiting clutch to protect the front axle from overloading should 'wind-up' occur between the two axles.

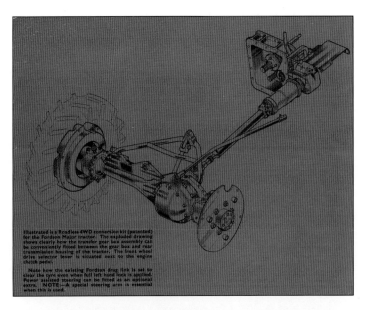

Illustrated is a Roadless 4WD conversion kit (patented) for the Fordson Major tractor. The exploded drawing shows clearly how the transfer gear box assembly can be conveniently fitted between the gear box and rear transmission housing of the tractor. The front wheel drive selector lever is situated next to the engine clutch pedal.

Note how the existing Fordson drag link is set to clear the tyre even when full left hand lock is applied. Power assisted steering can be fitted as an optional extra. NOTE:—A special steering arm is essential when this is used.

The MANUEL-ROADLESS 4 WHEEL DRIVE
FORDSON SUPER MAJOR

Two differentials give minimum turning circle without skid steering.
Unequal wheels give better forward visibility.
Torque control clutch eliminates transmission "wind-up". Front and rear loaders can be fitted.

AVAILABLE AS A CONVERSION KIT FOR YOUR FORDSON

ROADLESS TRACTION LIMITED
HOUNSLOW, MIDDLESEX. Telephone: HOUnslow 6421

The MANUEL-ROADLESS 4 WHEEL DRIVE
FORDSON DEXTA

It's twice the tractor

Günther Papenbroock (22c) Aachen Alfons-Straße 15 2.3. Dez. 1961

ROADLESS TRACTION LIMITED
HOUNSLOW, MIDDLESEX. Telephone: HOUnslow 6421

The Roadless four-wheel drive conversion for the Fordson Super Major was introduced in 1960 – the new skid unit offering the advantages of hydraulic draft-control and differential lock, which of course operated on the rear axle only unlike the County conversion. The four-wheel drive Super Major cost £1,230.

The Roadless four-wheel drive conversion for the Fordson Dexta was launched at the 1959 Smithfield Show. Roadless did not manufacture this conversion itself, but bought the parts in from Selene in Italy. It had a similar transfer box as fitted to the Major derivatives, but used a split-casing axle from a Dodge truck.

The 4 WD FORDSON DEXTA is a great little tractor

Similar in conception to the four-wheel drive Fordson Super Major, a transfer gearbox is inserted into the transmission of the Dexta. A coupling is placed between the output shaft of the tractor gearbox and the final drive pinion, and a further pinion integral with the coupling transmits the drive, via the transfer gearbox to the propellor shaft and thence to the front axle.

With the 4 W.D. DEXTA work output is increased and in most conditions the tractor can tackle 4 furrow ploughing with ease.

The 4 W.D. Dexta with deep digger plough.

Rolling with the 4 wheel drive Dexta.

The ROADLESS PLOUGHMASTER 6/4

6 CYLINDER
DIESEL POWER
PLUS
ROADLESS
4 WHEEL DRIVE

The new Roadless Ploughmaster 6/4 four wheel drive tractor is the answer to greatly increased tractor power in a compact form, without appreciably increasing the weight or overall tractor size. The ROADLESS Ploughmaster 6/4 develops 76 b.h.p. yet its wheelbase is considerably less than comparable models. Even the turning circle is identical to that of a tractor with lower h.p. rating.

ROADLESS TRACTION LTD.

The Roadless conversion of the Fordson Dexta was too expensive at £1,101 to sell in any great number. However several were sold against the Massey Ferguson 35 to market gardeners in the Surrey area who needed the extra traction for their soft and undulating land. The conversion was also fitted to the Super Dexta, but total production (Dexta and Super Dexta) was just 78 machines.

The Roadless Ploughmaster 6/4 offered more power from a 76hp six-cylinder Ford 590E engine mated to the Super Major transmission. Following trials in 1962, the tractor was launched in March 1963 and exactly 200 were built before production ended in October 1964.

THE ROADLESS PLOUGHMASTER 6/4

4 WHEEL DRIVE

All available engine power 76 b.h.p. is utilised by the Roadless Ploughmaster 6/4, enabling you to *plough* and *cultivate* faster and deeper even under conditions that would prevent an ordinary two wheel drive tractor from working. The short wheelbase ensures correct weight distribution and tight turning circles. Conventional design means good forward visibility and unrestricted access to the engine for servicing and maintenance, and with power assisted steering as standard equipment, maximum operating comfort and efficiency is obtained. The versatile Ploughmaster is the modern high performance "all round" tractor.

Four wheel drive on the Ploughmaster 6/4 converts all the available engine power of 76 b.h.p. into tractive effort. The short wheelbase results in a weight distribution of approximately equal proportions on front and rear axles, so ensuring that all four driven wheels produce the maximum tractive effort without unnecessary built-in weight. This results in a high power/weight ratio with a tractor that is sufficiently light not to leave heavy wheelmarks. Four wheel drive cuts wheelspin and soil smear to a minimum, the driven front wheels give positive steering in tight corners and increased safety on slopes.

(1) The compact design of the driven front axle allows the driver full forward visibility.

(2) All parts of the tractor are easily accessible for mounting to the driving position, and also for servicing and maintenance.

(3) The layout of the rear of the Ploughmaster is quite conventional, with normal 3-point linkage arrangement or swinging drawbar.

McCORMICK INTERNATIONAL
B-450
FOUR WHEEL DRIVE
Diesel Tractor

INTERNATIONAL HARVESTER

All over the world, the McCormick International B-450 Diesel Tractor is in use, where high sustained power output coupled with unmatched traction is called for. Now, in conjunction with Roadless Traction, International Harvester add a four wheel drive version to the B-450 range. In cases where extra traction is needed, such as steep slopes, sticky conditions and/or heavy ground the front axle drive enables the tractor to make the most advantageous use of the 55 h.p. engine. Severe testing for over two years has produced a four wheel drive version of an already universally accepted agricultural tractor giving an increase of up to 25% drawbar pull. When fitted with power steering, the B-450 4-wheel drive has outstanding steering ease, making it even more manoeuvrable and enabling the operator to work more acres a day.

When designing the Ploughmaster 6/4, Roadless's engineers moved the front axle back to shorten the wheelbase to 75in. This optimised the weight distribution over both axles and did away with the need for additional and unnecessary weights. The prototype, registered 7271 MD, and the first few production tractors were finished in green and yellow paint, but the company quickly reverted to a blue/grey livery after John Deere took exception to another manufacturer using its colour scheme.

In 1961, Roadless was approached by International Harvester to develop a four-wheel drive version of its B-450 tractor. The front axle was again based on GMC ex-military vehicle components with a side-drive taken from an aperture in the tractor's gearbox casing. The model was assembled at Doncaster using conversion kits shipped from Hounslow. Roadless also developed similar conversions for the later International B-614 and 634 tractors. No mention of Roadless's involvement was made in the sales literature.

TRUSTY

The Trusty was a product of Tractors (London) Ltd, which was formed in the 1920s by John C Reach in partnership with his wife, Marion, as a machinery dealership with close ties to the Rushton tractor. The Rushton, designed by George Rushton, bore remarkable similarities to the Fordson, and had a short but chequered history.

The Rushton tractor was launched in February 1929 and was produced by a subsidiary of AEC, the well-known commercial vehicle manufacturers. Tractors (London) Ltd, with premises at The White House on Dancers Hill Road in Bentley Heath, was appointed the distributor for Hertfordshire.

Sales were disappointing and AEC had bailed out of the venture by September 1929. George Rushton formed a new company, but only managed to keep production of the tractor going for another year until his business went into liquidation in late 1930. The liquidated stock of tractors and spares was acquired by the Huntingdonshire machinery dealer, Frank Standen.

Standen, trading as the Agricultural & Industrial Tractor Company, moved the operation to the former Crown Hotel in St Ives. Here he sold spares and continued to assemble a small number of tractors, most of which were built as crawlers fitted with Roadless tracks. The distribution, both UK and overseas, of these last few Rushton machines was entrusted to Tractors (London) Ltd, which shipped the tractors from a depot in Broad Lane, Tottenham.

By 1933 the Rushton venture had all but run its course. That year Tractors (London) Ltd began assembling the pedestrian-controlled Trusty garden tractor at its Tottenham premises. Incongruously, parts were supplied from Colnbrook in Berkshire by a British subsidiary of the American fire extinguisher manufacturer, Walter Kidde. Initially sales were slow and just 25 machines were sold during the first 18 months.

In 1938 Reach moved production of the Trusty to Bentley Heath and introduced an extensive range of attachments. The range of matched implements and equipment, almost a complete farming system in its own right, made the Trusty tractor an attractive proposition for the smallholder, market gardener or fruit grower – and sales flourished.

The Trusty tractor remained in limited production throughout the war and the 10,000th machine was built in 1947. The design was simple with a single-cylinder air-cooled petrol engine driving a single-speed transmission via a centrifugal clutch. The drive was via a single chain to a countershaft and then by two chains to the reduction gears on each wheel. Two sliding dog-clutches on the countershaft were used to disengage the drive to each wheel for turning.

Two models were offered in the immediate post-war years: the Trusty Model No.5 and No.6. The Model No.5, priced at £125, was powered by a 412cc JAP engine; while the No.6, costing £130, was offered with the choice of a 540cc Douglas or 633cc Norton power unit. Pneumatic tyres were £10 extra and later options included a reverse gear and a diesel engine. A three forward speed and single reverse Albion gearbox

The original Trusty — WHICH HAS BECOME FAMOUS AS THE **Light Tractor with the Big Performance**

Choice of three types of engine : J.A.P. 4.5 h.p., DOUGLAS 7.5 h.p. or NORTON 14.5 h.p. Patent swinging Drawbar. Impulse starting. Easy Maintenance. Foolproof handling. On standard, spade lug or pneumatic wheels.
Reverse gear fitted by maker £10 extra.

Ploughs (with G.P. or digger] bodies) From £18 18 0

Ridging bodies From £5 5 0

Cultivators From £13 16 0   Disc harrows (8.18 in. discs) From £32 10 0   Bogey units From £12 0 0
Many other implements also available for *every* job on farm or smallholding.

TRUSTY leads the way with
Ample reserve of the right type of power . Patent Automatic Clutch . Patent Swinging Drawbar . 'Silky' start, smooth running and self-steering . Scientific weight distribution . Torque-reaction for soil penetration . Adjustable width . Specially designed tool for *every* job on holding . Implements speedily, easily changed . Highest efficiency, versatility and reliability . Good after-sales service.

PRICE FROM **£125** to **£150** IMPLEMENTS EXTRA
There are over 14,000 TRUSTY TRACTORS in use throughout the world

By 1949, approximately 14,000 pedestrian-controlled Trusty tractors had been sold worldwide. The Model No.5 was powered by a 4½hp JAP engine, while the No.6 was offered with either a 7½hp Douglas or 14½hp Norton power unit. The machines were priced from £125 to £150 with a single forward speed transmission. Reverse gear was optional and cost an extra £10.

TRUSTY

The four-wheel Trusty Steed was a ride-on machine. Introduced in 1948, the Mark I model had the driver's seat in front of the engine. The power came from a 13.4hp Norton engine and the transmission gave a single speed of 3½mph or 8mph in forward and reverse depending on the size of sprockets fitted for the chain drive to the gearbox.

The Mark II Trusty Steed, launched in 1950, had a more conventional layout with a 600cc air-cooled petrol engine mounted at the front. The three-speed Albion gearbox gave forward speeds of 1¾mph, 3mph and 4½mph with 1¼mph in reverse. The final drive was via roller-chain and spur reduction gears, and the clutch was a Ferodo-lined automotive-type.

became part of the specification in 1951.

Sales of the pedestrian-controlled machines were eventually overtaken by those of the ride-on model. Tractors (London) Ltd had been experimenting with a ride-on design as early as 1943, but it wasn't until 1948 that a four-wheel tractor was put into production as the Trusty Steed.

The Mark I Steed was basically a pedestrian-controlled Trusty tractor in reverse with the driver sitting in front of the engine aboard a four-wheel chassis. The power source was a 13.4hp Norton engine fitted with a centrifugal clutch, and the transmission gave one speed in forward or reverse. A joystick was used to select forward or reverse and control the dog-clutches to disengage the drive wheels when turning.

Priced at £200 the Trusty Steed was advertised as a towing tractor for yards, factories, post offices, aerodromes and building sites. A matched single-furrow plough was also offered for an extra £22 10s.

The Mark II Steed, which appeared in 1950, had a more conventional layout with the engine at the front driving a three-speed gearbox via an automotive-type clutch. The tractor was fitted with a spring-assisted lift for a rear-mounted plough and mechanical lift for a mid-mounted toolbar. Norton or JAP 600cc engines

provided the power and the basic machine was priced at £177 10s. From 1960 the tractor was fitted with an enclosed bonnet and upright exhaust.

The Trusty pedestrian-controlled tractors were dropped in 1967, but Tractors (London) Ltd continued to trade until 1978 when the business was sold and reorganised as the Trusty Tractor Company.

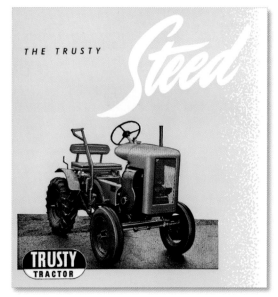

By 1960 the Trusty Steed had been given a slightly more modern appearance with an enclosed bonnet and upright exhaust. The single-cylinder air-cooled petrol engine was a 600cc unit developing 14½hp at 4,500rpm. The brakes could be operated independently via the dog-clutch levers and power take-off was optional.

155

TURNER

The Turner 'Yeoman of England' was the first wheeled tractor to be made in Britain with an 'own make' multi-cylinder diesel engine, predating offerings from David Brown, Ferguson, International, Ford and Nuffield. It was beaten to the marketplace by the Massey-Harris 744PD and Fordson E27N Major P6, but these used Perkins diesels rather than their own power units.

The tractor was developed by Turner Manufacturing; an illustrious Midlands engineering firm with a history dating back to the early nineteenth century when Thomas Turner began trading as a locksmith in Wolverhampton. In 1901 the company came under the control of the Dumbell family, expanding into the manufacture of railway equipment, bicycles, motor vehicles, marine engines and much, much more.

After building machine tools during the First World War, Turner diversified into commercial vehicle components and fairground equipment. The Second World War saw the company at full stretch manufacturing recovery winches and aircraft landing-gear. Not wishing to rely solely on its military contracts, a return to peace saw Turner explore several new avenues including a light delivery vehicle and a range of diesel engines.

The diesel engines were designed with a 'vee' layout in order to make the power units both compact and easily accessible for servicing. The layout also permitted a large degree of commonality of parts – the same piston, liner and connecting-rod, etc, being used for single-, twin- and four-cylinder units – allowing for simplified and low-cost production.

Designed for marine or industrial applications, the 1V95 single- and 2V95 twin-cylinder diesel engines went into production at Turner's Wulfruna Works in Wolverhampton in 1946. The 4V95 four-cylinder power unit was added to the range in 1948.

Seeking further applications for the engine, Turner came up with the idea of developing a diesel tractor, which seemed a shrewd move considering the growing post-war demand for farm machinery. The

Turner's 'V95 Series' of diesel engines all shared the same 3¾in bore and 4½in stroke. Production began in 1946 with the V-twin 2V95 model, rated at 17hp, followed by the 8½hp single-cylinder 1V95 engine. The engine family was completed by the arrival of the 3,260cc (199cu in) V4, designated the 4V95 and rated at 34hp, in 1948. Applications for the engines included marine use, generating sets, pumps, compressors, cranes, excavators, winches, concrete mixers, hoists, welding sets, road-making machinery, narrow-gauge locomotives and agricultural machinery. This leaflet also contains the only image ever released of the company's two-cylinder Mark 1 tractor.

man in charge of the project was the company's chief draughtsman, Tom W Graver. Working under him as tractor designer was Reginald Hill, and both reported directly to Turner's chairman and managing director, Philip Dumbell.

The first prototype tractor, known simply as the Mark 1, appeared in early 1948. Powered by the 17hp two-cylinder 2V95 engine, it was designed as a lightweight tricycle machine with a narrow-front twin-wheel arrangement. Much of the machine was hand-built with the front grille and bonnet made from alloy castings due to the post-war shortage of steel. No hydraulic lift or linkage was fitted.

While the Mark 1 was being evaluated on a local farm, Graver drew up plans in May 1948 for a second (Mark 2) prototype, which was a larger tractor fitted with the 34hp four-cylinder 4V95 engine, a three-speed gearbox and a conventional wide-front axle layout. Hydraulic linkage was also developed in conjunction with Adrolic Engineering of Scotland. At the end of the trials, the Mark 2 was chosen for production and the two-cylinder tractor was dropped.

Further changes were made to the design before the tractor was released for production in May 1949. The 4V95 engine was up-rated to 40hp and the gearbox was changed to a four-speed unit. The tractor was officially launched as the Turner 'Yeoman of England' at the Royal Show on 5 July 1949.

The tractor was only part of the story because Turner, in line with other manufacturers of the time, also offered a full range of matched implements and accessories. The 'Yeoman' equipment line was launched at a two-day demonstration held in May 1950 at Compton Farm on the outskirts of Wolverhampton. The equipment was supplied by several leading British implement manufacturers.

During 1950 an engineering consultant, Harry Aston, was appointed Turner's new chief engineer, and Tom Graver was promoted to assistant chief engineer. Aston's brief was to oversee a number of improvements to the 'V95 Series' engines, in particular a redesign of the cylinder heads.

The first of Aston's improvements was incorporated into the Turner Mark 2A tractor, which also featured a Donaldson oil-bath air-cleaner and a new two-tone green and yellow livery. Further revisions to the combustion process, as well as a change from dry to wet cylinder liners, were introduced on the Mark 3 model that was phased in during 1951.

Despite the changes, the 'Yeoman of England' tractor was plagued by a number of troubling reliability problems. It was also no match for the vastly superior and cheaper Fordson Diesel Major that was

launched in November 1951. The Turner tractor now cost over £700 and was more than £200 dearer than the Fordson, which proved to be a better and more reliable machine.

The overseas demand was more encouraging with sales to Australia, New Zealand, South America, Africa, Europe, Scandinavia and India. Argentina was a particularly important market and sales to that country inspired the final version of the Turner tractor. Fitted with a Perkins P4 diesel engine, a five-speed gearbox and a strengthened rear axle, this prototype machine was known as the 'P4 Argentinean' tractor. One was built for evaluation during 1955, but the design was never put into production.

Production of the 'Yeoman of England' continued until March 1955 and the tractor was listed until 1957 when the final stocks were cleared. The demise of the tractor coincided with Turner being awarded a lucrative contract by the Ford Motor Company to supply timing gears and oil-pump drives for Fordson production at Dagenham. There has always been speculation that Turner agreed to drop the 'Yeoman of England' and ditch the 'Argentinean' tractor in return for the contract, thus relieving Ford of one of the main competitors to its Diesel Major.

Turner wasn't short of work and it was still supplying winches to the British Army, as well as gearboxes, torque converters and transmissions for a wide range of applications. The agricultural connection was revived in the 1970s when the company developed synchromesh tractor transmissions for both International Harvester and Leyland. Today, the Wolverhampton concern, trading as Turner Powertrain Systems, is part of Caterpillar and continues to supply transmissions for numerous off-highway applications.

Pre-production models of the Turner Mark 2 tractor underwent trials on farms in Staffordshire and Northumberland during 1948. Following the trials, the engine was up-rated to 40hp with a three-bearing cast-iron crankshaft and alloy pistons. The gearbox was also changed to a four-speed transmission featuring a spiral-bevel differential with the final drive to the axle shaft via heavy-duty spur gears.

The Turner Mark 2 was introduced at the 1949 Royal Show. Initially, the model was to have been known as the Turner 'All-Purpose Diesel Tractor', but the company decided a more prestigious cachet was needed and so the 'Yeoman of England' identity was hurriedly overprinted on the introduction brochures in time for the tractor's launch. The list price of the tractor was £650 and the company charged £1 10s extra for the lubricating oil! Ancillaries included a power take-off unit (£11), a pulley (£12 10s), differential lock (£5), electric lighting (£6) and wheel weights (£3 15s). A power lift unit supplied by Adrolic Engineering of Coatbridge in Scotland cost £58, while for £4 10s Turner would water-ballast the rear tyres.

The Turner 'Yeoman' equipment line consisted of a full range of approved implements and accessories for the tractor. The equipment was supplied by several leading British implement manufacturers, including Adrolic Engineering (ploughs), Salopian (disc ploughs), H Leverton (toolbars, cultivators, steerage hoes and a front-mounted potato coverer), McConnel (saw-bench), Featherstone (mower), Steel Fabricators (loader), Bomford (dozer- and grader-blades), Dening (disc harrows), Stanhay (wheel strakes), Scottish Aviation (cab) and Belton Bros & Drury (pick-up hitch).

The 'Yeoman of England' Mark 2A tractor incorporated a number of revisions made to the 4V95 engine in 1950 by Turner's new chief engineer, Harry Aston. Other changes included the provision of a Donaldson oil-bath air-cleaner and a new two-tone green and yellow livery. Aston was an engineering consultant with great experience in military and automotive products, having previously worked for the Metropolitan-Cammell Carriage & Wagon Company, GKN and the Ministry of Supply.

The 'Yeoman of England' Mark 3 tractor, introduced during 1951, featured further improvements to the 4V95 engine's combustion system. A Turner-designed pre-combustion chamber with an oval air-cell was offset into the cylinder heads and the compression ratio was raised. There was also a change from dry to wet cylinder liners.

At the heart of the 'Yeoman of England' tractor was Turner's V4 diesel engine – the 40hp 4V95 unit, which had a wonderful and distinctive exhaust note. The engine was carried in a sub-frame, which supported the front axle and was bolted to the rear transmission. The transmission consisted of three castings: a clutch and coupling housing, the drive housing for the hydraulic pump and the five-speed gearbox. The gearbox also incorporated the differential and spiral-bevel reduction gear. Final reduction spur-gears were enclosed in housings bolted to either side of the gearbox. Borg & Beck supplied the 11in single dry-plate clutch, Girling the independent internal-expanding drum brakes and Marles the steering box. A Lucas 12-volt electric starting system was fitted.

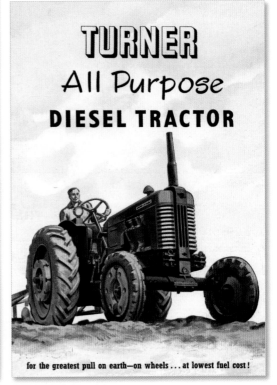

VICKERS

One area in which the British tractor industry was sadly lacking after the Second World War was in the production of a heavy crawler tractor for both agriculture and industry. The government was acutely aware of this, which is why heavy crawlers were exempt when a restriction on the import of American tractors was introduced in 1945.

For a time the needs of earthmoving plant operators and large-scale farming were met by a continuing influx of Caterpillar, International Harvester and Allis-Chalmers tracklayers from the USA. With the UK facing a severe dollar shortage, it was an untenable situation and before long a government-led initiative was put in place to stimulate the production of a British crawler that would meet the needs of both the construction industry and the British armed forces – still a major customer for heavy plant.

The scheme was first discussed in September 1947 with the proposals being put forward for a joint venture with Vickers manufacturing the tractors at its

Designed for heavy earthmoving operations, the Vickers VR-180 crawler was powered by a direct-injection Rolls-Royce C6SFL six-cylinder diesel engine supercharged to 180hp at 1,800rpm. This mighty 12,700cc (743cu in) unit had dry-sump lubrication, wet cylinder liners, aluminium pistons and twin cast-iron cylinder heads covering three cylinders each. The supercharger gear was driven from the timing gears, and cooling was by a conventional radiator with air taken through vents in the bonnet top rather than through a grille at the front. The transmission gave six forward and three reverse speeds.

Scotswood plant in Newcastle, Rolls-Royce supplying the engines and Jack Olding handling the sales and service. It was an ambitious plan involving over £1 million in investment.

Vickers-Armstrong was probably Britain's greatest armaments manufacturer with interests in shipbuilding and aviation. During the 1920s the organisation had manufactured a wheeled agricultural tractor, but this was no more than a short-lived venture. The post-war crawler project was said to be the largest in heavy tractor production ever undertaken in the UK, and Vickers threw itself into it with the highest confidence, despite the fact that it had far more experience in building tanks.

The engine chosen for the project was the Rolls-Royce C6SFL six-cylinder diesel; a four-stroke direct-injection unit supercharged to 180hp at 1,800rpm. Drive was via a single-plate dry automotive clutch to a six-speed forward and three-reverse gearbox. Steering was by clutch and brake with hydraulic assistance.

Vickers drew on its experience with tanks to design the running gear, which was a simple arrangement with no track frames. The three large idler wheels and sprocket, mounted each side on two separate swing-arms, had four rubber rings between the outer rim and inner hub. This provided a cushioned drive that relied on friction alone to transmit the power.

The track was a complex design for the time with sealed and lubricated pins, and was designed to flex in both directions. Much thought was given to ease of maintenance and Vickers claimed that the front half of the tractor could be parted from the rear in just two to three hours.

Worldwide distribution of the Vickers crawler would be handled by Jack Olding of Hatfield in Hertfordshire. Olding had been a Caterpillar distributor since 1937, but Olding's relationship with Caterpillar had become somewhat strained over its refusal to open a factory in Britain. Seeing the Vickers crawler as his company's future, Olding took the portentous step of relinquishing the Caterpillar franchise in 1950 becoming the first distributor ever to

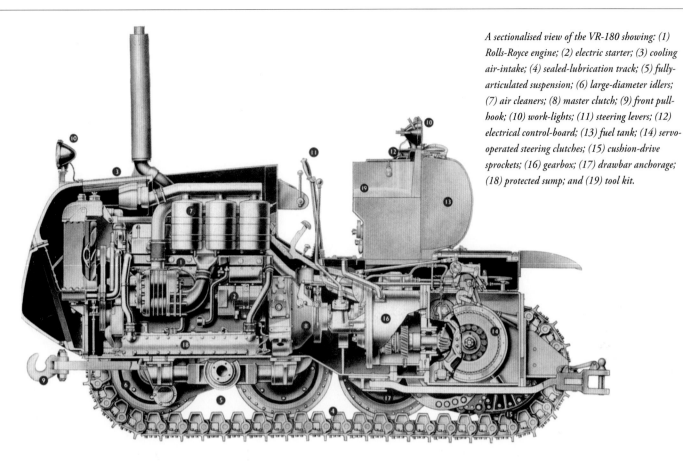

A sectionalised view of the VR-180 showing: (1) Rolls-Royce engine; (2) electric starter; (3) cooling air-intake; (4) sealed-lubrication track; (5) fully-articulated suspension; (6) large-diameter idlers; (7) air cleaners; (8) master clutch; (9) front pull-hook; (10) work-lights; (11) steering levers; (12) electrical control-board; (13) fuel tank; (14) servo-operated steering clutches; (15) cushion-drive sprockets; (16) gearbox; (17) drawbar anchorage; (18) protected sump; and (19) tool kit.

give up the agency voluntarily.

A total of 23 pre-production Vickers crawlers were already on trial across the world, and Olding's engineers were given the job of assessing their performance. Hatfield's experienced technicians went through each tractor with a fine-tooth comb suggesting numerous changes and improvements. Unfortunately their advice went unheeded as Vickers refused to implement their suggestions.

Full production of the crawler, designated VR-180, began in the spring of 1952, but the tractor – as Olding's men had predicted – sadly failed to live up to expectations experiencing a number of complex design faults and reliability problems. There was nothing fundamentally wrong with the design, but it was more suited to military applications than the rigours of prolonged earthmoving applications where tractors were double-shifted and not always properly maintained.

Vickers introduced a rolling programme of progressive modification, which was fine for military vehicles when the government was paying, but it didn't endear the company to the private operators who disliked being charged extra to rectify a product that should have been right in the first place.

Priced at £7,475 in 1952, the VR-180 was an expensive machine to buy and its spares were costly.

There were plenty of ex-military American crawlers on the market that were cheaply available and more easily maintained. Vickers had unfortunately priced itself out of contention.

The company attempted to fight back with the new Vickers Vikon model, which was launched in 1956 with a four-cylinder supercharged Rolls-Royce C4SFL engine developing 142hp. This scaled-down version of the VR-180 (now known as the Vigor) met with no greater success and just 21 were made.

Meanwhile, several batches of Vigor crawlers had been supplied to the British Army where expensive and prolonged maintenance wasn't a problem. Most saw service with the Royal Engineers. The British Army became the main customer for the VR-180 and was supplied with the improved Vigor Mark 2 and Mark 3 models, the last of which wasn't withdrawn from service until 1983.

The restyled Vigor Mark 3, introduced in 1959, was also available with a torque-converter transmission as the 6000 Series machine, or with a 210hp Cummins engine as the 3000 Series tractor. It is not known, however, if either of these versions was actually put into production. In April 1961, having incurred losses of £1.75 million on the venture, Vickers decided to withdraw from the crawler market after less than 900 VR-180s had been built.

The Vickers VR-180's running gear was both innovative and simple. The three large idler wheels and sprocket, mounted each side on two separate swing-arms, had four rubber rings between the outer rim and inner hub. This provided a cushioned drive, which relied on friction alone to transmit the power. However, if the bolts clamping the sprocket hubs to the rims weren't kept tight, the hubs would turn inside the rims and there was no drive to the tracks.

SPEEDING UP THE NIGHT SHIFT

FAST, POWERFUL, efficient, the VR-180 leads the field in earth-moving, by day or night. Its supercharged Rolls-Royce engine and fully reflexing track make light of the heaviest going in any climate of the world.

A wide range of Vickers-Armstrongs and Onions Ancillary Equipment has been specially produced to team up with the advanced-design features of the VR-180 and to take every advantage of the tractor's extra speed and power.

THE VR·180 AND ITS MATCHED EARTH-MOVING EQUIPMENT

DESIGNED AND BUILT BY VICKERS-ARMSTRONGS
POWERED BY ROLLS-ROYCE
DISTRIBUTED THROUGHOUT THE WORLD BY

JACK OLDING & COMPANY LIMITED · HATFIELD · HERTFORDSHIRE ·

Vickers offered a comprehensive range of equipment for the VR-180, including dozers (both cable and hydraulic), scrapers, rippers, root cutters, push loaders, logging winches, side-boom cranes and cable-control units. The attachments were manufactured as a joint venture operating as Vickers-Armstrong (Onions) Ltd from Bilston in Staffordshire.

The Vickers Vikon was introduced in 1956 with a four-cylinder supercharged Rolls-Royce C4SFL engine developing 142hp. This scaled-down version of the VR-180 had a five-speed transmission and weighed 26,300lb.

OTHER MAKES

Such was the insatiable demand for farm machinery in post-war Britain that the tractor market looked to be an attractive proposition for every budding engineer and entrepreneur. Everyone was jumping on the bandwagon, but for every manufacturer that made its mark, there were plenty more that fell by the wayside. Those that failed either didn't have the financial backing of the larger companies or it was a question of the wrong product at the wrong time.

More often than not, it was simply the wrong product altogether. Every engineering firm that emerged from the Second World War had spare capacity. Proprietary parts abounded and many motor manufacturers were keen to offer engines and gearboxes at attractive discounts. It was a straightforward exercise to cobble together a few parts to make a farm tractor, but automotive components weren't always suited to farm work, and a mismatch of proprietary units would always have its limitations in terms of suitability for agricultural applications.

Makes of tractors assembled from automotive or proprietary components included the Byron and the OTA, both of which were three-wheel machines powered by an industrial version of the Ford 10hp side-valve car engine. Byron Farm Machinery Ltd of Walthamstow announced its three-wheel tractor in 1946 and production continued until 1954.

Oak Tree Appliances of Coventry introduced its three-wheel OTA tractor in 1949. A four-wheel version, the OTA Monarch, was launched at the 1951 Smithfield Show. Two years later, the company sold the rights to its tractors to Singer Motors, which continued production of the Monarch at Birmingham until 1956.

These little tractors were only really suitable for the smallholder or market gardener rather than large-scale farming. Similar machines designed with the horticultural market in mind included the Carterson,

The Byron was the tractor with the poetical name, but there was little to wax lyrical about when it came to the specification, which was about as basic as you could get. The Mark 1 model was introduced in 1946 with an industrial version of the Ford 10hp side-valve car engine bolted to an automotive (Ford) three-speed transmission. It was designed as a tricycle rowcrop tractor with a single front wheel and the rear tread adjustable from 56-73in. It had independent brakes and a manual lift. A Mark ll model with improvements to the throttle linkage (Bowden cable), steering and brakes was introduced in 1949 with a list price of £247 10s.

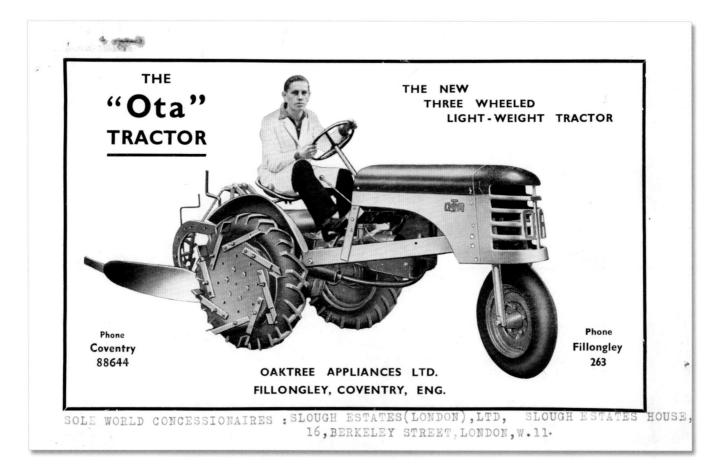

THE "Ota" TRACTOR

THE NEW THREE WHEELED LIGHT-WEIGHT TRACTOR

Phone Coventry 88644

Phone Fillongley 263

OAKTREE APPLIANCES LTD.
FILLONGLEY, COVENTRY, ENG.

SOLE WORLD CONCESSIONAIRES : SLOUGH ESTATES(LONDON),LTD, SLOUGH ESTATES HOUSE, 16,BERKELEY STREET,LONDON,W.11.

Introduced in 1949 and priced at £246 10s, the OTA was a lightweight three-wheel tractor built by Oak Tree Appliances of Fillongley, Coventry. Although rated at 10hp, its side-valve Ford engine actually delivered 17hp at 2,000rpm from a displacement of 1,172cc. The three-speed Ford gearbox was fitted with an auxiliary high/low ratio to give six forward speeds and two reverse. Extra equipment included hydraulic lift, belt pulley and power take-off.

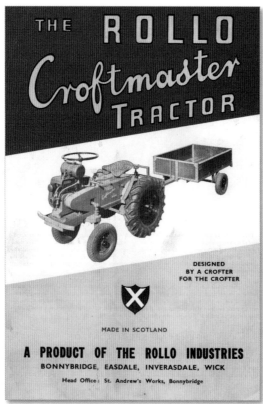

THE ROLLO Croftmaster TRACTOR

DESIGNED BY A CROFTER FOR THE CROFTER

MADE IN SCOTLAND

A PRODUCT OF THE ROLLO INDUSTRIES
BONNYBRIDGE, EASDALE, INVERASDALE, WICK
Head Office: St. Andrew's Works, Bonnybridge

Coleby Shire, Crawley, Garner, Gunsmith, Kent Pony, Lea Francis Uni-Horse, Martin-Markham Colt, Rollo Croftmaster, Trojan and Winget tractors.

Unfortunately, few of these compact machines could match the ubiquitous Ferguson TE-20 in terms of versatility or price. With a full range of equipment and an organised sales and service network, it offered a complete farming system. The all-conquering Ferguson was a proper agricultural tractor and was light years ahead of many of these other machines both in terms of design and performance.

One tractor that had a little more going for it was the Goldstar made by the famous stationary engine manufacturer, R A Lister of Dursley in Gloucestershire. Aimed at the overseas market, it was launched in 1958 with a twin-cylinder air-cooled Lister diesel

The Rollo Croftmaster was a lightweight machine that was designed by Scottish crofter, John Rollo, for smallholdings in the highlands. Several different versions were offered from 1953 by Rollo Industries of Bonnybridge in Caithness. The famous film actor, Richard Todd, was one of the customers for the Mark 7C model, which was powered by a 9hp Briggs & Stratton engine. The linkage for the single-furrow plough was raised by a hydraulic ram.

engine mated to a six-speed transmission, but even it couldn't compete with the Ferguson FE-35 or Fordson Dexta.

At the other end of the horticultural market were the two-wheel pedestrian-controlled machines, which trod a fine line between tractors and garden cultivators. We've already mentioned the models produced by BMB, Howard and Trusty in the previous chapters, but probably the best-known of this genre was the British Anzani Iron Horse.

British Anzani Engineering of Hampton Hill in Middlesex always referred to its Iron horse as a tractor. Despite being something of a 'man killer', it was a very successful machine. Designed by Charles Henry Harrison, the first tractor was built in 1940 and more than 10,000 were sold before production ended in 1956.

Many manufacturers felt that the key to interesting the small farmer in mechanisation was to develop one machine that did everything, but it was the old adage of jack of all trades but master of none. David Brown had tried but failed to envelop the concept with its 2D tractor. Similar but less innovative tool-carriers were marketed by Bean, Maskell and Opperman.

The Hertfordshire firm of S E Opperman Ltd, based at Stirling Corner near Boreham Wood, also felt that what the small farmer needed most was a motorised cart. The three-wheel Opperman Motocart, launched in 1945, was powered by an 8hp single-cylinder petrol engine mounted on the front wheel together with a four-speed gearbox. It was certainly novel, but being different doesn't necessarily translate into sales and production ended in 1952.

Another motorised cart was offered by E Boydell & Co Ltd of Manchester, manufacturers of Muir-Hill dumpers. The Muir-Hill Powacart with a drop-side body for farm work was introduced in 1946 to use up stocks of war-surplus dumpers that the company had bought back from the government.

The post-war frenzy to get on the tractor bandwagon saw several new names enter the crawler market. Rushed into the marketplace after a short development programme, several never reached production and most came and went almost overnight leaving little or no trace of their existence.

Glave Ltd of Northampton announced a crawler powered by a Morris 12/25hp petrol engine. Its main claim to fame was its LG1 regenerative steering system, which was developed by Gates & Hardy Ltd of London from transmissions used in British tanks during the Second World War.

A similar LG1 transmission, which used a system of gear ratios to steer the vehicle, was also fitted to the wheeled Powersteer tractor developed by Maxim

Engineering of Ladbroke Grove. Both the Glave and the Powersteer were introduced in 1947, but neither seems to have had any impact on the market.

Fraser Tractors of London launched its crawler in May 1950 with a price tag of £1,375. This was a fairly conventional machine with clutch-and-brake steering and a four-speed gearbox. Several engine options were offered, but the general consensus is that it was a one-hit wonder and only the prototype was ever built. Another obscure machine was the Bagnall-Burns BB90 crawler, which had a hydrostatic transmission and was powered by a Meadows 4DC420 engine. Announced in November 1958, it also seems to have disappeared without trace.

The Lanarkshire firm of James A Cuthbertson Ltd

The post-war Iron Horse was powered by an air-cooled Anzani-JAP petrol engine developing 6hp at 2,000rpm. Priced at £130 in 1949, it had a centrifugal clutch driving three speed and reverse synchromesh gearbox giving a top speed of 4½mph. Dog-clutches acting on the differential were controlled from the handles for turning under power. Petrol consumption was two gallons per day.

introduced its semi-amphibious Water Buffalo tractor in about 1953. Two models were offered with rubber-jointed tracks for working on soft terrain, peat or marshland. The 'large' tractor was powered by a six-cylinder Leyland diesel engine, while the 'light' model had a four-cylinder Albion power unit.

One manufacturer that we haven't mentioned thus far in the book is Caterpillar – probably the greatest name in the history of crawler tractors. Of course it's an American firm, but it deserves inclusion because satel-

lite production was established at Glasgow in 1958 when this British plant became the first factory outside the USA to build complete Caterpillar tractors.

The first machine to go into production at Glasgow was the 22A model Caterpillar D8, which was built in Britain until 1966. The 24A model D4 was also manufactured at the Scottish plant from 1959-64 when it was replaced by the 88A model Caterpillar D4D, which rolled out of Glasgow until 1968.

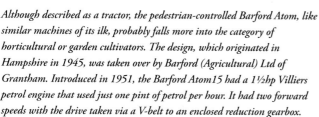

Although described as a tractor, the pedestrian-controlled Barford Atom, like similar machines of its ilk, probably falls more into the category of horticultural or garden cultivators. The design, which originated in Hampshire in 1945, was taken over by Barford (Agricultural) Ltd of Grantham. Introduced in 1951, the Barford Atom15 had a 1½hp Villiers petrol engine that used just one pint of petrol per hour. It had two forward speeds with the drive taken via a V-belt to an enclosed reduction gearbox.

A cross between a lightweight tractor and a motorised toolbar, the Garner was introduced in 1949. The machine was built by Garner Mobile Equipment Ltd of North Acton with a 5/6hp single-cylinder air-cooled engine mounted behind the drive. It had a centrifugal clutch and a three-speed gearbox. The mid-mounted toolbar was raised manually, and the tractor cost £202 15s on pneumatic tyres.

During the Second World War, E Boydell & Co Ltd of Manchester was awarded a government contract to supply the armed forces and civil defence units with thousands of its Muir-Hill dumpers. At the end of the war, surplus stocks of unused dumpers were bought back by the company to protect its own market. To find an outlet for these surplus machines the dumpers were fitted with drop-side bodies and sold into agriculture as the Muir-Hill Powacart. The power unit was a Fordson Model N tractor running on petrol/TVO. A Marles-Weller steering box was fitted to provide a forward-control driving position.

The Cuthbertson Water Buffalo was a semi-amphibious tractor with a hull made from welded sheet-steel that allowed it to ford 4ft of water. The flexible tracks were made from jointed rubber pads and exerted a ground pressure as low as 1½psi. The 'large' tractor was powered by a 165hp six-cylinder Leyland AU680 diesel engine with a five-speed SCG pneumo-cyclic gearbox operating through a centrifugal clutch. Steering was by clutch-and-brake. Albion supplied both the 81hp four-cylinder diesel engine and the four-speed gearbox for the 'light' model. The Water Buffalo was sold for forestry work, peat extraction and oil exploration.

The Fraser crawler, announced in May 1950, was a fairly conventional machine with clutch-and-brake steering and a four-speed gearbox. The tracks were an interesting design with flanged roller-wheels running around oval steel plates. The choice of engines included an Austin petrol/TVO unit or a Petter or Russell Newbery diesel.